Birth Cry

A personal story of the life of
Hannah D. Mitchell, nurse midwife

Shirley Roland Ferguson

WestBow
PRESS
A DIVISION OF THOMAS NELSON

Scripture taken from the King James Version of the Bible.
Scripture taken from the Holy Bible, New International Version®. Copyright © 1973,
1978, 1984 Biblica. Used by permission of Zondervan. All rights reserved.
Scripture quotations taken from the New American Standard Bible®, Copyright
© 1960, 1962, 1963, 1968, 1971, 1972, 1973, 1975, 1977, 1995 by The Lockman
Foundation. Used by permission." (www.Lockman.org)

WestBow Press books may be ordered through booksellers or by contacting:

WestBow Press
A Division of Thomas Nelson
1663 Liberty Drive
Bloomington, IN 47403
www.westbowpress.com
1-(866) 928-1240

Because of the dynamic nature of the Internet, any web addresses or
links contained in this book may have changed since publication and
may no longer be valid. The views expressed in this work are solely those
of the author and do not necessarily reflect the views of the publisher,
and the publisher hereby disclaims any responsibility for them.

Any people depicted in stock imagery provided by Thinkstock are
models, and such images are being used for illustrative purposes only.

Certain stock imagery © Thinkstock.

ISBN: 978-1-4497-2740-6 (e)
ISBN: 978-1-4497-2741-3 (sc)
ISBN: 978-1-4497-2742-0 (hc)

Library of Congress Control Number: 2011917273

Printed in the United States of America

WestBow Press rev. date: 11/04/2011

Contents

1930-1938

1938-1944

1944-1946

1946-1967

1967-1990

"For I know the plans I have for you," says the Lord.
"They are plans for good and not for disaster,
to give you a future and a hope."
Jeremiah 29: 11 (NLT)

Foreword

"I personally knew Hannah Mitchell for nearly 50 years. She was a great influence for good on generations of college students and young couples in our church; and the stories of how God used her as a nurse to the least of His children were an inspiration to those of us who sat at her feet. It is well, and fitting, that her story be told, and I would encourage you to read about her life. You will be moved by her steadfast faithfulness to the calling God placed upon her."

Terry Parker, Founder, National Christian Foundation

Preface

In 1972 Miss Hannah became our neighborhood Bible study teacher in Doraville, GA. Each year she offered a new Bible to anyone who had read the Bible through. After receiving several new Bibles, instead I asked for her life's story, and surprisingly, she consented.

In 1979 when our family moved back to Alabama, Miss Hannah and I began a delightful interchange. Over the years while she taught our Bible study, she had shown brief glimpses of her private self, but when we began the interview process, through phone calls, cassette tape recordings, letters and personal conversations, she allowed her life to unfold. As she began to reveal her thoughts, memories, heartaches and achievements, it became a labor of love for both of us. At home in her cottage she went through data, and at my house I pecked away on an IBM Selectric typewriter. Once, after a session she came home with me, bringing homemade peanut brittle and a sampling of her Miracle Fruitcake. Anytime our family visited her in Atlanta, she delighted in giving us the garden tour.

What you are about to read is a true story with actual events. I combined some stories, and created conversation that would have been difficult to recall, but Miss Hannah approved. To bring it up to date her journal entries were created from occasions re-told to me from friends who were with her during her final months in Atlanta.

Yes, this is an old manuscript. Although we tried over the years, Miss Hannah and I were unable to generate interest from publishers. But former members of the Bible study, who believe hers is a story worth reading, have continued to encourage me to pursue publication on my own.

Throughout this book I hope you will be inspired and challenged to realize that God is in control through life's ups, downs, twists and turns. May you find your own way and rest in His perfect will for you.

To the memory of
Hannah D. Mitchell
1907 - 2000

Hannah's Journal, April 1990

Last night the nightmare returned. I was lost on the farm in Missouri, where I had lived with my family as a child. In darkness, I groped blindly, and stumbled in swirling fog, as I searched for the house. Then, as I lost my footing and fell toward a dark void, I screamed in terror and clawed the earth to keep from being sucked into a bottomless chasm. My screams woke me, and I lay gasping for breath with a pounding heart. I had no idea where I was, until the moon slid out from behind the clouds. Then I could tell that I was safe, in my bed, in my little cottage in Atlanta. I clutched the sheets and tried to stop shaking. With this frequent nightmare, I sensed something terribly wrong. I felt that long fingers on the edge of darkness threatened to drag me into a terrible night, of which I could not return.

After several minutes, with a shiver against the chill of a spring morning, I got up and lit the space heater in the living room. I shuffled to the kitchen, and sighed with gratitude as the night terrors receded, and I felt the comfort of my little house, my home for the past forty years. Outside the window my garden showed off with huge azaleas, which stood in a riot of pinks and reds, with yellow jonquils clumped by the walk.

I glanced at the wall calendar and saw the date circled. April 6. Let's see. What is the significance of today's date? Oh, yes. Today is my birthday. I am eighty-three years old on this beautiful morning.

Back in the living room, I wearily settled into my easy chair with a steaming cup of tea. I remembered, that in my dream, I had screamed for my Mother. How odd. But even now, I wanted her presence, especially on my birthday. I needed her comfort and help in understanding my consuming fears, of the helpless feeling of being swallowed into nothingness. If only I could hear her voice again....

1907-1925

CHAPTER 1

Ozark Mountain Roots

Mother stood on the back porch with Marcus on her hip. "Hannah! I'm sending Paul out for you to watch while you weed the onion bed. Don't let him wander off! And do a good job!" I groaned as my younger brother ran to me. I was six years old, the firstborn, and Mother's appointed assistant.

One of my first tasks on the farm near Neosho, Missouri was to weed the seed onion bed in the springtime. I thought it insurmountable when Mother took me to the edge of the patch, and all I could see were green onions. They put up a leaf that I could barely detect from grass or weeds. No matter how many onions I pulled up by mistake, if the weeds weren't gone when mother came to inspect, she quoted, "If a task is once begun, never leave it till it's done." Disregarding my tired knees, arms, and back, I had to continue until I finished weeding row after row of the little seed onions. Plus, keep Paul entertained! When Mother said, "whether it be large or small, do it well or not at all," if I hadn't done it well, I sometimes replied, "I guess I'd better not do it at all, then!" She quickly convinced me with a swat to finish and to do it well.

Mother was one of thirteen in her family, so she knew how to delegate responsibility. My Father, an only child, pampered by his near-sighted mother who kept him by her side, didn't walk until he was three years old. When the couple decided to marry, Mother's family, the Moody clan, discussed it at length during one Sunday lunch after church. An old maid, who frequently snorted that it just wouldn't work, ended the discussion with everyone nodding agreement so they could delve into the serious business of homemade apple pie.

But Sarah Moody and Martin Mitchell, disregarding her family's skepticism, married anyway. They moved to the Mitchell farm in Neosho, where old Mr. Mitchell and his second wife, Martin's mother, lived. Mr. Mitchell's first wife had died earlier, and with their children grown, the old couple relied on the newlyweds to care for them.

Sarah and Martin moved into a house on the other side of a spring they shared with Martin's parents. Rocky soil made farming difficult, and they worked hard to make a living, constantly cultivating the land during growing season. When I came along in April 1907, Mother soon went back to the fields, taking me with her.

Grandfather Mitchell died when I was a small child, so Grandmother often entertained me while my parents farmed. Sometimes we met under the trees by the spring, and she kept me enthralled with old stories from the past.

"Hannah, see those markings on that old tree? Those are Indian blazes!" I inched closer to her side, looking for Indians. "You'll find them on the oldest trees. The Osage braves marked a trail that goes to the back part of our property. Near a cave lies an old burial mound."

I thought I saw movement in the trees. "Are Indians around here now?" I asked.

"Pshaw, no!" she snorted. "But one afternoon, an old Indian did come to the house, and asked to visit the burying ground of his people. Your Grandfather told him to go anywhere on the farm and he wouldn't be harmed. For several years the old man came, then he stopped coming."

"How come?"

"I reckon he died," Grandma said, as she stood and brushed herself off, to avert a discussion about death and dying with a six-year-old.

In the fall I would have entered the little country one-room school, but I stepped on a wheat stob, and injured my foot. A stubborn infection set in that took the entire school year to heal, so my parents and Grandma tutored me at home. They taught me from Dad's old blue-back speller dated February 1888.

When Grandma jumped on a misspelled word, it was like a hound on a jackrabbit's trail, and she sometimes, in her enthusiasm, sprayed the air with saliva. "Spell it by syllables, Miss-is-sip-pi!" I quickly grasped spelling and pronunciation, so Grandma wouldn't spit on me as she sounded out the words.

The next September Paul and I entered school together. Mother called out, "See that Hannah doesn't injure that foot again!" It turned into a rugged first day for me. I stayed in chart class from take-up to first recess; the teacher advanced me to the primer from first recess till noon, then on to first grade the rest of the day, with recitations in each class. After school, Paul dashed home ahead, to tell the family about our teacher's surprise at my progress. He carried a note complimenting my parents and Grandma on their instruction the past year. With a hug, Grandma sprayed her pupil with exclamations of delight.

The Mitchell family continued to grow. The inconvenience of living two and a half miles from school prompted my parents to look for a house in town. Up to this time, Paul and I either walked, or rode the horse in rain or snow. Just prior to the terrible flu epidemic of 1914, Mother found a house near the school. Marcus was three years old; she was expecting another child soon, so she kept pushing my Father to close the deal so we could move.

"What about me?" wailed Grandma. "I might die, and all alone!"

"Oh, it's only a couple of miles away, Mother! We'll be back and forth," said my Father.

He went to the bank to close on the house. We children skipped around the farmyard, chattering, and watching for him to return. As last he walked into the yard, but he looked solemn.

Mother wrinkled her brow. "Martin, did you get the house?"

"I have to tell you something. They included a fee we hadn't figured on. I came up short fifty dollars."

Mother's voice rose. "So, *you didn't buy it, did you?*"

"Well, I borrowed the money from Mr. Scofield," Dad said, to the look of disbelief on Mother's face.

"You borrowed money?" she gasped.

7

"It was the only way to get the house!"

"But, we still *owe* fifty dollars!"

Our family normally got up every morning before the sun at four o'clock, to milk the cows by lantern light. But the next day, with extra work assigned to everyone, by daybreak I trudged out to the winter onions, and pulled them all. I washed them in cold spring water, and wrapped them in large bundles, tied with string. Dad and I packed them in the wagon and went to town, where I sold them, door to door, ten cents a bundle. Dad sold the calf. By midmorning, the dew had dried on the strawberries, so we picked all three acres, and measured them by pints and quarts. This time, Paul joined me in the wagon. He and I peddled strawberries, while he whined and complained the entire time. Finally, by day's end, we counted over fifty dollars.

Dad paid off the debt.

In bed that night, I overheard Mother say to Dad, "Oh, Martin. Isn't it good not to owe anyone?"

I yelled out, "Well, you might feel good about it, but I'm so tired I can't go to sleep!" However, their short-term loan proved a valuable lesson for me to remember. To this day, I never want to buy anything, unless I can see ahead to pay for it.

Shortly afterwards, in September of 1914, my brother Russell was born. My parents' perseverance in raising their family became obvious to everyone, including Mother's skeptical family. Although no one admitted having doubted in the first place, they all concluded that this marriage might work after all.

Chapter 2

Dedicate It To The Lord

Both of my Grandmothers were godly women. On Grandma Moody's side of the family, circuit preachers worked their farms during the week, and lectured from the pulpit on Sundays. Mother's family claimed William McKinley, the twenty-fifth President, as their ancestor.

I am the tenth Hannah on my Father's side, with each one receiving the family papers, tracing our history. From deciphering the old English in a London Review dated 1788, we concluded that Warren G. Hastings, the English statesman and administrator in India, had done some missionary work there, and stood trial for it. Since he was a relative, the family had evidently followed his trial. Also, printers abounded on my Father's side. My Grandfather, Martin Rice, printer and poet, sold his books well during the Civil War.

Our community needed a church, so we gave enough land for it to be built on. The congregation found a pump organ, some songbooks, and invited a preacher once a month. Our family attended Sunday school, where Grandma taught a class for primary children.

"We need to dedicate the church," she frequently announced to the congregation.

"Soon," everyone agreed.

"Wait until we have more members."

But they never got around to dedicating the building to God.

One night a cyclone ripped through the countryside. At our place it hit the chicken house and turned it upside down, drowning the chickens and driving blades of grass through the baby chicks. It demolished the church. For years afterward, on that part of the farm, wherever we turned up the sod, we found fragments of the church – splintered pews, pages out of songbooks – all reminders of our meetinghouse.

"God destroyed it because we didn't dedicate it to Him," vowed Grandma. "No matter how good something is, if you don't dedicate what you have to the Lord, He doesn't want it, or need it."

At times, she could read the Bible, only if she held it close to her face, so we youngsters often read aloud to her. One evening, I had read her the story of Samuel, when he ran to Eli, because he thought Eli had called him.

That night in bed, I heard my name. *"Hannah."*

I went to my parents' room. "No," said Mother. "I didn't call you."

"Get on back to bed!" grumbled Dad.

In bed, again, I heard it.

"Hannah."

How could a voice, so audible in my mind, go unnoticed by my parents, or brothers, in our thin-walled farmhouse? Then, I remembered that Samuel had said, *Lord, if you want me for anything, I am here.* At church, and at home, I had been taught to listen for that still, small, voice that comes from inside us. *"You should yield, and not ignore the call, for it is God calling,"* my parents often said.

Does God call little girls my age? I wondered. *"Yes, Lord? Is that you calling me?"* I whispered.

In my childlike way, as best I knew how, I turned my life over to the Lord Jesus Christ that night. When I opened my heart to His calling, a peaceful joy enveloped me, because I sensed God seeking me out. From that night on, I knew I belonged to the Heavenly Father.

Just like Moses erected and dedicated the Tabernacle in the Wilderness, and the Lord filled the meeting place, and as the mother Hannah dedicated Samuel to the Lord, so the child Hannah dedicated herself to the Lord, when she heard His call. I wasn't yet ten years old.

CHAPTER 3

Girl Things

We kept the farm after we moved to Norwood. Dad worked for years in the general mercantile store with a lumberyard attached. He also operated a print shop in the building, which housed the only hotel in town.

"Look at these!" I called one afternoon, while my younger brothers and I rummaged around in a vacated room of the old hotel in town. "Doll dishes!"

Elated over finding them, I carefully picked up tiny saucers and cups, hoping they weren't cracked, and blew off the dust. As I rubbed the plates, underneath the grime a pattern of delicate blue and white flowers emerged. Paul, Marcus and Russell dashed over. They looked at each other, and wrinkled their noses in distaste as they watched me clutch my little treasure.

"Doll dishes? You want to play with those *girl things?*"

My face went slowly red, as I realized they didn't understand. I often entertained the boys, and played what they wanted because Mother stayed busy with James, our new little brother. I was tall for thirteen and rapidly maturing physically, so I felt varying emotions. One minute I behaved like a child, at other times I felt grown up.

11

"Be graceful and ladylike, Hannah," Mother encouraged often. "The name Hannah means 'Full of Grace'." But I was gangly, large boned, and neither felt, nor looked ladylike.

Confused about keeping the dishes or discarding them, I gazed at them lovingly, wondering what little girl they could have belonged to. They were like a prize to me, to be washed and dried, and carefully stored in a tiny, safe place, not to be discarded in a shabby room of an old hotel. I sighed, and reluctantly set them down.

"No," I shrugged. "I don't want them. Come on."

The boys dashed outside and started a game of tag. Keeping up with them seemed an unending task. On the farm, where I had spent my early childhood, we had few neighbors, and no little girls to play with. As a child, I had longed to dress dolls, not play cowboys and Indians. Chatting with girls at school now appealed to me more than playing hide-and-seek.

But I had little time for play and small talk with my friends. As the oldest sibling, in the afternoons, I helped Dad print sale bills. He called me, 'the printer's devil'. After he set and printed the type, I dumped the letters in a bin and replaced them in their proper boxes alphabetically. Dumping, and rearranging the letters, was called 'pieing' – my job as the printer's devil. Dad taught me to set type when I was twelve. He wrote out the sale bills, and I set the case, but if he found a misspelled word, he dumped the entire case in disapproval. I learned to patiently pi the characters and start over, re-setting the type.

We sometimes worked till dark, and had to light the large kerosene lantern that hung directly over my head, because customers came in late to have bills printed, or to pick them up. Exposure to small town gossip in the print shop revealed a world I wasn't aware of, until now. Not only was I maturing physically, but my thinking also changed.

Late one afternoon, a customer came in to pick up leaflets we had run off. He leaned over the counter.

"Mr. Mitchell, a terrible thing happened last night." He lowered his voice. "Someone going down the alley back here thought he heard a baby cry."

I easily overheard their conversation in the quiet shop.

"It was dark, and the man couldn't see," continued the customer, "so he stopped, and listened. Again, a faint little cry came from over by the privy."

Dad and I stopped working, and listened intently. "The fellow went over, and poked around in the refuse of the outdoor toilet. Sure enough, he found a newborn baby!"

"What?" Dad looked horrified. Thinking of our own new baby, I clasped my hand to my mouth.

"Yes, sir. It had been thrust through the hole in the privy seat, and was all covered with the fecal material." He shook his head. "It can't live, poor little thing."

"Oh, Dad! Who would do such a thing?"

The townspeople were outraged. "That mother should be put on a rail and run out of town! If the baby dies, she should be lynched. To think someone couldn't face reality, and would try to kill an innocent baby!"

The guilty mother, a young girl of fifteen, was soon discovered. She worked at the hotel, making beds, washing dishes, cooking meals, and had become pregnant by one of the tenants. When the townspeople confronted her, she collapsed in tears.

"I didn't know what to do!" she sobbed. "I know what I did was wrong. But it would be a *shame baby*! Oh, don't you see," she wailed. "I didn't know what to do!"

The girl had concealed her condition by tightly corseting herself, and wearing a thickly gathered apron over her dress. As time approached to have the baby, she quietly went about her duties at the hotel, where her labor began. Without crying out, she endured the pain, and in the last stages of labor, hurried to the privy outdoors. Alone, she expelled the baby, and thrust it through the hole behind the seat, hoping no one would find it.

A few days later the baby died. By this time, tempers had cooled. "Well, she *is young,*" the people reasoned. "We couldn't hang her for abandoning it out of fright." The ladies relented, "Humph! She can just try and live down the scandal!"

I was shocked at the townspeople's reaction, which had humiliated a hysterical girl, caught in a desperate situation. I grieved for the poor dead baby, with only the preacher, and a few brave mourners, at the cemetery. And the girl, too young to face motherhood, would have to live with this sordid event for the rest of her life.

It really touched me when I realized the girl was only a couple of years older than me. I wanted to visit her, and take her the china doll dishes blossoming with the tiny blue flowers. I imagined we could have a tea party.

"Would you care for some tea?" I would ask.

She would smile through her tears and say, "Why yes, thank you." In our minds, we would go back. Back in time, before she felt the first little butterfly wings of a baby moving inside her. Back before she gave up her virtue. She would offer me a cookie, and we would giggle like little girls.

Ignoring our changing worlds, I would pretend I wasn't too old to play with dolls. She would pretend there wasn't a dead baby. For a few short hours, we would revisit our carefree days of childhood. She could have briefly forgotten the pain of grieving for her child, and wishing the whole thing had never happened. She would have felt better because of my visit.

It would have been a lovely afternoon. And she would have understood about girl things.

CHAPTER 4

One Crime Calls For Another

Usually in raising children we want them to avoid any contact with crime, because it may impress on them that crime is advantageous. I am so thankful that the Heavenly Father, in my early teen-age years, used it to make me realize that God abhors evil, and that I should stay completely away from it.

During the summer months, my family moved back to the farm so we could work the fields, and can food for the winter. One night, I heard a cough from outside my bedroom window, so I peered through the curtains, and saw the red glow of a cigarette. Again, the cough came from someone standing in the barn lot.

Are Paul and Marcus smoking? Surely not! They've never done anything like this before! I decided to play the spy and catch them. Slipping out the back door of the house, I pressed myself against the wall, listening for the cough. A muffled spasm of coughs floated across the warm night air. Although a bright moon lit the night, I could scarcely make out whom it was, because he moved within the barn's shadow.

And, then I knew. *Why, it's Mr. Farmer! What's he doing here?* I heard the lock and chain scrape across the feed house door, and I sucked in my breath. *Oh! He's stealing from us!*

I darted across the yard to the feed house. Next to it stood a table, where we stored utensils used for separating milk. Heavy mosquito netting covered the utensils and was draped down the table, so, feeling very clever, I quickly crawled under the table, careful not to rattle the metal spoons and pails. I planned to reach across, slam the door shut, lock it, and run for Dad. My heart pounded with my smug little trap to catch a thief.

Just as I stuck out my hand to grab the partially opened door, out came Mr. Farmer. As his pants leg brushed my fingertips, I jerked back just in time, to prevent the feed house door from slamming on my hand. Feed from a half-used sack spilled on the ground while he redid the lock and chain. He went through the gate with the feed sack, to the back of the barn lot, got on his horse and rode away.

Rats! I slammed my palms on the ground in frustration. Feeling rather foolish now under the table, I crawled out, sneaked back to the house, quietly let myself in, and went to bed.

Before breakfast next morning, we all went about our chores, feeding the chickens, horses and cows. We did the milking, separated the milk, and then sat down to a big breakfast.

Before any of us started eating, Dad said, "Sarah, I just don't know what to think of these boys. When I went out to the feed house this morning, feed was all over the floor." He looked sternly across the table. "Someone will get punished for wasting food. Even though we raise part of it, it's expensive and shouldn't be spilled. Boys, how many times have I told you to take the feed out carefully to feed the animals?"

Paul glanced at Marcus, Marcus at Russell, both of them wide-eyed. They stared at Dad with their mouths open. His satisfied look showed that he had made his point.

I spoke up. "Dad, it wasn't the boys. Old Mr. Farmer went in and did all that."

Dad looked at me in disbelief. "How do you know this?" he demanded.

I explained about the cigarette cough, and grinned at my snickering brothers. I told how I had planned to catch Mr. Farmer, but failed. Exultant in my bright idea, I glanced at Mother, who had stopped feeding James; her face had gone white.

"Hannah! Don't you know that a person who steals, usually carries a gun?"

"No," I said casually, helping myself to sausage and eggs. "I thought it a good idea to lock him in."

When Dad went out to the barn, on examining the lock, he discovered that our neighbor had ingeniously loosened the hasp. Whenever he wanted in the feed house, he pulled out the hasp, and put it back when he finished. Mr. Farmer had been pilfering the entire time Dad thought the boys were being wasteful.

In a couple of days, Dad brought home a new lock and chain. He made two holes, one on the door, and one on the feed house. Through this he drew the chain, put the lock through the ends of it, and locked it.

Late one afternoon, we heard the large gate at the end of the driveway clang, and we looked out to see Mr. Farmer coming by the house. "Stay inside, children," Mother signaled, and went out on the porch to greet our neighbor.

When he came opposite the house, he called out, "Hello! How's everybody?"

"We're all fine," Mother answered, casually wiping her hands on her apron. "How's your family?" While they chatted, Mr. Farmer's eyes constantly went from Mother, to the new chain and lock on the feed house door.

"Well, guess I'd better get on," he said after a few minutes, as he kicked his horse and left.

Back inside, Mother said, "Children, I wish you could have seen the awful look of guilt on Mr. Farmer's face, when he realized we had found out about the grain pilfering." That night at dinner, she told Dad about the visit.

"Let this be a lesson to you," Dad said. "Crime doesn't pay. We've lost a lot of grain to Mr. Farmer, but he isn't happy about it. He feels guilty and frightened."

Glancing at the family Bible, Mother reinforced his statement. "It says in the Ten Commandments, that we are not to steal. Don't ever take *anything* that doesn't belong to you. You must work for things yourself, or have them given to you." Our parents forbade us to speak of the incident outside the family, for it was to be our particular secret. I didn't understand.

Mother explained. "We mustn't put Mr. Farmer in an embarrassing spot, so that he could be criticized. His children would be ashamed if some of the other children teased them about this."

I thought about that lesson on stealing every time I saw Mr. Farmer, or one of his children. Needless to say, no more thieveries occurred at our place.

* * * * *

Another incident happened in my late teens, which also made a deep impression on me. Mother's brother Silas, a sheriff in another county, discovered a large moonshine operation. He needed help to make a raid on it, so he came by the store and asked Dad to help him the next day. While he and Dad discussed their plans, the moon-shiners surprised them by coming in the store, for they had followed Silas at a distance. Furious, they glowered at Dad and Uncle Silas as a warning, and stomped out of the store.

Dad relayed the incident to Mother. "It's about time those fellows got caught. They've hauled liquor all over this county."

"But, Martin! That's dangerous business! Those men aren't playing games!"

However, resolved to make the raid the next day, Dad oiled his gun and laid out his clothes before we went to bed. During the night, we were awakened by the sound of a horse galloping into the yard, rousing the dogs. A heavy-booted man stomped up the steps, and pounded on the door. Dad jerked on his pants and went out to see.

"It's Mrs. Mitchell's brother. He's been shot!" Out of breath, he spurted, "He was home, playing on the floor with his little boy, with tinker toys, I think. Someone fired through the window."

"How is he?" Mom gasped from behind Dad.

The man removed his hat. "I'm sorry, Ma'am. "Your brother's dead."

When my parents went to the funeral, we all couldn't go because we were down with the measles. I had a lighter case, so I was responsible for my four brothers. "Stay inside now," Mother cautioned. "You don't want a relapse."

"Stay inside?" we screeched. "You're leaving us, with a killer on the loose? We wouldn't dare stick our necks out of this house."

"Oh, you'll be all right," Dad assured us.

The boys were sick enough to be entertained without any problem. When we pulled the curtains, it wasn't only to protect our eyes from the light. We were scared out of our wits, and jumped at every noise. When I heard the front gate clang shut, I peered out at a neighbor, who had come by to feed the livestock.

"Keep the milk, Mr. Allen. We don't need it today," I whispered through a slit in the door. Craning to hear what I had said, he looked puzzled. Usually, I talked his ears off. All day I watched for strangers, not trusting anyone. I even looked suspiciously at the mail carrier. When the sun went down, I felt my pulse pounding in my throat.

At last we heard our wagon squeak into the yard, and I dashed to the door and flung it open wide, all the while attempting to appear calm and natural. Behind Mother and Father in the wagon sat Grandma Moody. I was so glad to see her; I all but knocked her down. We rarely saw her, because Neosho was so far away. She had come to stay a few days, after attending Uncle Silas' funeral. Relieved, the more people we had in the house, the more secure I felt.

Next day, Dad saw to it that the murdering men got arrested, but they paid a high bail, and to our dismay, were released. Dad was disgusted. "Silas was the only one who knew the location of their still. They'll be selling liquor again before we know it," he said.

Within a few days, Grandma Moody left to visit some other relatives. After sleeping with her, it felt luxurious to have my bed all to myself again, so I stretched, and sprawled all over it. My fright over the murder was beginning to fade.

But the night she left, I heard a noise outside my window. My bed lay situated so that I could look directly at the window with a slight turn of my head. Scarcely breathing, I turned slowly, and saw a man's face pressed against the glass, clearly visible in the moonlight. I froze. *Oh, dear God! Is this one of the murderers?* I shut my eyes tightly. *Please! Protect me, and make this man go away!* When I opened my eyes, he was no longer there, as he evidently had seen that only a child occupied the bed.

In a flash I was at my parents' bedside. "Wake up, Dad!" I whispered loudly, shaking him. "Someone was at my window!"

He jumped up and looked out. Thinking it my imagination, he said, "Then, why didn't the dogs bark?" Next morning, we knew why when we tried to feed them; they only sniffed at the food. By the fence lay a bone, and remains of fresh meat, which had been used to lure the disloyal terriers and bulldog away from the house. So now, we children refused to go outside for *any* reason.

"You *must* go to school, and do your chores!" Dad said sternly. "Just don't talk to strangers, or leave with someone you don't know."

We moved Mom and Dad's bed to a safe corner of their bedroom, so no one could shoot into it while they slept. We also bought shades, and put them on all the windows, and pulled them at night for a long time afterwards.

Shortly after the peeping-tom incident, the men who killed my uncle went to the store where Dad worked in order to get revenge, and make sure no one found the still.

"How about coming out to the warehouse, and loading some feed," one of them snarled, slapping the money on the counter. The other man browsed around the store, to make sure no other customers were present.

"Bring your truck over here," Dad said to the driver, and walked to the back of the warehouse for the feed. In an instant, sensing something wrong, he realized he should never have turned his back on either of the men. He spun around just in time to catch one of them stealthily creeping up, with a raised axe in his hand.

"Now, I have you," the man growled.

Fortunately, Daddy remembered a door behind the feed stack. It was a long drop to the ground, but he plunged through the door to escape the axe. Their deed thwarted, the men ran. Back inside the store, Daddy shakily brushed himself off, and asked a waiting customer to stay with him awhile.

Finally, with all the evidence against them, the murderers received a sentence of life imprisonment. Not till many years later were they released on good behavior.

These two incidents with crime enlightened me in a valuable way. I saw how someone starting off with a small misdemeanor, like stealing food, could get away with it, but he suffers guilt, and the fear of having to answer for it one day. In the moon-shiners' case I learned that with each felony a person's character is corrupted, for usually one crime calls for another, then another, until finally a serious mortal sin is committed, such as murder.

Hannah's Journal, mid-April 1990

I feel again the anxiety of the law having to deal with those murderous men, and the terror of that man peering in my window! I shudder tonight, now that supper is over, and shadows lengthen. I am nauseous with fear as bedtime approaches. During my career as a nurse, I noticed that babies usually fuss, mothers' tempers are short, and fathers come home grumpy in the evenings. I had chuckled when a co-worker gave her explanation. "You know what it is. Everyone is afraid of the dark!" However, in the past, I harbored no such fear. I have always enjoyed seeing the day give over to twilight that softens my garden, with a welcoming lamp shining in the window.

But now, it isn't evening's darkness, or fear of a human intruder that I dread, but the enemy of my fading memory. As a nurse, I know too well the signs of dementia. At first, what I had discounted as normal signs of ageing, I am beginning to recognize as clinical symptoms of dementia. And I know that damage to the brain is beyond the control of the patient. The knowledge of the meaning behind growing lapses in memory, inability to recall names and faces, makes me weary. I truly fear the coming darkness accompanying the disease.

I sank into my chair, and with a shaky hand opened the mail. When a letter fluttered to the floor, its handwriting looked familiar. Hmmm. It reminded me of my brother Paul's hurried scrawl, remembering that Paul rarely wrote. Of course, any word from him always had its purpose, usually self-centered in nature....

1925-1930

Chapter 5

A Fowl Invitation

*U*nable to sleep, I lay in bed listening to the little house in Tulsa settle down for the night. Everyday noises magnified themselves in the dark, as dying embers sputtered and hissed in the living room coal stove, and floors creaked in the bare hall outside my room. I jumped when a rafter overhead cracked like a rifle shot, but across the hall, my Aunt Vada slept on, sighing occasionally.

Each time I closed my eyes, a gust of wind spattered rain against my bedroom window. A threatening feeling that had built for days permeated me, as my thoughts again gravitated to the letter on my bedside table. After repeated readings, I still didn't know how to respond to my younger brother, Paul. Only a couple of years separated us in age, and although we were close as children; since his disappearance from home, we had all despaired of hearing from him. I prayed for him daily, and watched the mail. *Now, this letter.*

Paul. I haven't heard from you in months! You have the nerve to send me a hasty note, asking me to help you start a chicken ranch in Denver. No explanations as to where you've been. Just drop everything, and come. I can't believe you're trying to involve me in one of your hare-brained schemes!

It was 1929, and I was twenty-two years old, working hard at a bookkeeping position at Renbergs in Tulsa, Oklahoma. I enjoyed sharing a rented house with Vada, who felt more like a sister, eight years older than me. Between our salaries, we had furnished the house with books and comfortable chairs. My independence in working, and living away from home not only gave me a sense of pride, but increasing reports of unemployment across the nation made me appreciate my job even more.

I protested four nights ago, when I first received the unwelcome invitation. "Oh, Vada. I like it here in Tulsa. Paul says that he plans to sell young fryers to the hotels. But, he doesn't say if he really knows anything about the market for chickens!" I looked at her imploringly.

That night, she and I had routinely made dinner, and set the table with our usual white cloth and napkins, but neither of us had felt in the mood to decorate with roses from the garden, or a centerpiece of goldenrods picked during one of our frequent walks. Often, while pots simmered, and bread browned, I would hum and sing softly; or we both made peace with the world as Vada played the piano, and I the violin. Now, the letter between us on the kitchen table disrupted our tranquility.

"What will you do, Hannah?"

"It isn't fair! Why can't Paul just settle down and live a normal life?" I sighed in exasperation. "Oh, I don't know *what* to do!"

"Let's send a night letter to your folks, and get their opinion," she suggested. "Since I work for Western Union, we could charge it to my account." We phoned the letter that same night. My parents' farm, and the store in Norwood where my Dad worked, had no phone, so we awaited a written reply.

"You know," Vada remarked wistfully, "I'll miss you if you go." She knew I enjoyed my job, friends at work and church, also that I felt gratified in continuing my education.

After classes in Spanish and accounting, I had enrolled in a class at the First Presbyterian Church in *How To Study The Bible*. I felt I could never have as full a life in Colorado.

For the past few days, I had furiously attacked the inventory books in an attempt to forget Paul and his offer. "Hey! Your machine is smoking," teased an office worker, giving me a curious look. "Hmm. You're so quiet. Are wedding bells in the wind?"

Another gust of wind sent me shivering under the covers, and the letter fluttering to the floor. I retrieved it from under the bed, and also reached for Mom and Dad's reply that had come today. I remembered some of the words, written in Dad's flowing hand. He started with the usual, *Dear Kitten,* and gave me news from home, yet he was non-committal about what to do about Paul, adding to my discontent. *Do what you think best. Give Paul our love.*

The bed lay in shambles from restless tossing, and my two large feet kept appearing from loosened covers, so in frustration I got up and tucked all the corners back under the mattress. I resented the chill of an early winter wind that kept seeping under the windowsill. It felt like a wind of change, not only uprooting me from Tulsa, but also attempting to dislodge me from all security and stability.

In the dark I tiptoed across a cold floor to the kitchen, and made a mental note to see about weather stripping for the kitchen door. A mothball fragrance wafted in from the hall shelves. The familiar house with its drafts and smells enveloped me. *This is home! I can't leave!* Even the drippy kitchen faucet sounded constant and reassuring.

Vada had fussed at dinner, as she watched me dawdle over my food. "Can't make decisions on an empty stomach, Hannah." In the dark, I smiled as I sliced a chunk of her homemade coconut cake. *I'll tell her a mouse must have taken it. Sweet Vada. So easy to live with, steady and dependable.*

I huddled in a kitchen chair, savoring the cake, and swigging on a glass of fresh milk. Hugging my knees against the room's chill, I watched as shadows faded and reappeared. In the distance a dog yelped, reminding me of a terrier on our farm in Missouri.

The farm. Mom and Dad. I wish they'd been more help about Paul. He was the one who had loved adventure stories. When I was a child, I had often read to my brothers and Mother till I was hoarse, but Paul, Marcus and Russell had never wanted me to put the book down. It was Paul who would bring me water, or a piece of peppermint candy, so, won over by my rapt audience, I read on. *Had those thrilling stories built a hunger within him that would take its toll from all of us?*

One day when I had brought him water from the spring while he worked in the fields, I looked at his tall, strong frame and realized that he was a grown man. Leaning on his hoe, he gazed into the distance. "Wonder what's out there, Sis." He looked out across the Ozarks while he drank the cool water, then he handed me the dipper and grinned, "Suppose your *true love* waits for you somewhere?"

To his delight I flared up and marched off. "Get back to work, Paul Mitchell! You'll forget those daydreams if the corn doesn't get planted!" But he didn't forget, and one day, he just left. My parents painfully accepted his rambling ways; they called him 'our wandering boy'.

After I graduated from high school, Dad had encouraged me to take the job in Tulsa. "We'll help all we can," he said. I often wondered how he managed his meager finances, with three large, hungry boys at home. Marcus, Russell and James, aged eighteen, fifteen, and nine, worked hard in Paul's absence. I sent things my family needed, and wouldn't buy – a new shirt, material for a dress. They sent picked out hickory nuts, and carefully packed, hard-shelled guinea eggs. Our parents' caring devotion for each of us created an example not easily forgotten by us children. Disconcerted as I felt by their neutral letter, I somehow felt close to them, knowing they shared my burden about Paul.

A blast of wind hit the kitchen door. *Wonder how cold it is in Denver. Has Paul repaired the chicken house? The small house he'll live in – what's it like?* I remembered the rest of his letter. *Let me know which bus you'll be on.* Frowning at his smugness, I wondered how he would react to: *Sorry. Can't leave the nest. Chicken farming isn't my idea of bringing home the bacon.*

As I nibbled at the cake crumbs, I pictured Paul working day and night, alone with the chickens. *Who will help him?* Glancing around in the semi-darkness at the walls I called home, I wondered if I was being too sentimental about this place. *Give Paul our love.* Dad's letter echoed in my mind. *I'm Paul's only tie to home and our family awaits my decision. Is Paul actually pleading for help with his nonchalant invitation?*

At that moment, the answer quietly came to me. *How else express love and concern to my brother? I suppose that's why I finished the inventory books, and mused over life here in Tulsa. Subconsciously, I've probably known all along.*

Out of habit I rinsed the glass and plate, put them on the drain, and crept back across the squeaky floor to the hall, where the fresh smell of clean linens and towels came from open shelves. I paused at Vada's bedroom door, where, undisturbed by wind, rain

28

and indecision, she slept on. Though I knew Vada would agree and understand, I wistfully thought *I'll miss you, too.*

I slid between sheets now crisp and cold. "Heavenly Father," I whispered, "Is this in your plan for my life, to change localities?" I was unable to see God leading in every area of my life – my bookkeeping skills, lessons in Spanish, classes in Bible study – all preparation for the future. Little did I know that a *drastic* wind of change was coming world wide – a Great Depression that would affect all of us.

The weight of warm quilts and peace of mind soon had me drifting. Funny how uncomplicated the night becomes, when a matter is settled; noises quiet down, even the wind wanes to a sigh. Yawning, I again thought of Paul. I imagined his apprehension on receiving my response, and then his big grin as he read it.

Stay put little brother. I'm coming. We Mitchells, with God's help, will stick together.

Then, committing myself to God's perfect will, I went to sleep

CHAPTER 6

The Calf's Trail

The flat lands of Kansas offered little to see. Ripened wheat waiting for harvest waved monotonously in the prairie wind. But as the bus entered the foothills of the Rocky Mountains, we encountered a rare and beautiful white stallion, with several mares and colts. They paused, then lifted their heads, and galloped down the valley where they would spend the winter. Already, the snow capped peaks of their summer grazing grounds looked cold and ominous.

Denver lay high in the mountains. I pulled my cardigan sweater around me; glad I had packed my warmest clothes. The mountains, like a dropping curtain, shut out the sun's last rays, and night came quickly. Although I felt a thrill about going to an unknown future because of my confidence in the Lord's leading, I still wondered how long it would last, knowing Paul.

"Denver's laid out like the trail of a little calf, who's lost its mother," said the bus driver, as we entered Denver's rambling streets and disorganized names. "You can wander around in these streets like you know where you're going, but first thing you know

– you're lost." I smiled, gazing out the window. *That's what I'm following – a lost calf's trail.*

I easily spotted Paul at the station, because he towered above some of the people. He always attempted to comb straight his dark brown, wavy hair, but it had already curled back across his forehead. His stern mouth broke into a grin when he saw me step off the bus.

He got right down to business. "I've found a good little ranch, Sis," he blurted out, studying my reaction. "Looks right out on a high mountain. I know you'll like it."

"I'm sure I will too, Paul," I said, as we hugged each other.

"I've ordered the chickens," he added, relieved at my light manner. "Oh, and we'll be staying with the Allens until I finish repairs on the ranch. You remember them, don't you?" he asked, motioning to a man and young woman who stood over by the station. I nodded in surprise at our friends, who had moved from our home community in Norwood. Their daughter, Charlotte, younger than I, volunteered, "You'll be sharing my room, Hannah."

We noisily renewed old friendships at the Allen home. The younger children told me about their interests in school, but the youngest cried at seeing a stranger, and hid behind her Mother. While Mrs. Allen, who didn't look well, talked of possible surgery soon, I felt an immediate welcome in their family's cheery clamor.

The following Sunday, Charlotte and I took her two brothers to their Quaker church. Charlotte introduced me to the friendly young people, and I smiled at the clumsy advances of the young men, who reacted awkwardly at meeting someone from another area. A lovely girl named Flora with curly brunette hair, and sparkling brown eyes, came over to us; her natural manner generated an instant friendship between us.

Next day, Paul took me aside. "The chicken house is large, with a stove to warm the chickens, and I'm almost finished with the repairs. By the way, the little house we'll live in is furnished, and an older couple lives next door, so we won't feel completely isolated." He watched my face for any misgivings, then left to complete his repair job.

A few evenings later, we went to the hatchery to pick up several hundred little chicks. "Ooh! Look at their soft, yellow down," I cooed. "But, they're larger than I thought!"

Paul laughed. "Did you think they would be newly hatched, and we'd have to keep them in incubators?" He started packing boxes of chickens in his rattletrap car, among feed and groceries. We put chickens everywhere – in the trunk, across the back seat, in the floor. I even held boxes on my lap.

Paul squinted into the darkness. "I've never been out here at night, but I think I know the way."

"Well, I'm no help," I said. I couldn't see a thing over the boxes. The last street light receded, and we started for the country.

"This must be the way," decided Paul, taking a turn. Immediately we plunged off the road, and with a bone-jarring crash, the car sat still.

After a long silence, Paul waved at a frantic, cheeping chick, and asked, "Hannah! Are you hurt?" Loose chickens scrambled for freedom out of crushed boxes, throwing broken glass from the windshield over us.

"No," I answered, spitting and brushing gritty fragments from my hair and face. "The chicks saved me from going through the windshield, but it's sure ruined." I peered out. "Where are we?"

Before he could answer, the doors of a nearby house flew open and several men soon surrounded us, shouting in broken English. At first they seemed as puzzled as we were until one of them laughed. "You jump the irrigation ditch and land in our asparagus field!" While they helped us out of the car, chattering to one another in broken English, an older man kept waving his hand toward the field.

"What those white things?" he asked, and then recognized them as some of our little chicks, lying motionless over the black soil; while the others ran, raising their new wings in vain attempts at flight. The men easily collected the live chicks, and carefully cupping them in their hands, brought them to me.

"I am Valente," explained the older man. "These my sons!" He motioned proudly to the five brawny men chasing the floundering chicks. "We Italian truck farmers!"

The men soon got us loaded again, picked up the car, and set it back on the road. While they carried us across the ditch I felt quite like a queen, or Oriental princess, being carried by her slaves. But I soon came back down to earth again when Paul was able to coax the little motor into action. Our escorts stood around us, gesturing in mixed English and Italian, as they directed us toward the ranch once more.

Slowed by the shattered windshield, we again bumped and cheeped along, until we finally arrived at the ranch, exhausted. A few more chicks died from the impact of the accident, but the rest ran to the feeder, and scratched around in their new quarters. The warm chicken house, with feeding, chirping chicks, brightened our weary spirits as we took one last look, turned to unload the car, and put away the groceries.

I found it difficult to comprehend, that a few days before, I had been in Tulsa working at a comfortable bookkeeping job, and fuming about my brother's nervy letter. Now, here I was with him in a cold farmhouse, helping set up a kitchen for our immediate use. I stared in disbelief as Paul brought me boxes from the car.

Oh, well. At least, the lost calf is back on the right trail again, I concluded, looking at the light from the warm chicken house. We're here, properly launched in the fryer business. Give Paul our love, I kept thinking, as I put the groceries on a bare, unpainted shelf.

CHAPTER 7

Chicken Duty

"We need to check on the chickens every two hours, night and day," instructed Paul. "I'll work from noon until midnight, and you work from midnight till noon."

"Okay," I yawned, glancing at my watch. "You take the first shift." I set the clock, to waken me for Paul to hand out orders, and give a report on the welfare of the chicks.

When the alarm went off at midnight, I thought I had just shut my eyes, but I pulled on a heavy coat over my pajamas, staggered outside to a cold starry night, and clattered across the yard to the chicken house.

Wide-awake by the time I opened the door to the warm coop, I noted that it was free from dangerous smoke. The chickens huddled against the boards around the stove, just as Paul had warned me they would. In fear that they might smother by piling on top of one another, I carefully separated them; then I couldn't walk, as they collected around my feet with incessant cheep, cheep, cheeps of mother-hungry chicks. After making sure their pans contained enough water and feed, I cuddled several irresistible, leggy powder-puff balls against my face, then gently put them down, and eased out backwards through the door. In a cooled bed, I plunged into dreamless sleep, until the alarm called me to chicken duty again.

The weeks went busily by as the restricted fowls quickly developed wing feathers, and lost the rest of their down, gaining weight rapidly. As they soon grew large enough for market, Paul sold them, and then replaced them with another order of chicks. In contrast, getting up every two hours at night soon wore me out, and I lost weight. Paul, who was responsible for marketing the chickens, buying the feed, and keeping up repairs on both houses, also often looked like his feathers had been plucked.

Our friendly, next-door neighbors came over often, sometimes with steaming dishes, and the excuse they had cooked a little too much. I suspect they noticed our sleepless eyes and cold suppers. At any rate, we welcomed their surplus. My new friend, Flora, and her brothers also came out to see us regularly, along with Charlotte Allen, and young people from the church. We sang and talked while the chickens grew and squawked.

Maria Valente, and her sister, came out to the ranch one day. "Father says we can go to church with you, Hannah," offered Maria shyly, "provided you first go to Mass with us." As we took turns alternating between the two churches, I began to feel more and more at home, thanks to the good people of both congregations. Maria asked many questions about the Christian life, and gradually came to the realization that Christ alone is the Power to reconcile us to God. After one of the services she prayed, asking to be forgiven of her sins. She then simply asked the Lord Jesus Christ to come in and fill her life. I was thrilled at the joy on her shining face, which revealed her inward peace with God.

Maria's parents soon noticed a radiant change, in her conduct with friends, and attitudes in family relations. In appreciation, her father brought a truckload of cabbage over one day, and dumped it in our yard. Paul and I dug a pit, lined it with straw, and stored the cabbages inside the mound. We ate many meals with fresh slaw or steamed cabbage after that. I even made Sauer kraut. Thanks to the Valentes, an abundance of at least *one* vegetable made up our diet.

Money got tighter and tighter, until Paul and I found ourselves in financial trouble, because the chicken ranch couldn't pay for itself like we had anticipated. One day during our routine we came to grips with our low funds.

"It's time for me to get a job," I decided. Paul agreed, but next morning at breakfast, he held up the paper. In bold type the front page read "20,000 PEOPLE OUT OF WORK!" The article also told of soaring unemployment throughout the country. Fear gripped the nation.

Dejected, Paul said, "Don't waste your time."

I hesitated, then said, "I think I'll go into town, and ask anyway." I felt rather foolish, as Paul watched me walk down the hill a quarter mile to meet the streetcar where it turned around. I prayed as I walked. *20,000 out of work? Why pursue this?* In an attempt to ease my doubts, I prayed all the way to Sixteenth and Champa. *Father. Please direct me to a bookkeeping job!*

The streetcar stopped near The May Company, so I went in and applied, although the man collecting applications gave me no hope as he pointed to a stack of papers just like mine. Many other businesses discouraged me too. Clusters of jobless people standing around filled me with dismay, so, tired and hungry, I went home.

When I stepped off the streetcar, I glanced toward the house and saw Paul standing in the yard, waving excitedly for me to hurry. I didn't feel up to it, but I raced up the hill, and he thrust a piece of paper in my hand.

"Call this number! They've called twice already!" My heart pounded as I dialed the number, and waited, gasping for breath. Finally the operator said, "The May Company." She connected me with the man I recognized as the same one who had discouraged me about applying for a job.

"One of the bookkeepers has had a sudden illness in her family. Could you come in tomorrow, to help in the foreign and eastern ledger posting?" I quickly accepted, and slowly put down the receiver, flushed from the run up the hill, and elated over our new source of income. *Thank you Father, for giving me the faith to follow through on your prompting to look for a job!*

Paul, watching my face, looked dumbfounded. When I explained about praying for the job, he shook his head. "You didn't even need to check the other places! This job was *waiting* for you, the first place you applied!" He repeated it over and over, all the while shaking his head in disbelief. His reaction both amused me, and made me glad he had witnessed answered prayer.

Easier and more interesting than my previous job, it required posting many different products sold to our company from foreign countries. One afternoon, I discovered an error on one of the big teacart-sized ledgers I had been working on. I glanced at the clock on the opposite wall. It was almost five and quitting time. I checked through quickly, but I couldn't find the error. The mistake puzzled me all the way home. I thought about it constantly during dinner, and while I helped with the new batch of chickens.

Later that evening, I set the alarm for midnight, and sank wearily into bed, welcoming the folds of my feather mattress and soft covers, to steal a few hours of sleep. But elusive sleep didn't come, because I kept thinking about the posting error. Finally, I prayed about it. During the night, I awakened with *The Amalgamated Silk Mills Company* ringing in my mind. I clicked on the light and jotted it down, then slept again until the clock crowed.

Next day, I carried the note to the office and looked in the ledger. There it was! A double entry in The Amalgamated Silk Mills Company! Hours of searching saved! *Thank you, Father.*

As the weeks passed, I perceived that I had gained entrance to a special school, where I was being taught important values about faith. I realized more and more how the Heavenly Father continually cared for one of His chicks. He sustained me while I worked long hours in my bookkeeping job, and caught snatches of sleep at night. He supplied a job, food, friends, and importantly, spiritual fellowship with others. Our financial needs were met. He answered prayer, even about posting errors.

Somehow, too wondrous for my small mind to comprehend, I knew that He heard - over the vastness of space and time, the cheep-cheep of a Father-hungry chick. It gave me a special feeling to know that He had covered me with His wing, and He never, not once, tired of caring for His own.

CHAPTER 8

cum

A Time To Cry

All work and no time off created a spiraling downhill drain on Paul. My absence all day made it lonely for him and he felt tied to the chickens. Advancing winter added to his discontent as nights grew long and bitterly cold, and short grey days dumped snow down the mountainsides. The walk from the house to the chicken coop took on an atmosphere much like an exercise yard in a prison, as a path in the snow soon formed - from the house, to the chickens, and back again, without any diversion. Paul often paced like a trapped animal.

One day at work a heavy snowstorm tied up all traffic, including the streetcars, and I found myself stranded in town along with most of the other office workers. "Happens at least once a winter," remarked an old timer good-naturedly, while the storm lashed snow against the windows in fury. "No need to concern yourself," he reassured me, as he started taking cots, sheets, and plenty of blankets from a well-stocked storage room.

"Might as well make the best of it," we laughed. I called to let Paul know that I was all right, then relaxed with dinner and breakfast provided by the company. Next afternoon I went home to a restless brother.

"You've been busy," I noted, glancing at a sink full of dirty dishes, and ignoring the tension in the air.

"Yep. Just me and the chickens," he moaned, rising from the couch. "Think I'll go to town for supplies; that is, if I can get the car started." A permanent gloom hung about him as he ambled out, eager to escape his routine.

A little warning that had begun weeks before now prompted me to invite our friends in more often. They braved the weather, in an attempt to create activity as we schemed to prevent Paul's discontent from growing. They praised him for the great job he was doing with the chickens, and for his skill in keeping up repairs on both houses. We kept conversation light, and sang our hearts out around the coal stove, while we sipped on hot chocolate. On a distant hill coyotes answered. As they howled from a lonely hill, under a black carpet of sky that permitted only a glitter of stars here and there, our noises must have sounded eerie to them.

"Remember when you were a little boy," I recalled to Paul at one of our gatherings. "You climbed the tree outside our kitchen window where I was busy helping Mother with the dishes. You had placed a rug across two tree branches, about two feet apart. Just as you started to sit right in the middle of it, Mother spotted you. She threw down her dishrag, and ran outside, yelling, 'you stay right there, young man!' She coaxed you down from the tree."

'This is my house!' you objected. When she finally got you down, she stung your legs with a little peach branch in frustration. But, you wouldn't cry. Instead, you looked up at her and grinned, 'I climbed up!' Remember, she laughed, and couldn't spank you any more."

Everyone grinned at Paul as I told the story, and he chuckled. But moodiness prevailed. When we were alone, he hardly spoke at all; he only went through routines.

One day a letter came from a friend in Wyoming, adding to his restlessness. He paced the floor all evening in a dark and pensive mood, occasionally glancing my way, as I avoided his disposition.

"He has a job for me. Wants me to come right away," Paul mumbled. He rambled about the house, in and out the door, checking on the chickens a dozen times while he looked at the weather, setting and re-setting the clock for midnight.

Finally he blurted out, "Sis, I'm tired of this."

I stopped my needlework, and dropped it in my lap. "I'm tired too, Paul," I hedged. "Maybe in the spring, things will get better. We'll be more used to our schedule by then." I went to the kitchen, and put on a fresh pot of coffee for him to drink during the night, then got ready for bed, to avoid any more discussion.

As I clicked off the light in the bathroom, and started for my room, a quiet, but determined voice said from the living room couch, "Hannah, I'm taking that job in Wyoming."

Though arguments rose in my mind, I knew they wouldn't change his. Disappointment welled up in me. We had only been chicken farming for a few months. It was too soon to give up! I felt so despondent because we were quitting, that we had failed, and the wanderlust had won.

"All right, Paul," I sighed.

Next morning, he gave notice to the owners of the rented house, and sold the chickens to another rancher. When he called the Allens about my moving back in with them, they suppressed their surprise, but graciously agreed.

"Hannah will be a good influence on Charlotte," Mrs. Allen laughed. "She's so boy crazy."

Paul threw his jeans in a bag while I rounded up his shirts and got them ironed. While he prepared his beaten up car for the trip, it occurred to me that he needed money. "Here, take this," I said, offering him half my salary check. "I'll get paid again in a few days."

"Don't worry, Sis," he protested, ducking under the hood of his car. "I'll be fine." Distant and anxious to leave, he at last seemed satisfied that the old car would get him to Wyoming, and slammed down the hood. I watched him leave as he squinted through the spider-web effect of the damaged windshield. At the last glimpse of him, as he rattled down the road that wound north to Wyoming, I suddenly felt deserted and alone. I wondered if I would ever see him again. No more ties with family. *The wandering calf is in your hands, Father, I prayed.* When he was out of sight, I slowly went back inside to wait for the Allens to pick me up.

Within a few hours, they came for me and let me cry all the way to their house without asking me questions. Immediately, frail Mrs. Allen began treating me like a daughter as they all welcomed me to their home. Charlotte allowed me to counsel her about changing her wild ways as she made me her confidante, and the younger children, including the baby, soon came to me for praise or comfort.

Even Mr. Allen confided his concern about his wife's upcoming surgery and the expense involved.

Newsy notes to Paul were returned unopened. 'Not at this address' the postman wrote on the envelopes. Mom and Dad sent me comforting letters trying to help me adjust. "Keep trying to locate Paul. He's showing his independence now after one little spell of dependency on you. You did right in helping him. He will remember that." They also encouraged me to continue with my new job and friends. Like a pat on the back, they sought to renew my self-confidence and calm my defeat.

Was it all in vain, my attempt to help my brother? Defeat accused me in the early morning hours. *You didn't protect him from the consuming wanderlust. It's entirely your fault.* While guilt hung over me like a heavy cloud, I tried to reason that I wasn't completely responsible for Paul. *After all, he's an adult now. It's up to him what he does with his life. But maybe our parents are right. Perhaps he will remember how I tried to help him, and he'll come home some day, like the prodigal son in the Bible. Then, we'll all welcome him.*

Gradually I put the situation out of my mind, and continued my own life. I was certain I *had* done the right thing in behalf of our family, and in spite of the failure, I was glad I had tried.

* * * * *

Spring came to Denver. Flora, Charlotte and other friends went with me on several trips to the mountains, where dormant wildflowers pushed through snowdrifts above the timberline in patches of brilliant color. Views of magnificent peaks rising in silent, breathtaking grandeur reduced any beauty of the Ozarks I remembered in Missouri.

When several of us went trout fishing in one of the streams, one of the fellows laughingly watched me battle a large, thrashing fish. "Here," he offered, wading into the water, "I'll help you pull him in." Dressed and filleted, it made a delicious meal when cooked over the campfire. I felt great contentment with a good job and nice friends; what more could I want? As happy faces smiled at me across the open fire, I wondered why I had fumed about having a full and happy life in Colorado.

Work continued at a steady pace and the hours flew in the pleasant atmosphere. Usually I left work at five, either to go straight home or out to dinner with friends from work. However, early one afternoon an uneasy feeling came over me. While I frequently glanced at the clock, time seemed to be standing still. I glanced at people working around me, and they either nodded or smiled when they caught my glance. Unable to figure it out, I shook my head and went back to work, anxiously watching the clock for quitting time.

Promptly at five I hurriedly gathered my things. A friend from another office stopped by my desk. "What's your rush, Hannah? Several of us thought about taking in a movie."

"Can't tonight, Irene. I have to get home." Without explanation, I headed for the door and left her standing with a puzzled expression on her face. I waited with the crowd at the corner, craning my neck for the streetcar, all the while looking at my watch, thinking the streetcar was late, but it arrived on time. I entered with a sick feeling in my stomach. The operator kept up his usual friendly chatter all the way, but I hardly responded. I only wanted to get home.

"See you tomorrow," he waved, as I stepped from the trolley onto rain-washed streets. I forced a smile although I didn't feel like it. I wasn't particularly tired, but inside something had gone wrong. A feeling of despair saturated my thoughts, like something was coming to take away my happiness. *Could it be bad news about Paul?*

The dread increased when I walked in the Allen home, and saw the telegram they handed me with anxious faces. "It's for you, Hannah."

I reluctantly took it and opened its brutal message with shaking hands. It said, FATHER KILLED TODAY IN ACCIDENT. PLEASE COME HOME AT ONCE.

"Father? Whose Father?" I said, and read it again. "Not my Father! No!" I cried, clasping my chest. I sank in a chair, and put my head in my hands.

I had pictured Mom and Dad growing old together. Years from now, they would live in a pretty white frame house, with flowers around the porch. Cared for by us children, they would sit in rockers and watch their flowers grow. Dad would keep honeybees, and putter in his garden out back. In disbelief, I stared at the paper again. Then, the image of my parents and their little house blurred and disappeared with my tears.

The Allens helped as I hastily collected my belongings for the trip home. I choked up again when I called the office supervisor. "I'm so sorry," she murmured. "I'll miss you." I knew after talking with her that I couldn't face my friends. "Will you tell them for me after I'm gone?" I asked.

As much as I dreaded saying goodbye to friends, leaving the Allens hurt more. They had become my second family. *But my own family needs me now.* When they saw me off at the train station I made a mental picture of each family member – from tall, lanky Mr. Allen down to the toddler.

The train pulled out and I made preparations for the long night ahead, but I couldn't sleep a wink. All night as I either stared out the window or tried to doze, I kept seeing the telegram, envisioning Mother's face when she asked a neighbor to send it. Everything seemed so unreal. Train rides were for happy occasions, like going to visit relatives, or to a new job, not going home to death. As the cars passed over the tracks, the rails replied mockingly: *"Father Killed. Come Home. Father Killed. Come Home."*

Next morning as the rising sun permeated the darkness, I noticed hawks high overhead, soaring gracefully in their search for prey. Their wings cast shadows on the ground as they hung on the air currents. While I watched a Bible verse came to mind. *"And in the shadow of Thy wings I will take refuge until destruction passes by."* Again, I valued the presence of my Heavenly Father. Death had come to my family, and although I grieved; in my sorrow God was with me. This realization comforted me while I cried and the train click-clacked on towards Missouri.

CHAPTER 9

Our House Will Stand

*I*t became the second death in a year for our family. My brothers adored a sister, who was born to my parents after I had left home. One afternoon, a gypsy woman carrying a sick child had come to our farmhouse asking for milk. Before Mother could stop her, our two-year-old, Mary Evalyn, went out to look. She contracted diphtheria from the baby and died a few days later. I went home for her funeral to find a family barren and despondent, and I also felt the loss of a sister whom I could have known and loved so much.

Once again, I was anxious to be with Mother and console her. The trip seemed endless while the train puffed across miles of mountains and open spaces, stopping at desolate towns in between. I could not fathom how Mother could endure the overwhelming grief of losing Dad so soon after her daughter. Recently, the family had moved from Norwood to Neosho, Missouri, to live near aging Grandma Moody. After school, the boys harvested grapes and strawberries on the fertile fruit farm she owned near the mining town of Joplin. Dad had found work as a carpenter, one of several trades he knew.

"I waited for Martin to come for lunch," Mother explained, as we embraced and cried. "When he didn't come home, I became anxious. It wasn't like him to be late. Finally, a workman came to tell me about the accident. He had fallen twenty feet off some scaffolding onto the concrete, and died instantly."

My Father was only forty-seven when he died. Standing by the coffin, I saw for the first time his youthfulness with dark, wavy hair. Those strong, rough hands that had held a plough for most of his life, had also written me expressive letters; supple enough to master type setting for his print shop, they were also skilled at carpentry. Now, those busy hands, which had constantly provided for his family, lay still.

Although Dad had taught us early on to work hard for what we wanted, jobs didn't sprout like blackjack oats, and I wondered how we would manage financially without him. I looked at my own hands, those of a twenty-three year old girl, who only knew how to keep books. As the oldest child, I suddenly felt a heavier weight of responsibility than I had experienced till now.

After the funeral, Mother gathered us around her. "We need to stay together as a family," she said. "Although our circle isn't complete without Paul, I don't want you children to go off and live with relatives.

Marcus agreed. "I graduate from high school in a few weeks, and then I can work full time."

"And I know what work is," boasted sixteen-year old Russell.

James, almost ten, piped in. "I can work, too!"

Mother patted James reassuringly. "Now, don't get so caught up with work that you forget I have always wanted you boys to get a college education. It's important. We can *all* work hard. I know Hannah will help." Taking a deep breath she added, "With God's help, I *know* we can do it."

For the next few months I helped with insurance papers, death certificates, and the disposal of my Father's things. As we grouped together, it became a special time for us as we re-lived the past and its memories. We could almost feel Dad's presence.

Mother's strength surprised us all when she decided to remain independent of other people, and keep her family together. Her key to courage lay in the simple statement 'With God's help'. As a Christian family, we had been taught to read our Bibles, and have faith in God. Now, Mother reached down past the pain of her new widowhood, and found real strength when she decided to put her faith to the test.

So many times, I had read the challenge of Jesus' words, "If you build your house on the rock, when the storms burst against it and the winds howl and rage, your house will not crumble, it will stand." All their lives my parents had built their lives on the bedrock of faith in the Lord, and now that the storm had come to test us, we felt assured that the Mitchell house would stand. I had misjudged Mother. Instead of collapsing under grief, she decided to continue living, and give encouragement to her children.

Yes, the Mitchell house would stand, with its faith in God.

Chapter 10

From Roots to Life's Realities

Although we enjoyed reminiscing about out family, we lacked the resources or time to linger long over our Father's death. He had left a small insurance policy, so with it and what we all scraped together, we set about re-organizing our lives. I kept a few books for people on a short-term basis. The boys divided their time between studying and jobs after school, with Marcus saving everything he could for college.

Before Dad's death, he and Mother had bought a little place in Schell City, Missouri, and had planned to move there. Grandma Moody's neighbors had agreed to watch after her, so we moved from the rented house in Neosho, in an effort to cut down on expenses. We left as soon as Marcus graduated from high school, and I spent most of the summer helping Mother settle us in.

I knew Marcus missed having Dad at his graduation, but my heart really went out to James. As the youngest, he had enjoyed a special position in the family, especially with Dad.

Hopefully, he would retain memories of their times together.

James and I also shared a rapport often evident between the youngest and oldest in a family. Thirteen years older, I had held him on my hip when he was an infant, and sang to him while I washed the dishes. For years I had been the big sister away from home, writing often and exchanging little gifts in the mail. Now we sometimes played in the floor, or read a book together. I prayed for a way to help him in his grief.

We felt the terrible void most in the evenings when we all gathered in the living room. After a few games of checkers, James and I set the board aside, and sat together against the wall with our feet stretched out, his reaching my knees. "I want to talk with you about something," I ventured. James looked up. "Remember how we've been taught that God plans our lives and knows all about us?"

"Yep," he said, watching our feet.

"Well, I believe that God knew about us before time began. It says in the Bible that He designed and shaped us in our mother's womb, and that He envelops us before we are born. He decided you would have brown hair, and your eyes would look like the Mitchells. What do you think?"

"And my mouth like Grandma Moody's, and my body would have to catch up with my big feet?"

"Yes," I laughed. "God planned all that. In the Psalms, it says that you are fearfully and wonderfully made. Long ago, the all-knowing God knew the kind of home you needed to influence your life, to shape you in His image. It says that your days are numbered that you are to live."

"Oh." A sad look came over his face. We sat in silence until I spoke again.

"See," I continued in a shaky voice, "none of us knows how long we'll live, so we should make a practice to live pleasing to God. He gives us His protection, but when death from sickness, or an accident takes away someone we love, we need to accept that. If we allow Him, He will gather us under His wing, and help us through that time." I put my arm around my little brother. "You see, we don't know the whole picture, like God does." We watched our feet move back and forth in a little game of rhythm before I went on.

"You don't realize it, but one day your legs will be longer than mine, and I'll be looking up at you. We can't see one bit ahead to the future, but God can. He wants to guide our lives, just like He guided the formation of our bodies, but we must yield to His wisdom and leadership. Do you understand any of this?"

"I...think so," James said, a new look in his eyes. "But will God help me with all that?"

"He sure will. He'll help you, always." We hugged each other and he gave me a special squeeze. "Why don't you get on to bed? It's getting late." I prayed for James' comfort as I pulled myself off the floor.

About that time, Marcus came through the front door, spry after a long day at work, waving a letter. "I just learned where I'm going to college!"

We all talked at once. "You mean, this fall?"

"Yes! This is from John Brown University!"

"How is that possible?"

"I'm going on a work/study program. They offer financial help to students like me who need it. School starts next month."

He looked at me abruptly with a fresh idea. "Say, Sis. Why don't you come, too?"

My mouth dropped open. "What do you mean? How could I possibly come with you?" Marcus knew that college was one of my desires, because I had wistfully mentioned it in the past. Even though bookkeeping paid well, chasing inanimate figures and working mathematical equations all the time had begun to bore me. I wanted a job working with people.

Marcus pursued it. "Mom! Don't you think Hannah should come with me? This is as good a time as any!"

Mother studied my reaction. "Well, if you really are serious about it, check with the University," she commented, and continued mending a shirt.

I didn't dare get my hopes up. "I suppose you both know that we're in the middle of a Depression. And there probably aren't any more education funds," I said. But Marcus had just fanned the flame of a long-standing dream, so at his insistence I wrote the college, all the while fretting about the lack of money while I waited to hear from them.

A week later they wrote me back! They offered me the position of dorm matron, since I was older than the other girls. I could supervise our living quarters, and sandwich classes in between.

"What do you think?" I asked, chewing my lip.

Mother thought for a minute. "Oh, go ahead. I think we can swing it."

"Remember, we're all in this together," my brothers said, with an affectionate pat on the back.

I was elated. The truth of my conversation with James took on a new personal meaning, as I realized once again that we *don't know* all that God has in His plan for our lives. We had emphasized the importance of my brothers' educations, but I thought college would never become a reality for me.

Financially it still looked remote, but we would just have to trust our Heavenly Father to provide the means. So, it was with deep gratitude that I made preparations to enter the first of many educational doors that would continue opening throughout my life.

Hannah's Journal, May 1990

My thoughts about God opening a door for education are interrupted, as I hear the rain beat against my door on the side porch of my little house. A spring rain is driving dogwood blossoms from the trees. Unable to venture outside, I have watched a bird huddle over her young in the azaleas along the fence, her eyes closed and feathers ruffled, determined to protect her nest. It saddens me, for I can still see my young brother James, gazing into my face so trustingly, while I comforted him about our Father's death. With my arms around him, I wanted to protect him from life's dangers.

As the youngest, I thought he would have outlived all the siblings, but he has been dead for several years, from a malignant brain tumor. He is buried in one of the three plots in Louisiana, that he had purchased for himself, his wife Nancy, and me.

A couple of years ago my doctor had told me that time was approaching for me to move near family. I assured him that my friends at church looked in on me often, but he removed his glasses and sat down.

He firmly said, "Hannah, friends are fine to have. However, there comes a time when family is needed. You should think seriously about your safety, and future care."

Looking back at that conversation, it occurs to me that he had made a keen observance. I now use a cane, and I watch my step when I walk, but my doctor had also commented about my unsteady hand, and hesitance in speech.

Tomorrow I will write my sister-in-law, Nancy, in Opelousas, to see how much time she needs to get my room ready. It was James' plan for me to come and live with them in my later years. How I would have enjoyed his company. But now, it will be just us women. And it would have been more pleasant for Nancy had I made this decision earlier. As it is, it will be an old, worn-out woman coming through her door. I sighed. My, but facing facts about ageing comes hard.

Heavenly Father, I prayed. Once again I don't know your plan for my life. I don't wish to burden anyone with having to care for me. Could you not just take me in my sleep?

While the wind blew against the door of my little cottage, and it remained intact, I thought of the many doors that had opened and closed during my lifetime....

1930-1938

CHAPTER 11

A Burning in John Brown's Breast

"Let me tell you about the Department Heads," said a student who met our bus at the college. "To get a quarter, go to Mr. Smith, to see about a fine, go to Mr. Shaptain, for final permission on something, ask Mr. Hodges, but when your heart is burdened, go to Brother Brown."

John Brown's dream to educate young people in a Christian manner had appeared foolish to many people when he spoke about funds for the college, but he had scraped, slaved and prayed it into reality. In 1919, he founded the high school and college at Siloam Springs, Arkansas, with an enrollment of sixty students. The private grade school named in honor of his wife, Julia A. Brown, was located at nearby Sulphur Springs.

Everywhere on campus, pretty girls strolled in attractive blue gingham dresses, with white peter pan collars, and boys in blue shirts and overalls. "We have six hundred students now," boasted one of the welcoming parties, "and the staff has increased from a dozen to almost forty. Not bad for a school just over ten years old, is it?"

The vine-covered dormitory for girls, constructed with money sent from patrons in California, lay on old Spanish lines. Students had made the furniture in the carpentry shop from native Arkansas walnut, wild cherry, apple, cedar, oak and pine.

The school supported itself amazingly well. Students harvested food in acres of fields surrounding the campus, and brought it to the Alumni Building, which housed the cannery with the heating plant in the basement. The second and third floors contained a bakery, laundry, pressing shop and dress factory, where they measured us for new uniforms. Machines in the print shop and publishing office noisily issued copies of Brother Brown's books, the monthly school paper, and articles from off-campus customers. Table after table of typewriters lined the extension office. The white house, which had originally housed dormitories, now contained classrooms, the dining room, and kitchen. Two quaint houses: the log cabin, and band house, produced musicals.

"We're rarely allowed to visit these departments," stated the girls, showing us the mechanics, electrical, and plumbing, furniture and construction sites. "The men's dormitory is off-limits, too," they teased, shaking a finger.

We went to chapel each day the first week; thereafter, it met once a week. All students worked four hours a day, half of us attending morning classes and working afternoons, the other half working mornings and going to class in the afternoon. We all attended study hall at night.

I saw Marcus again one day after the first week. "I'm getting up early to milk the prize Jersey herd," he said wryly.

"And I thought we'd left milking far behind!"

"It's not so bad," he grinned. "The old leaky barn is being replaced with a new one. Besides, we get special meals because of our irregular hours."

"As dorm matron I have a feeling my schedule will be unpredictable, too," I said. "Many girls come up with one problem after another, from misplaced books, to lost money. Some of them have never been responsible for themselves before."

In the months that followed, I met a group of young preachers, teachers and singers that went out each Sunday morning to hold services in the community. I joined the band of missionaries and lay church members, meeting many precious Christian men and women. One dynamic and dedicated young man in particular caught my attention. His name was Joe Jennings.

Joe and I developed an instant friendship. On Sunday nights, students gathered in our dorm lobby. It fell part of my job as dorm matron to chaperone, and Joe became my usual date for the evening. When the freshman class hosted Thanksgiving dinner, he and I worked together on decorations, so our friendship attracted attention and teasing from the younger students. Written across the corner of my menu a note read *November 27, 1930 'Those were happy days – everything was so rosy – when sitting by him so cozy'. Signed, your best pest, Eliza Jane.*

Part of my job also included attending staff meetings relating to discipline problems of both sexes. At one meeting, the night watchman shared a perplexing situation.

"Every night at eleven o'clock, I make rounds through the boys' dorm to make sure everyone is inside. When walking down the hall one night I noticed a light shining from underneath the shower door. I checked it out, and found a student sitting in one of the shower stalls, working with pencil and paper. I sent him to bed, but in a few nights I caught him again, working away."

"Who is this boy?" asked Brother Brown.

"Joe Chicol. You know, the one from Central America."

"I'll send someone to talk with him," Brother Brown said, noticing our grins, as we visualized a student hunkered down in the showers with his books. "He shouldn't have to do homework in there."

Next day a staff member approached Joe about it. Embarrassed, he looked at the ground. "I wasn't doing homework."

"Well, explain yourself! You know curfew is strictly enforced!"

Joe said, "As you know, I come from an Indian tribe in Central America, and I'm here mainly because of the missionaries who work among my people."

"What does that have to do with breaking curfew?"

Joe continued, "When the missionaries come, they bring Bibles written in English. Although they taught me to speak and read it, no one else in my tribe can. I was just trying to translate the New Testament into my tribal language."

This story made a deep impression on me and many other students, in particular, Cameron Townsend. He and his brother worked in the campus print shop, rolling out book after book for people already flooded with the written Word. It reinforced their theory that missionaries needed to learn spoken tribal languages, so he and his brother started a school of linguistics.

Little did Brother Brown realize how God would bless the dream that burned within his breast. John Brown University, foolishness to some, proved hope for many. Here, Christian concern crystallized, not only for the lost people of a local community, but also for savages too hostile to care.

Cameron Townsend, printer, later founded the Wycliffe Bible Translators and undertook the mammoth job of producing literature in the languages of naked headhunters, who would injure and kill some of the people who brought it to them. Today, Wycliffe translators fly their missionaries into these remote areas.

John Brown's prayers would still be answered far into the future, his dream coming true, as his Christian beliefs reached out in far-widening circles.

Chapter 12

A Homecoming and
a Home Going

About halfway through our second year at college, one of the girls came upstairs, and told me Marcus was waiting for me in the dorm lobby. I didn't think much about it, because he came over frequently. By the time I got downstairs though, he was fidgeting nervously.

"What's up?" I asked.

"I got a letter from Mother today. Paul's home," he blurted out.

An angry flush crept up my neck. *So, the prodigal returns just as abruptly as he left. He wanders from looking after no one but himself, while we buried Dad, moved Mother, and struggled to meet everybody's needs, without a word from him.*

"Where's he been?" I asked sharply.

"In the Army. Here. You read it."

Mother's letter glowed with tidbits of army stories, and joy that her wandering boy had come home at last. It hinted at no accusations about his devil-may-care past, just an open-armed welcome.

How long will he stay this time? I wondered bitterly. I suddenly felt akin to the older brother in the parable about the prodigal son in the Bible. All this time, I had done the right things for the family, and shouldered Paul's responsibility, now this will-o-the-wisp receives a royal welcome! How I sympathized with the eldest son's feelings in the story.

Mother's letter bubbled over with plans for a family reunion. She wanted to cook all our favorite dishes. Such joy exuded from those pages that I hadn't read in ages. After all the heartache he had caused her, how could she forgive and forget so quickly? While I fumed, a timeworn voice echoed in my mind. *She rejoices because she has regained that which she lost. At one time, you prayed for your brother's safe return. Or have you forgotten?*

But, so much has happened since then, I retorted. So much pain and grief! I've been so faithful to my family. I tearfully looked at Marcus, and handed him back the letter while I agonized over a reply. But the Lord continued reprimanding me. *The older brother also did the right thing by his family. And, did he have the right attitude when the prodigal returned? Do you? If you were the errant one, would you want a similar welcome? How many times have I forgiven you, for wandering from Me?*

I walked over to a window and looked out, my chin trembling, while Marcus waited patiently. The Lord continued dealing with me. *The story of the prodigal son is a perfect picture of My love and forgiveness, but if you refuse to forgive your brother, I won't forgive you.* I took a deep, laborious breath.

Well, I did pray for him to come home. But it's so hard after all we've been through.

That's what forgiveness is all about, child.

Looking back and forth to Marcus, I tried to let it all go. Finally, I prayed. *Thank you for answering my prayers about Paul.* Then with a heavy sigh I continued, *forgive me, and help me show love to my brother.*

By the time I turned to face Marcus, the turmoil in my heart was fading, and I saw relief in his eyes.

"Well, let's go help them kill the fatted calf," I said.

Marcus and I went home a few weekends later to find Paul looking mature and content, and even happy. He kept mysteriously slipping out the back door. "What's he up to?" I asked Mother. She looked like the cat that had eaten the canary.

"He's met Lucille Hardie, our neighbor," she said with a twinkle. "It looks like a real romance. They go out quite a bit."

"With what? Does he even have a job?"

"He learned to cut hair while he was in the army. He's about to open a little barber shop."

So, it looked as if his wandering days were over. Mother was right on target. After a brief courtship, Paul and Lucille married; he settled down to a profitable barber business, and became a good husband. The longer he stayed put, the better I felt about him.

I studied hard at school, staying up late at night like the other students, but I refused to study on Sundays, my literal day of rest. And, I believe the Lord blessed me for it, because I mentally outlasted those who studied constantly, and made better grades than them. Due to my good marks, the administration asked me to also teach for two summers at the grade school in Sulphur Springs. I enjoyed the children, and the extra money helped with my tuition.

* * * * *

With special interest, the student body watched a house being built across the road from the college. It was the home of our favorite newlyweds. Helen Brown, daughter of the College founder had married Dick Hodges, the head bookkeeper, and auditor of the school.

One evening, Joe Jennings and I walked across the road, and inspected the cottage. He glanced my way while he rubbed one of the timbers, and said nonchalantly, "Wouldn't it be nice to own a nest like this someday?" My heart skipped when he said it, because I realized his serious nature wouldn't allow him to make such a remark carelessly. "Yes, it would!" I replied warmly. He said nothing more at the time, but I felt a glowing happiness, thinking of where our relationship could lead. Joe's spiritual strength and dedication had made it easy for me to fall in love with him.

After the house was finished, Dick and Helen moved in, and turned it into a real home. But their happiness was short-lived, because Helen mysteriously fell ill, and died within days. Her death numbed the student body and the staff so that they cancelled all classes.

Brother Brown was in California, conducting a revival when she died. Before rushing home, he wired the family relaying his wish for no outward signs of mourning to be evident, no wearing of black garments indicative of death. He had often reminded us, that death is only the door through which we must all pass, into real life. At his daughter's funeral, he wanted us to honor the Lord by celebrating the memory of her life. Mrs. Brown was in agreement, so it was in this spirit that the student body made its plans.

A lovely morning unfolded the day of Helen's funeral. The Ozark hills, filled with dogwoods, and red bud trees, were bursting with bud and bloom. The apple orchard stood like a bank of snow with its solid coat of white fragrant blossoms against the new spring grass.

The students assembled in two columns in front of the girls' dorm. Dressed in fresh blue gingham uniforms, the girls held in their arms a sheaf or wreath of spring flowers. I led one group, and the Dean of Women led the other. The young men walked similarly behind, wearing fresh blue shirts, and clean pressed overalls. We proceeded to the chapel, singing hymns as we went.

"What a friend we have in Jesus" filled the apple orchard. Our voices blended in harmony with "It is well, it is well with my soul," "Amazing grace, how sweet the sound," and "A might fortress is our God." As our songs of praise ascended, the angels must have rejoiced at Helen's welcome to Heaven and our praise to God. What a glorious way to be honored as alive in Heaven.

When Brother Brown had wondered from the onset of the young college just who would be the first to die, he had no indication that it would be his own daughter. She was first from his family, first from the student body, first department head from the dress shop, and first from the faculty, where she taught sewing and fashion design.

As our forerunner, her death showed us that neither youth nor position are immune to its awful clutch, but her funeral taught us the Christian way to respond when a loved one goes home to eternity, and the open arms of the Heavenly Father. Here, *temporarily* my family celebrated the homecoming of my brother, but the family in Heaven had gained a new member, as Helen went to her *permanent* home, and the presence of the Lord Jesus Christ.

CHAPTER 13

The Ambulance Ride

I hurried on my way between classes, back to duties as Dorm Matron. Inside the dorm students dashed upstairs, or loitered in the hallway; those due in classes scurried out the door, yelling and teasing. I continued absent-mindedly to the second floor, when a girl in her nightgown pushed past me on the landing and stumbled down the stairs. It jolted me back to reality.

"Where's Louise Clarke going in her night gown?" I shouted to the girls.

"Home!" yelled someone from the railing. "That's all she'll say!"

Louise's roommate appeared at the top of the stairs. "Going home is all she'll say! She's talking out of her head, Mother Hannah!" It still irked me that these girls, only a few years younger than me, insisted on calling me Mother. But I reacted quickly.

I dropped my stack of books and ran after Louise, catching up with her just before she opened the front door to a blast of cold air. When I placed an arm around her quivering shoulders, I drew back at the touch of hot skin that smelled sweaty and feverish.

"Louise! Where's your coat?" I asked while I held her, and shielded her from the door.

"I don't know!" she snapped, with frantic, unfocused eyes blazing in a flushed face.

"Come on," I coaxed gently with an arm around her. "I'll help you find it." I led her back up to her room and sat her on the bed, where she lay down momentarily, shaking.

"Please! I want to go home," she pleaded through chattering teeth.

While I covered her and held her down, I called to a girl going past in the hall. "Lisa! Get Miss Patterson!" One look through the half-open doorway at her friend thrashing frantically sent Lisa racing to the Dean of Women. While we waited, I stroked her arms and back to calm her, but she suddenly flung me backwards with amazing strength, and threw off the covers.

"I'm going home!" she shrieked. "You can't keep me!" With all my strength, I fought her back to bed, speaking quietly and patting her.

Miss Patterson soon appeared in the room. "She's delirious!" she gasped, and ran to the telephone to call the doctor from Siloam Springs, a few miles away. My back ached during the eternity it took for him to arrive, while I restrained Louise in the low bed, and counted her rapid pulse. In her quieter moments I took her temperature rectally.

Finally, he entered the room, his short rotund figure half kneeling, to examine his patient. "Tell me about her illness."

"She's been sick for several days with a head cold, but she had improved. A little while ago, she went wild, and started screaming about going home," I said, observing the doctor while he made the examination. I added, "Her left ear seems to bother her. The area behind it is terribly red."

"Uh, huh. What's her fever?"

"104."

"Here's a pill to lower her temperature," the doctor said, straightening with a groan. He glanced at me. "Are you a nurse?" I shook my head, keeping an eye on our patient.

"Well, you ought to be," he remarked, slapping me on the back. At the door he said, "Your friend has a mastoid infection, and I'm sending her to the hospital at Ft. Smith by ambulance. A nurse will accompany her, but she also needs a friend. I would appreciate it if you went along."

The ambulance created some excitement when it backed up to the dorm steps, drawing a crowd. Joe and Marcus ran up while the attendants loaded Louise, and I briefly explained the emergency. "That's a two hundred mile trip, Hannah," Joe protested, squeezing my hand.

I reluctantly pulled away, acknowledging his concern for me. "Just pray, Joe. We need to reach the hospital, and start medication before the infection reaches her brain."

"I will!" he called, as I climbed in the tiny space reserved for me.

We pulled away from the crowd, and sped along a clear road until we entered the Ozark Mountains, where heavy patches of snow and ice lurked in the shady spots. The continuously curving, and winding, bumpy roads forced painful moans from Louise, and she attempted to sit up until the nurse finally restrained her with straps. While the nurse moved about I noticed a slowed unsteadiness, as she frequently swallowed gulps of air, and within thirty minutes she looked as green as the interior of the ambulance.

"Here, Miss Mitchell," she managed, clutching her stomach. "You sit by Louise. I don't feel well." I moved over and she collapsed in the seat I had occupied. *A carsick nurse? This will be a long trip.*

We crisscrossed in and out of mountains, plummeting down valleys, and up hills abruptly. The nurse lurched and groaned, hugging her stomach, that came up each time we went down. For Louise, the change in air pressure sent excruciating pains to her ears, for she groaned, and rolled her head from side to side. The pill we had given her earlier had little effect.

"It's all right," I purred constantly. "I'll hold your head against the turns." She only moaned, oblivious to any conversation.

After hours of my trying to make both patients comfortable, the drivers at last stopped for gas. I crawled out and stretched with relief. The men came to the rear of the ambulance, munching sandwiches. As they handed me one, they grinned, "Guess you're the only one back here able to eat."

Winking, one leaned inside the ambulance. "Who's the nurse back here?"

From her seat, the reeling nurse clutched an emesis basis, and mumbled, "I'll admit, Miss Mitchell is a better one than I am today."

"Hey, that's an idea!" agreed the attendant, turning to me. "Why *don't* you become a nurse? You'd be a crackerjack!"

I grinned.

We resumed the grueling ride to Ft. Smith, and finally pulled into the hospital grounds as a cold sun dipped behind the landscape. After admitting Louise to the hospital, I walked down the street, and found an overnight room in a tourist home. Stretching tired, cramped muscles, I deeply inhaled the crisp air, invigorating after the sickening ambulance smell.

After finding a room I trudged back to the hospital, and opened the door on a sleeping Louise. Her blond hair was laid in soft curls on her pillow, apparent that it had been brushed, and she wore a fresh, hospital gown. Even with restraints on her wrists, and side rails on the bed, she looked like a little girl asleep in a crib.

A soft voice came from behind me. "I'm the head nurse," it said. "Dr. Stephens saw Miss Clarke, and gave some orders."

"She looks better already, and peaceful," I noted, as we walked down the hall.

"Are you a nurse?" she asked. When I replied, no, she smiled. "Oh, sort of thought you were. I hear you took good care of both your patients on the way here."

I walked back to the motor court in dusky darkness. *What will they do for Louise during the night?* Other than making her as comfortable as possible, I didn't do much, didn't know how. I reflected on their comments, how the doctor from Siloam Spring emphatically told me I should be a nurse. The sick nurse in the ambulance thought I filled the spot well. The ambulance attendants had even kidded me about it. And the hospital nurse thought I really *was* one. To top it off, I had enjoyed taking care of both Louise and the sick woman. I felt a satisfaction that we had successfully gotten them both to the hospital.

Ridiculous! I'll soon receive a teaching degree. My summers teaching at the private school in Siloam Springs, and my job with the girls at college had strengthened my goal of working with people. Both the children and the college girls sought my advice. A knock on my door often preceded a homesick girl, or I usually knew by the way they floated down the hall, if they carried happy news about grades, or a boyfriend. I reflected on how they approached me with many situations, sometimes to pray. I shrugged off this new idea, and decided to discuss it with Joe back at school, since our relationship was becoming personal.

Next morning, I found a much-improved Louise, sitting up and eating her breakfast, with restraints and side rails gone. Her response to the medicine pleased her doctor, and her notified parents were on their way.

"Thanks for taking good care of me, nurse," she smiled. "I must have been a rotten patient. But I'm glad you caught me before I paraded through the campus in my night gown!"

With the crisis over, I caught a bus back to school. Sleeping most of the way, I often woke with a start, each time thinking someone needed medical attention. Then, I realized the carsick nurse, and delirious Louise were on the mend. Yet, I still felt the urge to care for sick people. *But, why? Why at this late date in my education, at age twenty-six, would I consider changing vocations? To win esteem and admiration? Or is it a deeper calling? Is the Heavenly Father again trying to direct me?*

When I arrived back at the dorm, I ran up the steps and immediately resumed the role of student, and 'Mother Hannah', where the girls bombarded me with questions about Louise. Happy back in school activities, I again pushed the niggling conflict about studying for a nursing degree into the background.

CHAPTER 14

White Dresses

Will you marry me?" Joe said, holding my hand as we walked around campus. I looked at him, wondering if those magic words had really come from his lips - so many times I had imagined it. "Hannah. I just asked you to marry me." He was smiling.

Dogwood blossoms suddenly blazed white in the full moon. Over Joe's shoulder, I noticed the little white chapel across the way. It wasn't just a simple architecture, I realized; with its steeple pointed in exclamation, it was a shout of joy.

"Oh, yes! Yes," I breathed into his shoulder. We were soon to graduate that spring of 1934. I glowed with happiness while we talked of our future. Together. Married.

"We'll have to wait until after I graduate from Seminary, since my parents have the arrangements made," I heard Joe say. "But after that, we can go together as missionaries to India." He had often told me of his desire to go as a missionary.

Then, I remembered the growing conviction I had tried to ignore. "I haven't mentioned something to you," I said, coming down from my cloud. "That ambulance ride to Ft. Smith did something to me. Since then, an urge to care for sick people has grown, and won't go away. I think I want to become a nurse." To his surprised look, I continued. "I realize it requires additional schooling and hard work, but I feel more strongly about it every day."

I still remember his reaction. "Hey! I'm getting the picture, too. You'll get your nursing degree while I'm at seminary. That will be a tremendous help in India, with the high birth rate. Think of the medical needs they have."

"Only thing. It will be a long engagement, Joe. But it will be worth it. Afterwards, we can work together, for the rest of our lives." The future looked perfect. I had never been so happy.

Mother beamed about my engagement plans, dispelling fears of her only daughter becoming an old maid. She liked my descriptions of Joe, which she had heard often. Too, prospects of her family growing again pleased her, since Paul and Lucille were now parents of a little girl. I told her about my winding ride to Ft. Smith, and comments about my becoming a nurse. I also shared my bewilderment as to what had provoked it.

"You had a few years experience taking care of your brothers," she teased. "But, I suspect you get this desire naturally. Your Great-Grandmother Calhoun took care of sick folks out farther west, when doctors were scarce. People called on her all the time." Mother recounted many stories about Grandma's success at nursing. "She just had a way with sick folks, and you probably will too."

"But can we *afford* for me to get another degree?" I had noticed how all the hard work in helping educate us was taking its toll on her. She looked exhausted.

"Well, write some nursing schools after you finish college," she said, straightening her shoulders. "God, in His Word says that He takes care of widows and the fatherless, and I'm sure He will continue providing for us. We will all just have to help you become a nurse, and keep His promises in mind, for encouragement." I remembered those words of faith. They often cheered me as I finished college, and waited for direction toward selecting a nursing school.

* * * * *

For commencement the girls at John Brown always wore new gingham uniforms, duplicates of their everyday outfits. The boys wore whatever they owned in a suit, or jacket and pants, much better looking than their overalls. But only four weeks before graduation, we learned that the girls were required to wear simple white dresses, to match the boys' more formal attire.

The staff didn't anticipate the pandemonium this change in dress created among some of the girls. Our student body contained a mixture of wealthy girls, with oil money from Oklahoma, and sharecroppers' daughters, who came on scholarships, or small loans. Teary-eyed girls from society's lower ranks soon confronted me.

"Mother Hannah, we can't graduate!" Wringing their hands, they all talked at once. "Our families can't afford to buy white dresses for us. What will we do?"

I felt so sorry for them. Whatever *would* they do? So I said, "Come to my room, girls, and we'll talk about this." While I tried to console them, it suddenly occurred to me to test all our faith.

"Do you believe in a Heavenly Father, who can give you what you need?" I asked abruptly. "I'm not talking about frills, but what you really *need*."

They looked at one another. "Yes, but:.."

"To me, this looks like something He would consider a need. Don't you agree?" They nodded. I gained enthusiasm. "Then, let's pray about it."

"But...we don't have much time!"

At my insistence, we knelt by my bed and prayed; asking God to give us nine white dresses, the exact number of girls kneeling with me. After awhile, they rose from their knees, and began the process of waiting for God to answer.

Nonetheless, in a couple of weeks they drifted back to my room, one at a time, or in pairs. "Mother Hannah, what if our dresses don't come?"

"Well, I have a little white dress that I've worn for two summers," I said confidently. "But if you don't get your dresses, then ten of us will graduate in our uniforms."

"But, that would look horrible!" they said, with panicky expressions. "Everyone else will have on *white!*"

"No, that wouldn't look right," I agreed. I called the girls to prayer again. Once more, we asked for nine white dresses.

One week before the ceremonies, no dresses. We prayed. Many of the wealthy girls had called or written home, when they found out the requirements for commencement, and they soon displayed beautiful, white frocks. Our anxious prayers increased.

While we waited, my own personal prayer had been answered, by acceptance to a nursing school in Kansas City, Missouri.

One day during countdown week, I received a call from the main office. "Miss Mitchell, we have a large box over here, addressed to you. It isn't too heavy. Could you, or some of your students, come for it?"

Could it be? I got word to the girls, and several of us brought the box from across campus, and pushed it upstairs to my room. We waited till all nine had gathered inside before we opened it. First, we read the letter taped to the outside.

"Miss Mitchell, you do not know us, but we have heard of you, as the Dorm Matron at the University. We are a group of women in a Sunday school class in Anaheim, California. Our daughters have gone to many functions this year, requiring white dresses. After praying about it, we decided to send them to the college, since our girls no longer need them. Could you use them?"

We tore open the box. A girl squealed while the rest of us held our breath, for we saw nothing but white showing underneath the tissue papers. Gently, we took out and lined up, not nine, but ten white dresses. In the bottom of the box lay necessary accessories – slips, hose, and even some shoes. Unbelievably, when we tried them on, they fit perfectly, and needed no alterations, even down to the hems!

The story of the dresses, and how God had provided them, exploded across the campus. At commencement, a joyous group of ten girls filed in, dressed like everyone else, because our Heavenly Father, in His marvelous Providence, had moved upon those women in California to send the exact number and sizes. As far as we could determine, no one had requested them.

I looked across the aisle at Joe, and caught his admiring gaze. Blushing, I breathed a happy prayer. *Oh, Father, this is only the beginning of white dresses for me. Soon, I'll be working toward a nursing degree, and a white uniform. I want to learn, but I love Joe so much. Please, let the time pass quickly. Then, I'll wear another white dress, down the aisle of a church, as I go to meet my bridegroom.*

Chapter 15

Student Nurse

With my acceptance to St. Luke's School of Nursing, the first steps toward a degree that would determine my life's work had begun.

The School, Hospital and Nursing Home, lay sprawled luxuriantly in a well-manicured setting of trees, shrubs, and grassy lawns, at the entrance of a beautiful residential area in Kansas City, Missouri. Known as the country club district, it also offered convenient shopping in an attractive nearby mall. When, in 1935, I entered these lovely surroundings, anticipating three years of learning, and work, I had an idealistic view of nursing.

We students immediately became absorbed in learning anatomy, pharmacy, techniques of surgery, and symptoms of disease. We practiced on one another the art of bathing a patient, giving back rubs, and changing a bed with the patient in it. When we finally went to the floor in our new student uniforms, we took care of the less ill patients, and soon grasped the importance of bedside manner.

"Roll over!" commanded a fiery redhead named Pollard, marching up to a bed in a men's ward. As an assignment she needed to give a young man a back rub.

"No, thanks!" he snapped, modestly clutching his sheet. "I don't need one!"

Undaunted, Pollard persisted. Their arguments grew louder, attracting attention from all over the ward. In desperation, she shouted, "Once, and for all. Roll over! I'm getting a grade out of this!"

The helpless patient relented and turned over on his stomach. Pollard jerked open the bedside table drawer, pulled out a can of powder, and lavishly coated the boy's back. She was working him over when he rose up, sniffing.

"That smells funny. What are you putting on me?"

She sniffed the can while he looked on. Together, they read out loud, "Medicated Dental Powder!" The other men, who had been watching the scene, guffawed as she fled the ward with face and hair aflame.

Patients also refused Payne's care, a girl with the I.Q. of an Einstein. She amazed us with her exact textbook recall and outstanding grades on quizzes, but application of this knowledge with patients eluded her. Instead, everyone asked for those of us who couldn't remember the names of bones, nerves, and muscles. Like a gigantic game of jigsaw, we put together the pieces learned in class against needs of hospital patients.

I wondered which part of nursing would most appeal to me. Each service appeared interesting, some more than others while I assessed them all with their practicality of use in India.

"Mitchell, be glad you're in surgery," groaned Milliken, my roommate.

"Why? What's wrong with obstetrics?" I grinned, knowing she despised the long, hard hours of attending women in labor.

Milliken flushed a little. "I almost fainted today when I saw my first birth."

"Aww, don't let it bother you. Someone else collapsed yesterday."

"I already know that obstetrics isn't for me," she said.

After eight weeks in general surgery, I took a short vacation to recuperate from a tonsillectomy, all the while looking forward to obstetrics assignment. However, the nursing superintendent, because of my successful assistance in a brain operation, thought

I possessed a flair for surgery, so she scheduled me for eight weeks in orthopedic surgery.

When at last assigned to the delivery room, I was fascinated with it. Individual reactions to labor surprised me. Some women faced it with radiance, others loudly cursed and blamed their husbands; a few were silent and stoic, and one or two showed interest in their labor and delivery.

I constantly marveled at the miracle of childbirth, and hounded the interns and residents with questions, like how the fetus could rotate and flex, to pass down the birth canal. I noted that many babies did this with ease, but when difficult delivery occurred, what caused the trouble? And how are complications prevented? How can you right a baby when it is turned the wrong way? Some of the doctors explained, while others brushed me off with a shrug. When the obstetricians couldn't, or didn't answer, I dug in the books, marveling all the while at God's perfect creativity in making a mother and baby.

Occasionally, when a patient came in for delivery during late evening hours, the waiting obstetrician slept at the hospital. Even then, many a time an intern caught the baby before the doctor arrived in the delivery room. Watching intently, I tabulated the intern's skill and its effect on mother and child, or what a lack of skill might incur for the two.

Then, *my* turn came when nature decided it was birthday time. Alone with a patient in advanced labor, I buzzed the desk. But it was too late for anyone else to help, for the baby's head appeared. *Oh! Help me. Dear God!* I silently screamed the most panicky prayer I have ever uttered. By the time the doctor came on the scene, a new baby had come into the world. The patient beamed.

"Miss Mitchell! That was the best delivery I ever had. No fuzziness from medicine, no pain from the baby coming. Just one good push!" She patted my hand. "I hope you're my nurse next time!"

I stood there waiting for the doctor's reaction for taking over his patient. *Would he reprimand me? Yet, what else could I have done?* He and the mother laughed together over her quick delivery.

I can still see his expression as he glanced my way. "Yes, I see I'll have to watch Miss Mitchell," he commented, while he examined the newborn. "If I'm not careful, she'll be taking my business away from me."

Ideally, I envisioned caring for mothers and babies, in a country far away from the civilized surroundings in which I now worked and learned. Even then, I thought his words sounded prophetic.

Hannah's Journal, mid-May 1990

It is odd that I am unable to recall recent events, but memories of Joe from long ago, easily surface...

Joe had enrolled as a seminary student in California, while I studied nursing at St. Luke's. One July, when I had three weeks vacation, I boarded a train that sped me toward him, and to meet his parents. He had met me in Lake Tahoe, and we continued by car on scenic highways. Pictures and descriptions of scenery reveal my happiness in being with the love of my life. One of the few pictures I have of him, he is standing beside our car and a Yosemite tree. Tanned, wearing dark trousers, his dark hair blends into the tree trunk. I wrote underneath his picture:

"I ride on mountain tops. I ride.

I have found my life and am satisfied."

On Sunday, July 11, we went to hear Joe's father preach twice during the day. We stopped at a picturesque old mission just as the sun set, and a few tourists were leaving. I felt a blessed feeling of worship, as I stood on the mission's threshold, worn deep by many feet.

While we toured Los Angeles, we got lost on highways several times, but we didn't care. We were a couple in love, together on vacation.

On July 22, Joe remained in California, and I reluctantly boarded the train for St. Luke's. I wrote in my journal: 'I am spent on the way home. The hours drag while the miles flee. Waiters pass food that doesn't appeal. Life seems rather dull.'

I stopped in Colorado to visit with Marcus, Russell, and his wife. Then, back to work and school as student nurse the night of the 27th. Time away from Joe was agonizing, and I longed to hear from him, to talk about our wedding.

But none of it was to be....

CHAPTER 16

Man Makes His Plans...

"Mrs. Mitchell," the voice on the telephone said to Mother. "One of my pigs just gave birth to a piglet with two heads. You all want to see it?" My brothers and I, at home in Schell City for Christmas, piled in the old jalopy and went out to the farm. By the time we arrived, the piglet had died. "Sorry. Knew you medical people were interested in such things," the farmer said in apology.

Russell examined the little pig and appeared reluctant to leave. "Sis, I'd like to take this pig back to school." Because of his good scholastics in high school, he had been invited to enroll in a wealthy boys' college, to 'leaven out the lump'. In order to stay in school, Russell held down three jobs. He fired the furnace, mowed the lawn, and washed dishes twice a day, for meals at a dorm. He later assisted a biology teacher, and had him in mind while he debated about the pig.

"Okay!" I said. "I know the formalin recipe. Let's go to the drugstore for the ingredients." This was just what he had in mind; so, together we pickled the pig, and put him in a stone jar.

After the holidays, the entire family drove Russell to the train station, with him protectively cradling his prize in the back seat between his knees. "Phew!" complained James. "I'll be glad when you're out of the car!"

Once on the train, we saw Russell pleading with the conductor, who pointed him out! They argued on the platform, but the conductor stood his ground. "Son, I can't let you ride inside, with that foul thing sloshing all over the place. Other passengers are already complaining." So, we waved goodbye to Russell as he stood between the cars in supreme cold, with his pickled pig. He wrote us later that he almost froze!

Struck with a theory for twinning, he dissected the brains on the pig's two heads, and wrote up his theory. At the biology professor's encouragement, he published it. Russell received all the credit for the well-done article, with necessary pictures, and on the last page of the paper, a footnote stated it had been edited and reviewed by the professor. Soon after its publication, Russell was put in *Who's Who In American Colleges and Universities.*

This incident occurred toward the end of my nurse's training at St. Luke's. We felt tremendous family pride at Russell's new fame, and hoped the notoriety would gain him some financial aid to finish school.

I was scrubbed in with brain surgery one day, which had lasted many grueling hours. Shifting my stance, I happened to glance out the operating room window, and noticed Russell pacing by his car, waiting for me to finish.

What has happened now? I wondered wearily, turning back to the delicate operation. Ordinarily I listened attentively to my brothers' problems, but my back ached from the duration of the surgery, and my head from lack of sleep for the past few days. But none of the physical pain compared with my agonizing, emotional agony. My heart felt open and bleeding, as if someone had cut it with a scalpel. All because of a disappointing letter I had received from Joe's parents.

When at last I was free to see Russell, I felt a stab of guilt. *It must be really important for him to drive all the way from school.* I tried to perk myself up, and went out to his car.

"What's up?"

He thrust several pieces of correspondence into my hands. "See what you think about these, Sis!"

"Scholarship offers?" I leafed through offers from Rhodes, England, Harvard, Yale, and several other places. I sank down on a nearby bench, and sighed. "These won't do," I said with a sharp edge in my voice.

"But, think of the opportunities at *any* of those schools!" He was taken back by my attitude.

"They're only partial scholarships, and they don't offer enough money!" I snapped. I was on the verge of tears. "The other boys need to finish their educations too. We just can't swing it!"

Russell's anger showed in his even reply. "I know they need help, too. That's why I wanted your advice about the offers. They're the best I've had." His hurt showed in his eyes. "Besides, it won't be *your* problem much longer. It won't be *us* carrying the load. *You'll* be married and *free* from the burden of us."

That did it. My chin quivered and tears slid down my cheeks. "Oh, Russell. It isn't going to happen! There won't be a wedding!"

He came toward me. "What? But...you were making plans just last week!" He sat down beside me, as the reason for my ill-tempered mood hit him full force.

"I know, I know!" I wailed. "But a letter from Joe's parents just came, breaking the engagement. They said that Joe is very sick."

He hugged me close. "Oh, Sis. I'm so sorry. Sick? Sick, with what? I just don't understand!"

"I don't, either." I said, sobbing into his shoulder. "It must be really bad. Their letter was so formal and terse, like they didn't even want a response from me. It's all over! I know that I'll never see Joe again!"

Russell stayed with me, and let me cry my heart out. But no matter how many tears I shed, the pain wouldn't go away. When at last, Russell rose to leave he looked hurt and defeated also. "Sis, I'll turn down the scholarship offers. You're right. Maybe something else will turn up." His voice was hopeless, as he turned and walked slowly to his car.

I lingered in the afternoon sun until it slipped behind the hospital and imposing shadows stole the last light. The day had calmly ended, maybe with a brilliant spring sunset; I don't know. Full of gloom, I trudged back to the nurses' quarters, thinking of Russell and his long drive back to school. *We've both worked and studied so hard, for years. Now, nothing makes sense. Instead of more education for him, the way is blocked. Life with the man I love is gone forever.* All our plans had evaporated like shimmering heat waves under a blazing, merciless sun. Now, I could only hope for God's intervention.

Take care of Russell's situation, Father. Like mine, it's come to a dead end.

I hid in my room for the rest of the evening, and for many evenings thereafter when I got off duty, not wanting to answer any questions. I almost got my hopes up again, when a student called me to the house phone a few weeks later. It must have shown in my voice.

"It's only me, Sis. Russell."

"Oh, okay." My hopes fell.

He couldn't contain himself. "It's happened! Something *did* turn up!"

"That's good," I sighed.

I have an offer from the University of California! They'll not only pay all my expenses, but they've agreed to pay my fees! Guess what else!"

"I don't know," I murmured.

"They're throwing in six hundred dollars a year!"

"I'm happy for you, Russell," I said dully. "The Lord has answered, hasn't He?"

"He sure has! And Sis, thanks for your help. I wouldn't have gotten this if I had accepted any of the other offers."

"I know."

"What about you? Has, uh, anything changed?"

"No. Nothing's changed." I hung up the phone, thinking of a verse in Proverbs. *The mind of man plans his way, but the Lord directs his steps.* Although Russell was exhilarated about his scholarship, I felt nothing. *What about me, God? Why would you bring me this far and then cut off all purpose for my life and education? Soon, I'll be a nurse. With no direction. No place to go. If not to India with Joe, then where?*

I slipped back into my room again, to attempt studying for my upcoming exams. Injured beyond feeling, I moved like someone drugged, or in a dream world. I felt abandoned and rejected, unloved; and nothing anyone said brought me out of my depression. Nursing became a mundane routine, as I went into my last few weeks of instruction and patient care. Instead of looking forward to receiving my diploma, it now mattered very little. In fact, it didn't matter at all.

Lord, when I lay down my head and cross the bar, Will you explain how I've come this far. Without a love to need me, to hold me. With only you to mold my eternity....

CHAPTER 17

A Need Like a Trumpet Call

"Get up, Mitchell," prodded Milliken "We have another boring speech today. Don't see what difference it makes," she grumbled, slipping into her uniform. "I just want to work general duty, and make some money for a change."

I delayed getting up, wondering how long I had been awake, or if I had slept at all during the long night. I forced lead-like limbs out of bed. "Who is it, today?" I asked, more out of politeness than curiosity. Toward the end of training, various speakers came to inform us of opportunities that awaited graduates.

"Somebody from Kentucky, I think. About nursing in the hills, in the middle of nowhere," Milliken said, pinning her cap in place. "Who cares?"

We filed noisily into the auditorium, and routinely settled into seats we had occupied for numberless lectures. Coughs and bored yawns greeted the speakers. I, too, sat dully through the introduction, and forced myself to listen as a woman began speaking.

"Students, I'm here today on behalf of The Frontier Nursing Service." She paused, as if she expected this announcement to profoundly affect her audience. "It was founded in 1925 with financial support from the Kentucky State Board of Health." Another pause. Clearing her throat, the speaker continued. "With this money, a woman named Mary Breckinridge, and two trained nurse midwives from England built a hospital in the isolated town of Hyden, Kentucky. Here, they began caring for the slow moving, low voiced people of that area, who at first didn't trust 'these brought on women'. But, because the nurses offered good medical care, the mountaineers gradually accepted them and sought their help."

The lecturer glared at a dozing student, then plunged into the heart of her speech. "As you know from medical history, the maternal death rate during childbirth in America in the early twenties, was the highest in the civilized world. Two hundred thousand babies died at birth, or during their first month, and nearly twenty thousand mothers! These statistics, higher than any war casualties in this nation, multiplied in the eastern Kentucky Mountains, where unnumbered women and babies died."

Her voice laced with concern, the speaker continued. "Also, epidemics of smallpox, diphtheria and typhoid raged across the hills. Hookworm and tuberculosis plagued the mountaineers in everyday life. Together, Mrs. Breckinridge and her two brave helpers suffered fatigue and danger, in extreme weather, as they battled these killer diseases. And, it is all for their love of humanity."

Someone behind me said, sarcastically, "For the *love of humanity*. How noble."

The speech rolled on. "In only seven years, this work has grown, extending to cover seven counties, in a region of eight hundred square miles. Today, a railroad ends at Hazard, twenty-seven miles from Hyden. A few mountain trails and a rutted road continue from there to Hyden, and the hospital. Yet today, twenty-eight nurses and three supervisors stubbornly care for nearly eight thousand people in that isolated world!" She paused again, for us to comprehend the situation.

"Thirty-one to eight thousand?" whispered student Houdek to Grinstead. "That's not work! That's slave labor!"

"Ladies," the woman continued plaintively. "These people are scattered up and down creeks and rivers with few towns, separated by canyons and ridges of dense forests. The only doctors they or their ancestors have known are quacks, or old granny women, who nurse the sick with superstitious remedies. When someone dies, they simply say, 'It was God's will."

Ignoring the other students, who whispered to one another, I strained to listen. The speaker's words contained conviction. She believed in her speech and her mission in nursing.

"These mountaineers, desperately poor descendants of English, Scotch and Welsh settlers during early days of colonization, have lost the hope and stamina of their pioneer forefathers." She paused, her voice rising. "Nurses! I challenge you to witness life in its fundamentals. I invite you to join those who care for a tired and ignorant people on an old frontier. I offer you no comforts of civilization. Life there is hard, the work harder. I might add - that Appalachian Kentucky resembles a foreign country - unlike any other area in this beautiful land of ours."

A foreign country. An intriguing choice of words.

"I must warn you that real danger is involved along these rocky, and often icy trails. Mrs. Breckinridge is recuperating from a broken back, caused by a fall from a horse during a rainstorm. But, when she regains her health, she intends to continue her campaign for financial support."

"Let me share her philosophy with you. 'Maternity is the young woman's untrumpeted battlefield. Who is helping her tonight, while her baby is born? The vigor and youth of a nation is born again in its children. Therefore, we *must* give these mountain children their chance.'"

The talk ended with scattered applause, and everyone left to catch the noon rays of a sunshiny day. I just sat, moved by the lecture. Something about hard work and isolation had appalled the other students. But I had known hard work all my life. I thought about Mrs. Breckinridge, and her courage to begin this work. *Now there's a woman I'd like to meet.*

Throughout the remaining afternoon speeches, I envisioned cabins perched on mountainsides, with a thin waft of chimney smoke curling into a cold wintry wind. I saw discouragement and despair imprinted on faces. I could relate. I thought of the hopeless faces of men who had fathered children, wondering if they would live or die. Unlike any living conditions I could imagine, the hills of Kentucky sounded like a post in a foreign country to me.

In the lobby I picked up an application form. The more I read, I wondered, *could this be my calling?* Although I still ached from my break-up with Joe, I thought about the way the Lord had directed me into nursing. My mind churned as I searched for objectivity. *Had it not been for the hope of marriage, I would probably be teaching school now, instead of pursuing nursing.* A thought surfaced. *Why not apply to Frontier Nursing Service?* I hesitated. *Is this compliant with the Lord's direction?* It was too far-fetched for me to unravel. *Why not apply...* the urge continued. From somewhere, a need like a trumpet call softly pierced my mind and penetrated my injured heart, my inert spirit absorbing the melody.

I leaned over a table, filled out the application, and deposited it in a nearby mailbox. The soft call remained at the outer rims of my consciousness during those last weeks before we received our pins.

One afternoon after I got off duty, I walked back to the dorm to check the mail. My roommate, Milliken, casually glanced my way when I picked up a letter she had tossed on my bed. She had already seen the return address.

"Well?" she asked lightly, while I slowly read the letter and held it out to her.

I smiled tremulously. "It says I've been accepted," I said, past a lump in my throat. "Looks like I'll be heading for the Kentucky hills."

As I folded the letter that contained my future, strangely, a peace that had eluded me for weeks rolled in. Although it would take time to heal all my aching heart, this was a new beginning. I no longer felt totally abandoned. I began to understand that when my prayers and plans failed in misdirection, that God would step in, and reveal his *real* direction.

Hannah's Journal, June 1990

The past few days are a blur. Yesterday, as I came down from the upper slope in the back yard, when I reached the kitchen door, I slipped on pine straw. Wide-eyed and stumbling, I fell face downward onto the stones. Stunned with pain, I lay there for several minutes, before I managed to get to my knees and push open the door. I crawled into the living room, and pulled myself onto the sofa, where I spent a sleepless night.

Today, stiff and sore, I crept to the bathroom, to relieve myself, and wash my skinned knees. I must look like a witch I thought, with my hair sticking up, one eye closed, and only a slit to see out of the other. Thankfully, nothing is broken. But what if I had knocked myself out, and sustained a concussion? When would someone have found me?

Dot Townsend called and brought lunch, but I could only eat a few bites. After she made us a cup of tea, she helped me bandage my knees, got me undressed, and into bed.

After she left, I turned to the lesson I am to teach on Sunday, but I cannot concentrate. I also need to deal with the doctor's warning about no longer living alone...and his advice on leaving Hannah's Haven...But I must rest...

I dreamed. I was on a train again, asleep in a berth. I was on my way to meet Joe. But even in my dream, I realized it was not to be. He is gone. Lost forever. When I woke, my pillow was wet with tears.

1938-1944

CHAPTER *18*

Send-Off To The Hills

On a crisp autumn day in 1938, I took a taxi to Union Station, accompanied by nurses Houdek, Milliken and Grinstead. As the cab pulled away, I looked back at the hospital and nurses' dorm, with an overwhelming sense of leaving security.

When we passed the two-story house where Grinstead and I had shared a room as we studied for state board exams, I recalled our conversation the night before. She had come home from working the night shift, bubbling about wedding plans with a fellow she had met in college. She paused when a wistful look stole across my face.

"Oh. Mitchell, I forgot about you and Joe marrying, and going as missionaries to India when you finished here," she said quietly.

I nodded, with the sinking sensation of never seeing, hearing, or touching my beloved, or being touched by him again.

"You'll be a missionary, just the same," she said.

"But, I'll be *alone* this way," I cried. "*So alone!*"

"Well, how about a mountaineer to go along with those horses you'll be riding!"

I was relieved that she had turned away so I couldn't see the pity in her eyes. The other nurses had also offered sympathy mixed with admiration, as they gave me hugs, and talked about my future as a nurse on horseback.

How good of these three special friends to see me off. We went early to the station, and had our pictures taken in a booth – four poses for a dime. We drank a coke, bought my ticket and checked my Gladstone bag, laughing good-naturedly while we waited for the train.

My friends helped me settle in the Pullman car, and 'All Aboard!' from the conductor came too soon. They scurried out to watch from the station platform as the train lurched forward. When I pressed my face to the window, Houdek's face crinkled up like she might cry. Milliken, my roommate through all our training years together, turned her back with her handkerchief to her face. Then, they vanished from sight.

The porter soon came through making up my berth. Exhausted, I crawled in. I had worked till midnight the day before, washed last minute articles that dried quickly on the line, and finished packing. Before that I had stopped off to say goodbye to undergraduates, the housemother, favorite long-term patients, head nurses and doctors.

Feeling the finality of things, I attempted cheering myself up. *You're on your way to a new life, one of adventure and challenge. Leave those painful memories behind.* But now I was alone and missing my friends, home and family. Snuggling down under the blankets, I fleetingly wished for my Mother to say goodnight with maternal love.

I had gone to see her the weekend before, and we had talked till after midnight. She praised me for my good nursing grades, and how my continued interest in family had bolstered her over the years. "But how far away *is* Kentucky?" she had asked cautiously. "Is it dangerous country?"

I avoided telling her of rumors of feuds and fighting. Instead, I surmised, "The mountain-folks are probably much like we once were in the Ozark Mountains, hard-working, just to scratch out a living."

I slept fitfully with startled awakenings, as the train repeatedly flung me forward when we started moving again after station stops. The curtains swung out and back, in spite of safety pins I had used for privacy. Porters called to one another, or to delivery boys about fresh linens, and people chatted and laughed with friends. Even with all the people nearby I felt isolated, till at some point during the swaying and jerking hours, a Bible verse came to mind. *My presence shall go with thee, and I will give thee rest.* Only then did I slowly relax and nap with the comfort of Christ's presence, until jolting and screeching brakes woke me again.

The dark screen that was my window began to reveal a grey dawn, and a few snowflakes on the window ledge mixed with coal dust. Silt was sprinkled on my sheet and pillowcase, even underneath they looked grey. In the washroom where I washed my hands, advancing light disclosed a sooty face peering back at me in the mirror.

At breakfast in the diner, the tablecloth showed coal dust also, with egg and grease stains from previous diners. Ignoring the waiter's greasy apron, I ordered breakfast. He brought me strong, steaming coffee. "We're out of eggs, ma'am," he said, serving me cold biscuits, with limp and undercooked bacon - a far cry from St. Luke's standards.

I sipped my coffee, wanting the miles to slip quickly by over Illinois, Indiana, through Louisville, Shelbyville, Frankfurt and into Lexington. I suddenly became aware of someone standing by my table. I looked up at the conductor.

"Ma'am, are you a nurse or a doctor?"

"I'm a nurse. Why do you ask?"

"The other conductor noticed your ticket envelope had St. Luke's Hospital written on it, and he reckoned you for a nurse or doctor. A sick woman in your Pullman car is screaming her head off, and upsetting everybody. Would you see about her?"

"Show me the way," I said laconically, setting down my coffee. *Nurse's work is never done.* Following him back to the platform, when he opened the door, I knew where my patient lay by her hysterics, and the voice of another female rose who seemingly had lost all patience with her. When I was introduced to the friend, she looked at me skeptically.

"Did you give her any medication?" I asked, gesturing toward the berth.

"She carries a lot to make her sleep," the friend admitted. *Hmmn. A high from too many pills, plus a hysterical temperament.*

The berth lay in shambles. Tousled hair and a swollen tear-stained face featured a woman in her late forties, behaving like a spoiled adolescent. Her wailing grew louder as she pushed the younger woman away with angry looks.

Signaling to the big-eyed porter, I asked for a fresh berth and towels. I guided the frantic woman into the clean berth while I spoke in a soothing manner, and after dampening the towels in the nearby ladies' room, I washed her face and patted her like she was a child. I shushed her shrill companion, and closed the curtains around the two of us, shutting out curious passengers. A massage with talcum powder from my small train case relaxed her stiff muscles, until at last she fell asleep.

Quietness and order settled in, so I walked toward the door to explore the rest of the train. But an anxious crew and passengers barred my way, so for the rest of the trip I was confined to the Pullman. Curiously, everyone except the two women thanked me; they never did.

We neared lovely Lexington, the famous bluegrass country of large horse farms, stately mansions, and spacious barns. Acres of white fences paralleled the train track, where horses trotted in the stiff breeze, or were exercised on training grounds. Miles of emerald grass and white fences stood in sharp contrast to the clinging coal dust from the train. *I hope some of my horses will be from here,* I thought, watching the estates roll by.

At the hotel room in Lexington I headed for the big bathtub, and soaked away the grime, but I remained clean for only a few hours. The night train from Lexington to Hazard was again a coal-fired locomotive, this time without the luxury of a Pullman.

In the day coach I saw rural Kentuckians for the first time. With few vacant seats, the people boarding the train looked me over, only to walk past, and sit, or stand up front with others of like dress and speech. Most of the men wore ragged, faded overalls, or rough trousers covered by old, bulky jackets. Loose coats on the women revealed worn out cotton dresses, buttoned at the front or pinned together.

One man said to another, jerking his head toward me, "I figure she's one a them brought on foreign women going to Hyden." Then they settled in to conversation, the weather a starting point.

"Doggies! It's colder'n thunder!"

"I know it, brother. I'm satisfied that the worst will be walking up that creek bed early in the break of day. Say, whose boy are ye, and how far up the holler do ye come from?"

As I listened to their speech, and that of the other passengers, I recognized old English mixed with local slang. Their mouths full of tobacco, occasionally a blast of cold air hit me when they raised a window, and sent a stream of ambeer outside.

I nodded during the night until a window slamming shut awakened me, followed instantly by a child's scream. I sprang to help, thinking a hand or arm had been caught. Several minutes elapsed before his mother and I discovered what hurt him. He kept rubbing his eye, evidently where a flying cinder had lodged. The mother held him with his head over her shoulder, his arms pinned against her. While I teased out the cinder with a soft handkerchief from my pocketbook, his father assisted me by shining my flashlight in the boy's eye. Either the easing of the pain, or my strangeness stopped his crying.

"Now! Doesn't that feel better?" I said, with a smile. He shyly hid his face in the fold of his mother's coat and peeked out again. He was a handsome boy, with fair skin and dark brown hair, like the other children on the train. Many of them appeared to be in poor health, but neither undernourishment nor poverty hid their angelic beauty. The little one thanked me with a smile, an opposite reaction from the two ungrateful women on the previous train.

I thought about what a Bible teacher had once told me. "Hannah, every life that touches yours, God has either sent or allowed to come." I gave my little friend a wink. Little did he know that, so far, his smile was the first amiable gesture from any of his people. I pulled my coat around me again and settled back into my seat, wishing the stove up front would send a little heat to the rear.

Early next morning the train braked to a stop in Hazard, the end of the line. A poll of grey smoke that hung over the big mining town made me cough. Snowfall during the night already showed dirty coal dust, and muddy footprints that led up to yawning, black mouths of the mines on steep hillsides. Here and there, cabins clung to sloping terrain, supported by shaky stilts.

As the sun broke through the blanket of smoke, I stiffly stepped down from the cold coach. "Could you direct me to a place for breakfast?" I asked a woman in the street who looked older than her years. With a toddler on her hip, her stomach bulging with another pregnancy, and pushing stringy hair back from her face, she eyed me carefully. Then, she silently pointed across the street to a café. Afterwards, while people watched me with sidelong glances or ignored me altogether, I caught the bus for Hyden, twenty-seven more miles away.

CHAPTER 19

A Girl Called Mitch

The bus lumbered along to Hyden on a crude road that had been cut by gashing out places in the sandstone cliffs. Raw bluffs with trickling streams of water, scrubby mountain laurel, rhododendron, and wild azaleas peeping out from the snow reminded me of my home in the Ozarks. Flooding had washed out parts of the roadbed, and we bounced jarringly, with the bus almost tilting over.

The mist cleared as the sun rose, exposing rough unpainted shacks with a ribbon of smoke curling from each sandstone chimney. A man led a mule to water in a nearby stream, chickens scratched at barn doors, lonely dogs scavenged at dismal door yards, and skeletal hogs rooted under the snow for food. But I saw no cows. My father would have disapproved; he thought every family should own a cow.

We passed men on the road going to work with miners' lamps in their caps; other men carried hunting rifles. Bus passengers opened the windows to spit, and called *howdy* each time we passed a group. Further along, poorly clad children of all ages came to the open doorways to watch the bus go by. The driver let people off at any spot they indicated, and as a man walked toward his cabin, the children gathered listlessly at the door; I saw no happy waving on their part. *How odd. We always ran to meet our Father when he came home.* Looking closer, I saw the younger children had no shoes. All looked underfed.

We entered Hyden where clusters of cabins, dirty muddy dooryards, and more children greeted the oncoming bus. The driver constantly honked the horn to clear the ruts of dogs, hogs, children and adults. They moved slowly, as if they mentally contested the entrance of a mechanized vehicle foreign to their usual way of life. The bus stopped in the middle of the road outside a drugstore, where the people piled off ahead of me. The driver helped with my bags and escorted me into the store.

As I started inside, while glancing across the street at the courthouse, I noticed a pig sedately walking up the rickety courthouse steps to the open doorway. People automatically stepped around him. I stared. *Hannah, you've come a long way from civilization at its highest to this place where animals have precedence over humans in the courthouse!*

The bus driver introduced me to the druggist. "I picked up this woman in Hazard, and she's going up to the hospital. Will ye see that she gets there okay?"

The druggist nodded. "Come here, and I'll show ye where ye're going." Outside, he pointed up the mountain, while I tried to pinpoint the hospital on the landscape. First, I saw a swinging bridge, over which cars or horses crossed. Squinting, I picked out a long, rocky path up the side of the mountain, which passed one house on the right, then many more steps up another rugged part. My mouth hung open, and when my gaze at last rested on the hospital near the top, I gasped.

"Think ye can make it?"

"I....I don't know. Could I leave my bags here?"

"Sure. I'll keep them till someone comes for them. I seen Clint come into town a little while ago. Come in and set awhile. When he comes by, ye can go up with him."

Inside, the storekeeper cleared a place for me to sit, among the supplies and mountain men that either milled around inside the building, or hovered near the coal stove in the middle of the room. They continued talking or playing checkers while they kept an eye on me. Finally, the druggist shouted, "Yonder he comes. Hey, Clint!" All conversation ceased when a burly looking man appeared.

"Clint, this nurse come in on the bus. Can ye take her up the hill?" Clint glanced my way and nodded. The druggist continued. "She's got two bags. Ye want to take one?" The slow-moving man negatively shook his head, and mumbled something to the storekeeper. With strong forearms, he picked up a shotgun he had leaned against the wall, and placing it across his thick shoulder, he motioned me outside.

I shakily walked out, with rumors of fighting and feuding racing through my mind. As we hiked up the mountainside, he shifted the gun from one shoulder to the other, or carried it with the barrel pointed to the ground. "Turned out to be a nice day, didn't it?" I offered. Clint only grunted a reply, and pulled his rumpled felt hat down further over his brow. Sometimes he stepped a little closer to me, as he looked around and shifted his gun. I also looked around for any signs of hostility. *Who is this man? My bodyguard?*

We passed by the fence opening that led directly up to the hospital, and I stumbled. "Just let me stop and catch my breath," I panted. "This air is so thin!" My heart was pounding from exertion, and also from fright of the surly, silent man who walked so briskly behind me.

When at last we entered the medical building, Clint ushered me into a living room and motioned me to sit down, and left without a word. I could hear patients' voices from a clinic area at one end of the building, and pots and pans clanged from the kitchen area, but I saw no one. Everyday sounds droned on and I nodded off. I jumped when a heavy-set woman bustled in. She looked surprised to see me. She tilted her head and spoke in a Scottish accent.

"Are you the new nurse?"

I sat up straight. "Oh, yes. I'm Hannah Mitchell."

"How'd you get here?"

"One of the men walked me up the hill. Clint, I think."

"Wonder why Clint didn't tell me you were here," she blurted harshly. "That man! Oh, well. Why don't you go on up to your room. Go on and get some rest till lunch is ready." She hurriedly pointed the way across a screened-in walk that bridged a rocky canyon between the hospital and nurses' quarters. "It's called the Bridge of Shivers. Even in summer, it's drafty and cold to walk through," she remarked on her way out of the room.

I walked out to the partially boarded and roofed Bridge of Shivers, where a cold updraft of wind constantly blew, and quickly agreed that it had been properly named while I paused in the cold, surveying my new surroundings. From here I could see across the valley where cabins dotted the landscape, each one depending on this tiny complex of medical knowledge. I wondered if it had purposely been built at the mountain's crest, offering hope to the townspeople and families across the valley. The only new facade in view, every other building or shanty looked as though it had occupied its spot for fifty, or a hundred years. Down the hill, I noticed Clint walking back to town still shouldering his gun, but now at a lethargic pace.

Surveying the horizon, I realized with a sinking feeling that St. Luke's and civilization were already becoming a part of the past. I didn't linger on the Bridge of Shivers.

Remembering the nurse's directions, I found my assigned room at the far end of the second floor of the nurses' building. Plain and simply furnished with a bed, chest, and single curtained window, it overlooked the town below. I stretched out on the bed, grateful for a few minutes rest. Too soon I was called to lunch.

After a curt introduction at the table I seated myself, and discussion immediately arose among the staff about what to call me.

"The doctor's wife is Hannah. We don't need two."

Someone agreed. "Chicken looks good today."

"I know. We'll call you Mitch."

This problem solved, they next instructed me as to proper uniform.

"On district, we wear the English riding habit. Hospital duty calls for regular uniforms. Pass the peas, McKennon."

I detected from their accents that most of the nurses hailed from Scotland or England, yet I felt like the unwelcome foreigner, as they discussed me without asking my opinion. The sinking feeling in the pit of my stomach now affected my appetite. The chicken didn't look so good to me.

"Off duty, everyone wears slacks. Hope you have some. Here, boy." All the time we ate, two owners fed a couple of dogs from the table.

I picked at my food throughout the meal, while the others, and their dogs ate heartily. After about thirty minutes, with their appetites sated, they promptly dismissed me. "Get some sleep, Mitch. You'll be on duty tomorrow night." I meekly smiled, quietly put down my fork, and left the room while their everyday conversation resumed. My absence or presence made very little difference.

Back in my room, I fell across the bed with my clothes on. I had never felt so unwelcome. Now I even felt deprived. Not only had I left my friends and family, but my identity was lost as well. Homesick and forlorn, I reflected on how Mother had told me when I was quite young, that I was named after a wonderful woman in the Bible. In my teens she had reminded me that Hannah means 'full of grace'. "You should always behave in a graceful manner," she often said. *Now I'm ungraceful Mitch.* I disliked this masculine, intimate name. People sometimes called my brothers Mitch, but never me. I was known by my last name at nursing school, but never, 'Mitch'.

Father had often called me 'kitten' because he usually found me curled up somewhere, reading. I thought about the evening he had commented to us about our family name. "You should be proud to carry it. Never do anything to dishonor what your Grandfather and his Fathers tried to keep clean, honest, and honorable." This shortened version of my name sounded cheap and meaningless to me.

I didn't bother to undress for the long night ahead. *Welcome to the hills, Mitch,* I thought with a heavy sigh, as I rubbed my hand across a bedspread that was probably woven by one of the mountain women. *Here you are, a girl with a new name in a strange culture, the only symbol of the Mitchells.*

Silent tears fell while Mitch stared out the window that first night in Hyden, at a strangely foreign sky.

CHAPTER 20

They Don't Have Much Feeling

One morning, while I slept after having worked all night on the unpopular shift of night duty, yelling and noises that sounded like gunshots awakened me. I stumbled out of bed to the window, opened it, and looked out over the town.

Two men were lying in the road, and smoke from the discharge of their dueling pistols hung in the air. Minutes seemed hours before anyone ventured out from behind a building to see about them, but finally a few townsmen crept toward the felled men, and turned over one motionless body. Then they bent low over the other, and signaled for help. Someone ran to the drugstore to phone about bringing the wounded man up to the hospital, while the others loaded him in a wagon, and started on the road that led the long way around the mountain, instead of the perpendicular way we usually climbed.

I threw on my uniform and rushed to the hospital to set up for surgery. Only one nurse was on duty to run the clinic; the others were out riding district, and couldn't be reached.

Heavy-footed men soon burst through the hospital doors, carrying a man bleeding from a stomach wound. "Miss Mitchell, this one's in a bad way. The other man's plumb dead." They spoke to me without expression.

"We'll do our best," I assured them, and started tearing away the injured man's bloody shirt. Though Dr. Kooser, who was Head of our clinic, usually did little surgery, he and I went immediately to work looking for the bullet. We had no time to wait for a surgeon from Hazard, which would take over an hour if the roads weren't blocked by rockslides. We cut and sutured about ten inches of torn intestine in a long and bloody operation, as we worked to prevent the patient's hemorrhaging to death.

"Get back to bed, Mitch," ordered the day nurse. "You'll have night duty again. Dr. Kooser and I will attend him now." The doctor nodded in agreement, so I left the sick man with them. I admired our doctor, who worked long demanding hours. He could have chosen a comfortable, well-paying practice in a large city; instead he had courageously moved his wife and two pre-school children to fortuneless, obscure Hyden.

That night on duty, I carefully nursed the patient as best I could, but the cruel bullet had done its work. Just before daylight he died. Next morning, when the day nurse came on duty, she helped me bathe him and change his bloody bandage.

"Go up to the attic and get some fresh clothes from the grab room," she directed. I went upstairs, and rummaged among rows and stacks of hanging clothes, donated by committees from cities in the north, until I found fresh trousers and a clean shirt. After we dressed him, bathed his face, and combed his hair, I stepped back to look at him.

"Why, he's only a boy!"

"Oh, yes," she agreed. "That's part of the sadness of life here. Families often fight one another, for reasons long forgotten. Men are quick to duel when defending their honor, no matter what age."

"Where do we put him now?" I whispered, glancing toward the ward of men.

"Soon as Clint comes to work, he'll help us take him to the wee hoose. For now, we'll just wheel him out in the hall."

"Clint?" Suddenly my eyes widened. "He walked me up from town the day I arrived, carrying a gun, and he hardly spoke a word. Do people shoot at us when they start fighting?"

The nurse looked puzzled, then chuckled. "You thought Clint was your bodyguard? Oh, my! No! The people never harm us, and Clint wouldn't swat a fly. He's the barn man! You know. He shoes the horses, and cleans out the stables."

"But, he's huge! And he carried that gun!"

"He eats a lot of hospital food, that's why he isn't lean like the other mountain men. He probably borrowed the gun to use for butchering hogs."

"Oh." I relaxed. I was learning.

Clint soon arrived and helped us put the body on a stretcher. Somehow we all got the boy down the stairs, and outside to the entrance to the wee hoose. It was a small, windowless room underneath the hospital, which measured about ten by twelve feet, and served as a morgue. When we opened the door, a damp, musty smell emerged from the darkness. Stooping, we entered the low-ceilinged room, where a large pine box sat on sawhorses. Into this crude casket we placed the boy's body.

"Make sure the lid is on tight, so no rats can get to him," the nurse warned, hammering the lid on one end. With goose bumps on the back of my neck, I hurriedly nailed down my section, imagining gophers lurking to swarm all over the casket as soon as we left. "Not too tightly, now. The casket belongs to the hospital. His relatives will remove him, and carry him on a stretcher to a wagon, if they don't live too far up the creek." She paused. "But, I don't remember this boy. They may have to stretcher him all the way."

I loathed the indignity of the makeshift morgue. Shuddering, I asked, "What about children? Do we put them down here?"

The nurse nodded. "When a child dies, the father carries it to the hospital in his arms, and holds it on a mule or horse. Oh, you'll see them die," she said to my look of dismay. "Many are almost dead when they arrive, because their parents delay in bringing them. After an eight or ten mile trip here, it's too late for a few."

We firmly shut the door on the wee hoose, and walked around to the front steps of the hospital. Lest she appear too accusative, the nurse further explained. "Too, treacherous weather often keeps people away. In spring, the Middle Fork River floods, and the only way to cross is to swim a horse. Boats can't be used then, because of rocks and swift water." She looked down the mountainside. "At one time, Hyden flooded and some of the houses washed down river."

"Those poor people," I mused.

She glanced my way. "Mitch, don't waste a lot of emotion about life here. People accept with stoicism, what others in the outside world consider tragic, or scandalous. These hillbillies live, and die, with a fatalistic outlook. Believe me, I've been in the States long enough to observe that they don't have much feeling. Giving birth, and burying their dead are commonplace incidents."

I realized our conversation was to educate me to this culture, yet hers, and similar deductions by other British nurses seemed insensitive to the mountainfolk's emotions, and it disturbed me. I found this attitude difficult to accept. *Not much feeling? All humans have feelings!* I admitted I had seen little display of sentiment in the patients, yet I wondered, if they in turn, sensed any callousness in the nurses. Somehow, I felt they would be offended if they knew they were classed as without feeling.

And what about their founder, Mrs. Breckinridge, whom I had heard so much about? From the primary speech I had listened to about Frontier Nursing Service, I had gathered that she valued the mountaineers. Still, the work had been established for years now. Had her philosophy slowly changed? I walked back through the Bridge of Shivers to return to my room and a few hours sleep, thinking on the way of how I had been taught in nurses' training to mask my emotions. But so far, my profession hadn't required purging myself of sensitivity to my fellow man.

* * * * *

Often volunteer nurses from other parts of the country worked at Hyden during their two-week vacations, in order to allow the regular nurses time off. Because of the constant stress of being on call, night and day, we received six weeks vacation a year. However, if a patient's delivery date neared, a nurse sometimes postponed her holiday because she wouldn't want to leave her patient.

Jane Reeder came down from Cincinnati, Ohio, to work shortly after I went to Hyden. "I want to see how these mountaineers live, love, and bear children," she announced. She received a full two weeks of nursing duty. In fact, she arrived the day of the duel in the streets, and chattered about it for hours. Someone took her to clinic by horseback on an eight-mile trip over Twin Mountain. She even went on a night call, with a home delivery on Bull Creek. For fun, she went to a syrup stir-off on Thousand Sticks Mountain. "I loved watching the mule grind the cane; then we dipped the stalks in the

syrup, and licked them while the women stirred and skimmed it."
She almost drooled telling about it.

Work kept Jane busy in the small hospital, which covered the
top floor of the medical building. Patients came in with pneumonia,
malnutrition, mining accidents, and snakebite or gunshot wounds.
All fifteen beds of the ward were usually filled, including a glassed-
in porch area, which could only be used in summer. Patients didn't
seem to mind being separated by gender, with only a curtain; at
home entire families often slept in the same room.

At one end of the floor thrived the maternity ward, with new
mothers and crying newborns. Jane was fascinated with their low,
drawled speech and fortitude in childbirth. The babies with velvety
skin and long lashes captivated her.

"I've never seen lovelier babies," she cooed, cuddling a dimply
one. "And none quite like this little darling."

"Orpha," she said to the mother, "I think you should let me
have it."

"Why?" smiled the young mother.

"Because it looks like me, with these black eyes, and hair.
Besides, you can have another, and I can't. I'm not married."

The mother blushed deeply, and then gazed back with stolid
features. She said quietly, "I ain't either."

All eyes watched Jane's reaction.

"It's a woods colt," the mother softly clarified.

Jane's face turned dark. She looked like she wanted to disappear,
moistening her lips as if thinking of something to say, but nothing
came out. I took the baby and re-wrapped it in its receiving blanket,
remembering the baby born out of wedlock to the girl in the hotel
during my teen years. *At least this baby wouldn't be abandoned to
die, I thought. It might even find acceptance, and a chance in life.*

"She *is* a lovely baby," I cooed, breaking the silence. I gently
tucked the sleeping beauty back under the covers beside her mother,
and spoke nonchalantly to a few other patients as we left the ward,
followed by their inquisitive looks.

Jane busied herself helping in the clinic. On certain days,
when nurse midwives all rode districts, she helped worm children
and adults, treated burns from fireplace accidents, or scalding. I
wondered if everyone appeared the same to her. *Were they only a
mass of faces that she saw every day? Did she also think they had
no feelings?*

Shirley Roland Ferguson

For a moment in the ward, I had caught shame and embarrassment from the mother, when Jane spoke so loudly about the baby. I noted the momentary relief from other patients when the situation was minimized; even in their uneducated way they recognized tact and appreciated it. And when I had taken some men to the wee hoose to show them the shooting victim's body, I distinctly heard a low moan escape the father's lips as they put his son on the stretcher.

I decided these mountaineers had feelings, all right. It just took a bit of listening, and reading faces, to catch it.

CHAPTER *21*

God's Little Lambs

One day, around noon, I went into the kitchen to remind the cook of a special diet for one of the patients. "Mattie, when you take trays up, make sure Annie gets only soft food," I called from the kitchen door.

"I'll get to it soon as I can," she muttered, hurriedly dishing up food and throwing it on the trays. "She'll be here any minute!"

"Who's coming?" I asked. I had never seen Mattie disgruntled before while she prepared meals. Before she could answer, I heard patients behind me rushing to the clinic door, as nurses in the dining room rose to look out the window. I headed for the door to see what was happening.

A group of children approached, following a horse up the hill. As the rider passed, townspeople threw up hands in greeting, calling Howdy, or Afternoon! "I'll take ye'er horse and turn him over to Clint," offered one of the men, stepping up to catch the reins.

A nice looking woman in middle age dismounted in front of the clinic, beaming at the children and patting heads approvingly, as she complimented them on their growth, or how well a broken arm had healed. They all looked to her for attention, each one expecting a greeting. Then, satisfied, they all cavorted back down the hill.

Our guest stamped her boots at the door, brushing trail dust off her riding pants, and pinning up escaping gray hair strands. Everyone moved aside to allow her entrance to the living room, while the clinic nurse advanced to greet her. I had no doubt as to her identity, but our hostess verified it when she said, "Come on in, Mrs. Breckinridge. We've been expecting you!"

"I've just been making my rounds," Mrs. Breckinridge told her audience. Stretching, she headed for the dining room. "Mattie! How about lunch?" The waiting cook gladly hurried to fetch it, while Mrs. Breckinridge joined the nurses at the table. To my surprise, she motioned for another new nurse and me to join her. Janie Burton had come to Hyden about the same time as I, and she had never met Mrs. Breckinridge either. We eagerly took our seats.

"Welcome to Hyden," she smiled to Burt and me. During lunch, the founder of the Service recounted a brief personal history. Her ancestry was from an old, wealthy Kentucky family, and she had studied in our best schools and abroad. Since her father had served as Minister to Russia during Grover Cleveland's presidency, she had grown up in Washington, D.C., overhearing national discussions. It was there she developed a concern for the health and welfare of people in rural areas. Her first husband had died, a second marriage failed, and when her two children also died, she reclaimed her family name.

On her property in Wendover, a few miles from Hyden, she built a summer home in memory of her children. Soon she became aware of many mountain children's deaths in their second year due to 'summer complaint', or diarrhea. Appalled at the severe lack of medical care for the area, she went to New York and obtained nurses' training. Since there were no midwifery schools in America, she went to England and recruited two nurse midwives to help her. Later, more nurse midwives from England and Scotland completed the present staff of twenty-eight.

"Mrs. Breckinridge," I said, "I'm curious as to how the staff here knew that you were coming. I don't recall anyone ringing us on the phone."

"By the grapevine, Mitch. You'll soon learn that no one stirs in these hills without the mountain folk knowing which creek you're on, or which hollow you've crossed. Somehow they relay information, either by the children, by whistles, or bird-calls."

"By the way," she said, getting back to her subject. "You and Burt are pretty familiar with hospital and clinic routine by now. Why haven't you been fitted for riding uniforms? It's time you both were given a horse to ride!" This news came surprisingly soon to us. We thought our initial service would be at home base, in the medical compound.

"Ladies," she continued, "As you know, war is spreading daily in Europe since Hitler's attack on Poland. Some of our overseas nurses have already left for home, and I feel others will soon follow." She glanced across the table at Annie McKennon from Scotland, and Betty Lester from England, who evidently would soon depart. "This imminent nursing shortage compels us to open our own midwifery school here." She looked at Burt and me, her eyes twinkling. "You two will be our first students. Betty Lester, and Nora Kelley, both from England have agreed to stay long enough to teach the course."

Burt and I grinned, sharing elation over going out on horseback so soon. While she sipped hot tea, Mrs. Breckinridge looked at our hands. "From now, on your hands belong to the FNS. You must do nothing to get sores or infected scratches on them. Any woman going out to deliver, with the possibility of infecting a mother or baby, is the same as a murderer. The death rate here is now the lowest in America. We've come far in thirteen years, and we don't intend to go backwards." She set down her teacup. "See to it that you girls get measured for uniforms this afternoon."

With lunch over, Mrs. Breckinridge rose abruptly and left the table. "Have to finish checking on my little lambs," she said. Turning to Burt and me before she left, she quoted from the book of Isaiah, in the Bible. "'He gathers them with His arms, carries them in His bosom, and gently leads those with young'. We should do the same." She limped to the door, with a permanent injury evident from the fall from her horse, but she carried charm and strength in each movement. As if on cue Clint appeared, leading her horse from the barn, and after mounting, she soon left the hospital area.

I watched her leave. As her horse trotted down the hill and nodded to people in her path, their deep respect was evident in the way they greeted her. *She's burning her life out for these people! She rides the rounds of all eight centers with never-ending concern!* Now I understood why nurses gave up salaries when funds ran low, and vacations when pregnancies were about to terminate, why committees donated clothing and medicine, why our doctor worked long hours, to save an ignorant people from starvation, disease and death. With her sacrificial life, she challenged others to demonstrate a love for the least of God's children, or as she put it, the love of God's little lambs.

I rather liked her term. While they were vulnerable to outside thinking, lamb-like in their trust in us, the mountaineers made me feel a responsibility to carefully nurse them. I especially found myself wanting to care for and protect the young mothers with babies.

That afternoon Burt and I followed instructions and were fitted for our custom uniforms, which were made on the English style. We pulled on jodphurs, the tight-legged pants that bloused at the hips, and pushed them into heavy boots. A black tie dressed up a long sleeved white shirt to be worn underneath a grey-blue coat that reached to mid thigh. On my head I perched a little grey cap with FNS embroidered in black. Fully dressed, we admired our attractive outfits in a full-length mirror.

Similarly, a firm-threaded light blue twill pair of pants, and sleeveless vest over the shirt, made up a summer uniform. Lightweight English boots completed it.

"Now, for a horse. Have you ridden often?" asked Lester.

"Only work horses," I confessed.

"You need a good, safe horse that rides well. Come out to the barn and meet Lady Ellen."

Inside the barn I patted a small mare. "She's lovely. I had hoped for one like this, from the blue grass country."

"Her beautiful running walk covers long distances," Lester said admiringly. "Seated on her back, you don't even move in the saddle, she's that smooth."

"Humph. She's no lady," said Clint from the next stall. "She's a little vixen. If you're riding together, she's a real flirt."

"Oh, a Scarlett O'Hara, huh?" I scolded. Lady Ellen responded to our teasing and patting with good-natured nuzzling.

* * * * *

Soon, I went out on district, to train with either Lester or Kelley. "We each have about a hundred and twenty-five families, and we do *everything* for them; take care of the mothers before and after delivery, deliver the babies, counsel the fathers and old people.

We immunize the children. We've even treated whole families for worms."

Sometimes when we went out on delivery, a mountaineer came for us, to chip the ice off the trail. Our loaded saddlebags were too valuable to risk losing by swimming a horse on a routine call, but in spring when the rivers and creeks flooded, it became necessary. We were exposed to the same diseases and maladies that affected the patients. One little boy's head was festered with lice and I undertook the job of getting rid of them. When I complained to Kelley about a furiously itching scalp, she examined it. "You have nits!" she said. I nearly scrubbed my scalp off, treating it for the eggs.

When we held clinic over on Thousand Sticks, we passed an old woman's house along the creek bed. She usually stood in the doorway and waved.

"Lite-a-wee!" she called one morning.

"What did she say, Lester?"

"It's old speech for, 'get off your horse and sit for awhile.'"

"Can't," I called back. "We need to get to clinic."

"I'll shear ye a flower pot," she called in her light, high voice.

"She'll cut you a bouquet."

I couldn't resist her invitation. "All right. Just for a minute."

"You been eating right, Granny?" asked Lester.

"I reckon. I hate them shucky beans, though." She cut a few flowers that she had coaxed out of the shaley soil and handed them to me, displaying a new friendliness from the mountainfolk. "Ye gonna be our nurse now, Miss Mitchell?"

"Yes. I'll check on you often," I replied amiably.

"I'll be a lookin' for ye," she grinned, showing a mouthful of snuff.

However, I shunned the overt friendliness of one of the mountain men. While riding up a creek bed one day, I ducked under a tree limb that had brushed against me, and I lost my St. Luke's nursing pin from my tie. Word soon reached me that a young moon-shiner had bought it from a child, who had found it lying in the sand.

"Guess I'll have to get the nurse this belongs to, now that I've got her pin," he bragged.

Horrified, I told Dr. Kooser.

"Mitch," he said, amused. "Send word by Clint, that if he'll bring me the pin, I'll have some cigarettes for the man, and I'll pay him what he gave the child for finding it."

A couple of weeks later, I got my pin back. Not long afterwards, the same fellow was shot and killed in a drinking brawl. I thought of Grinstead and her proposal of a mountaineer to go along with the horses. I shuddered, imagining the grubby mountaineer's amorous advances.

However, a new love had awakened inside me, and a new affection budded from the mountain folk. Already, in town husbands of the women I visited nodded, and said howdy. Townspeople I didn't know smiled briefly in acceptance. Often, in the grocery store I heard a soft, "Hey, Miss Mitchell." Turning to look, a little blond head would peep around her mother's skirt, or a little boy would playfully dart by.

With each trip up a mountainside, whether on delivery or routine clinic, the outside world receded further away. I became locked in another time and culture with sweet people and their winsome ways. Responding to needs night and day, like Mrs. Breckinridge, I began loving His little lambs. Even at night, while my body renewed itself with sleep, I carried lambs with me in my dreams.

CHAPTER 22

Born Before Arrival

War clouds grew blacker in Europe and with each mail, letters from home raised anxiety for families and war conditions, increasing the uneasiness among the English and Scotch nurse midwives. Many nurses had already left out of loyalty to their countries, when pressure from families and government increased. The mass exit of nurses all but wrecked FNS. Mrs. Breckinridge, quite concerned about the mountain work, didn't see how we could continue with such an exodus of help, so she intensified the midwifery course for Burton and me. As tension mounted with Kelley and Lester, they sometimes took out their frustrations on us. I restrained my tongue from angry retort many times.

One wicked night, when icy patches lay scattered over the frozen ground, a man walked several miles to reach us in a bitter, steady wind. He had left his wife in hard labor.

"We know the way," Kelley curtly told him. "Get on back, we'll be along soon." Our horses objected at leaving their warm stalls, particularly Kelley's big horse; he kept turning in circles to evade the bridle.

When at last we started out, our horses made slow progress breaking through the crusty ice. I thought we were lost in a forest of icicles until a familiar barbed wire gate barred our way. Being the student and youngest, I politely dismounted to open the gate. My feet ached with the cold, and when I moved they felt like dead weights as I carefully stepped around the ice. I clumsily worked at the closed gate with stiff fingers.

"Can't you hurry?" Kelley snapped from her horse, which stood at least sixteen hands high. She was a short woman all bundled up in coats, and with a woolen scarf around her neck she looked like a little toad perched on the horse's back. Her persistence in prodding me to hurry made me clumsier than ever, but at last the gate swung free from the post at top and bottom. After leading my horse through I stood to the side waiting for hers to pass, but Kelley's horse wouldn't budge.

Impatiently, she kicked him hard. He lunged forward, slipped on the ice, and in the process of regaining his balance he lost Kelley. Off his rump she slid and scooted down the icy hill like a little dumpling. Finally skidding to a stop, she tried to get up but couldn't because of so many clothes. She clambered around and then fell, looking like Humpty Dumpty, who couldn't get up again. I couldn't keep from laughing out loud.

"You bloody American! You'd let me die! Get my horse!" she screamed in rage. I quickly composed myself, put my horse's reins over the gatepost, and caught her horse. I hurried down the hill to her. "Are you hurt?" I asked, bending to help her, giggles escaping no matter how tightly I held my mouth.

"Let me alone!" She let out another angry stream of words against the bloody weather, bloody horse, and bloody nurse. I held her horse for her to mount, and we were soon astride again, her leading the way, and me following at a distance while I stifled the giggles.

When we approached the cabin, it looked dark and the dogs began to bark when we called out. Coming to the door, the man said, "I've jest been here a bit." He had no lamp burning, and a very poor fire sizzled from wet wood. "The fire ain't caught yet."

Kelley went straight to the fire to rub her bruises while I unpacked my saddlebags. The student is to do everything on delivery, while the supervisor only watches and advises.

My flashlight revealed a huge mound in a bed of heavy comforters, made from old coats and pants. Only a bit of frosty breath coming from a peephole revealed the patient. "How are you?" I asked the patient, and when I raised the covers she shivered from the cold. "Are you still having pains?"

"I've done had it," she replied through chattering teeth. *Under all that cover! It's bound to be dead.* With dread I tucked the covers back around the woman, and felt down lower to find the baby. Bending down beside the bed I pushed the quilts slightly aside, and surprisingly, shone the flashlight on a lovely pink infant that lay against her leg with the placenta still attached. I touched the baby and it stretched and moved its lips as if nursing.

"The baby's here," I reported to Kelley, who sat by the fire in silence. I rubbed my cold hands to warm them before I palpated the mother's abdomen; when I did her uterus contracted nicely. During the examination of mother and baby, I noticed the mattress had no sheet on it. "The baby's fine. But if I bathe it in this cold house, it'll take pneumonia."

"Do as you bloody please!" Kelley responded.

I boiled water at the fireplace in order to sterilize the scissors, and the water froze within minutes after placing it at the bedside. *I'll get a lecture about this, but I'm not bathing this baby.* I made a teepee from the quilts and placed the newborn under the tent, then stuck the upper half of my body under the tent. While I held the flashlight in one hand or let it prop against the covers, I put silver nitrate in the baby's eyes, tied and cut the cord, thereby loosing the baby from the placenta.

"You have a fine boy, Cora!"

"Hot diggity!" crowed the father from the shadows.

After hastily dressing the infant, I moved him up through the covers from the foot of the bed to the comfort of his mother's breast. Fortunately, the mother needed very little bathing.

"Take this medication now, and it'll all be over," I said, as I broke the ice in the bucket with a dipper, and handed her a drink. I threw the placenta on the burning logs and it popped three times. The mother laughed.

"I've got three more times to go through birthing."

"Is that a sure sign?"

"Never fails! I jest hope it's never this cold again." Her husband and I agreed.

After I repacked the saddlebags, Kelley moved from her spot by the fire, and strode out the door without a word. The waiting horses stomped and neighed impatiently for their feed waiting in the barn.

"I'll be back, day after tomorrow," I promised. The father propped a chair against the door after we left to keep out the wind, but there was little difference in the temperature, inside the cabin or out.

I hurried to catch Kelley who had already mounted, and was heading off down the trail. Not one word of conversation passed between us on the long ride back to the hospital.

CHAPTER 23

The Matriarch

"Mitch, your first assignment is Thousand Sticks on Bull Creek," informed McKennon, the hospital supervisor. "You're to ride the district around the mountain, visit the new mothers and babies, and check the children for worms and disease. If anybody needs to come to the hospital, either send them, or bring them when you return."

Burt and I had just completed twenty-seven classes in nurse midwifery. The course included more than a hundred prenatal visits in the homes, a hundred postpartum visits, and assisting in sixteen special clinics. I had helped with over thirty deliveries, including several BBA's (born before arrivals). After the stiff course ended, our instructors hastily left for Europe. Burt and I passed the Kentucky State Board Examinations, but our midwifery exams were delayed. Meanwhile, we filled two of the five staff vacancies.

"We've received word that Annie Smith is about ready to deliver, so you can begin your duty on Thousand Sticks by paying her a visit," suggested McKennon.

"How do I get there? I haven't been to Thousand Sticks many times, and the forests still look the same to me."

"Just go up Twisting Sourwood Creek past Hell-Fer-Sartain Mountain. She lives on a hollow up there."

I started out, carefully studying the trails, looking ahead to find my way, while I constantly looked back hoping I could remember how to return. All the creeks and mountains had interesting names. Twisting Sourwood Creek wandered and twisted among groves of shrubby Sourwood trees. I had once climbed rugged Hell-Fer-Sartain Mountain, and decided it was appropriately named. Its forests dropped down to winding ravines to the creek, which was friendly at first, but narrowed to a deep gulch. Broken rock and mammoth boulders made dangerous going for horse or man. Kingdom Come Mountain, some distance away, invoked the expression, "It's as far as Hell-Fer-Sartain to Kingdom Come!"

Along Bull Creek, children saw me studying the hills and ridges. "Thar's our nurse!" they called.

"Where does Annie Smith live?" I asked, hoping they didn't know I was hopelessly lost. They pointed the way; farther along the younger ones ran to ask their parents. As I made my way trying to remember directions, people came out on their stoops, or suddenly appeared among the trees to lead me. I could hardly have been lost at any time, with all the eyes and ears of the mountain grapevine alerted to my presence in their forest.

Thousand Sticks Mountain received its name from two stories. A heavy cyclone had come through and uprooted many trees, so that the place looked like a thousand sticks had fallen upon each other. The other story was that of a forest fire that had felled many trees as they burned. When they built the post office in the area, the employees rode through the fallen trees, and one fellow remarked, "This looks like a thousand sticks!"

The other man agreed, "That's a good name for the post office."

The trip to Annie's proved a false alarm, but one night just at the edge of dark, her husband came for me. The term 'edge of dark' was used because Thousand Sticks, Pine Mountain, and nameless hogback crags cast twilight among the trees before dark descended. The man's mule, homeward bound went at a steady gait. He guided me through the trails, slowing to rest my horse.

"Watch for low limbs that might trip ye'er horse," he reminded me, the inexperienced nurse. Bull Creek was down, so we forded it easily. I knew we had arrived at his cabin when the hounds started baying.

"Hurry in while there's light," said the nervous father. He added proudly, "I'll put ye'er horse in the barn." The crude-structured barn was taller than most - which were usually too low to house a horse, and were used only for pigs and chickens.

A low kerosene lamp with no globe, and a burning log in the fireplace offered the only light in the room. While I stood for a few seconds adjusting my eyes, I glanced around at a room freshly papered with newspapers covering the cracks, in order to keep out the wind. In a corner stood a clean, made-up bed. My patient sat by the fire. Then I noticed two other women also present for the birthing, one I guessed to be the patient's mother, another appeared considerably older.

The neat room looked like a play about to begin, with the furniture like props, and the women poised like actresses. It suddenly occurred to me who the older neighbor represented. She was The Matriarch, the boss of all the women on that part of Bull Creek. A mother figure, she governed the raising of children. For instance, if a woman wanted to visit her people on another ridge, she got the matriarch's permission. If a matriarch decided she didn't like a woman, she could even do damage between husband and wife. My mouth twitched in a smile as I turned my head, and draped the saddlebags over a chair. *So! The new nurse is on trial.*

"How are you, Annie?" I asked the patient.

The oldest woman answered, "She's tolerable."

"Do we have any hot water?"

"I got a kettle boiled," curtly replied the matriarch. I made preparations for delivery, while she eyed me suspiciously. She threw at me, "You ain't had any man or raised up any children?"

"Noo," I replied, keeping conversation simple.

"Ye're mighty young to be catching a baby," she allowed authoritatively. I smiled and said nothing. The other two women nodded and exchanged smiling glances. *So far, so good.*

"Mmmm," moaned Annie. "Pains getting a little closer."

"Would you like to get on the bed?" I suggested, provoking surprised looks between the older women. In their day, getting on the bed or birthing chair, meant the time for pushing and expelling the baby, not sleeping.

Annie spoke her first words to me. "I took the big eye last night, couldn't sleep a wink. Reckon I could get a bit of slumber?"

I knew she wouldn't sleep much, but replied, "All right. Why don't you try?" I helped turn back the covers, and Annie reclined in the bed.

While she dozed, the older women crossed their arms and sat by the fire, where I joined them. Glancing at the newspapers that lined the cabin walls with blaring headlines about the war, the stories marching upside down or sideways, I commented, "The room sure looks nice and clean, and the fresh newspapers make it real cozy." The women warmed a little to my compliments. This was usual décor for a birthing, or when they wanted to brighten their sooty cabins they came to the hospital for the papers. They made a paste of flour and water, and glued the papers haphazardly to the walls. Although it did keep out the wind, making the cabins warmer and cleaner, they also became firetraps. Many families got burned out this way, a fire catching quickly when a spark touched the walls.

Annie awakened with a sudden moan, her membranes rupturing with the intensity of the contraction. I quickly scrubbed while I made a decision about the spectators, which I usually didn't allow; but since my expertise as a baby catcher had been questioned, I decided to let them stay.

I was busy with the mother and didn't look around at the other two, but I felt their eyes watching my every move. Soon, a squirming baby boy arrived. They watched me cut the cord and sponge the baby in front of the fire.

"Annie, I'm leaving most of this white stuff on the baby's body. It's what I call God's cold cream, because it contains Vitamin A, and is good for his skin. When I get back day after tomorrow, it will all be gone and he'll look like a little peach blossom." Again the older women looked at one another like I was 'touched in the head' for leaving it on.

Nursing rules required that we wait an hour after the placenta came before leaving a case. I also had to wait till daylight before starting for the hospital alone, so we passed the time discussing the weather and the nice cozy room.

Heated discussion rose about the baby's name between the father and the two older women. The husband, usually lord of his household, was the only person who could successfully disagree with a matriarch. Even then, a matriarch sometimes wielded enough power to boss him. Annie kept her mouth shut till she was certain her husband had won the argument, and then she agreed with him. I waited all the while, pen in hand to complete the birth certificate. At that point the matriarch said, "I allow I'll go now."

"I'll stay with Annie while you show them home," I volunteered to the father, smiling goodbyes to the women as they left. It provided me an opportunity to discuss diet and the baby's care.

"Annie, is there any poke salad around?"

"Yes'm, but I didn't know it was good for a body in my condition."

"Oh, yes. The wild greens are full of vitamins."

"I reckon I could eat a bait of it," she hungrily replied, while she munched on cold cornbread and sipped coffee, the only food the matriarch told her she could have.

At first glimmer of light in the east, Annie's husband brought my horse from the barn. He put on my saddlebags, and then counted out the fee in silver, rubbing each piece as he placed them in my hand. "Ye took good care of my woman. Ye be careful now, it's a far piece back to the hospital."

On my way to Annie's, I had passed a cabin in the creek bed where an elderly couple lived. As I neared it on the way back, I saw the woman waiting for me on the porch.

"What'd they get?"

"A boy! They're doing fine."

She said the polite, "Come spend the day with me."

I replied the correct, "Can't. You just better come with me."

It turned into a glorious ride. I noted every trail, hoping I wouldn't get lost again. Budding beech trees bursting their brown jackets revealed new twigs with leaves, and a clump of hepaticas grew at the foot of one magnificent tree. I stopped and dismounted to view the delicate blossoms at closer range.

"Steady, girl," I told Lady Ellen who stomped and snorted for her oats. "Look at that mossy mound of green velvet. No, you can't eat it." I said, as I walked along leading my horse. Saddle sore from the day before when I had ridden far, visiting new babies and sick folks, I was now weary from the ride to the Smith cabin during the night. I paused to look at grey lichen on a rotting log by the trail. I looked up through the trees to a blue sky and inhaled the scent that ascended from the forest floor. I called out, "Heavenly Father! I praise You for this lovely day!"

I re-mounted Lady Ellen and she adjusted to the leisurely descent on Thousand Sticks Mountain. My view out across the miniature village of Hyden revealed smoke rising from cabins as the day began. How I looked forward to a day of rest.

* * * * *

Back in the barn, Lady Ellen stamped impatiently while I rubbed her down, her head submerged in the oat bag. After I removed stable dirt that clung to her hooves and legs from the Smith barn, I went to the dining room and my own late breakfast.

"Mitch," interrupted Audrey Dyer, "a photographer from the Courier-Journal in Louisville is waiting for you at Wendover. He wants Sybil Holmes' picture as the British nurse going to the war front, and your picture depicting American nurses taking over."

I groaned, "But it's *five miles* to Wendover!"

"Sorry. Mrs. Breckinridge says to hurry."

I reluctantly dragged Lady Ellen from her oats, saddled up and rode to Wendover. The photographer posed Sybil and me in front of a barn, while we rode a mountain road, and forded a stream; we even visited a cabin where I bandaged a scratched knee. "Now, just one more. How about a picture of you assisting a student in delivery."

"That's another five miles back!" I said wearily. "Oh, all right, since I have to return there anyway." At the hospital I scrubbed once more. Fortunately, a woman's delivery was imminent. Then I mumbled to the photographer, "If you want any more pictures, you must take them without me. I'm going to bed." I calculated on the way to my room that I had traveled a total of forty miles since the day before.

I almost fell asleep putting on my nightgown. I reviewed the day in my mind's eye, the scenario with the mountain matriarch and the patient in her jurisdiction. *Had I won her approval?* Then my drowsy thoughts centered on the glories of creation that I had reveled in earlier that morning. A smile traced across my lips as I inhaled again, as if to recapture a trace of the damp odor of the leafy forest alive with spring. The last thing I remembered before I fell asleep was the close-up of hepatica blue against a grey beech trunk.

Hannah's Journal, mid-June 1990

With a heavy heart today I dressed for church to teach the Sunday school class that I have taught for years. From this class, on How To Teach the Bible, students have left prepared to lead others in Bible study after several months under my tutelage. But now, my familiar Bible has become a jumble of words whenever I attempt preparing an outline, making it unfair to those attempting to hone their spiritual gifts. God, in his wisdom, has revealed it is time to relinquish teaching the class.

The decision at last resolved, while I drove to church, I prayed for poise and dignity.

I simply told the class, that for a few months I have considered going to Louisiana to live with my sister-in-law, and that the time had come. The room grew silent as class members sensed what I was about to say. With a trembling voice I told them, that although I would miss them, I had resolved that today was to be my final lesson. Somehow, I made it through, hoping the lesson was taught with clarity.

With the matter settled, another incident occurred to assure me that I had made a sensible decision. I became disoriented on the way home after church, and only arrived safely because a stranger let me follow his car when I told him my address.

My hands shook with fright when I unlocked my front door. I am nauseous with worry! How could I remember my address when I was unable to find my house?..I collapsed on the sofa. Would the time soon come when I wouldn't know my name?... My name...Hannah Druscilla!

CHAPTER 24

My Namesake

After my first initiation to Thousand Sticks, riding district gradually became routine in the months that followed, with each trail more imprinted in my memory and the cabins more familiar.

In the middle of a summer night someone came to me. "Mitch, you have a call on Owl's Nest. It's Molly Butler." At three o'clock in the morning I belonged to the world of the unconscious, and memory of creeks and mountains ran together. I dressed quickly while I tried to recall the patient.

Let's see. Molly Butler. Oh, yes. Her husband abandoned her. Wonder who came for me....Jackson, or Fred from down below, probably. Put on my black tie. Where's my nursing pin? Bet her mother, who said she has delivered many a baby, sort of wishes I wouldn't hurry. Strap to the right boot. Wonder how the river is. It was pretty high yesterday.

Within minutes, I had saddled up and started out for the delivery under an early dawn sky that looked grey among the stars. A pale late quarter moon hung unsubstantial and thin as Lady Ellen and I set out down the hill. A committee of dogs met us in the road at

Pig Alley, challenging our advance, while others bayed in defiance from houses along the way. Then, no sound except the splash and gurgle of water under Lady Ellen's feet, as we forded the river at Owl's Nest on the lower part. I looked back at the man walking far behind with his swinging lantern as the forest closed in, and only the gleam of my flashlight showed the way.

I finally arrived at the Butler cabin that offered only the light from a six-inch lamp without a globe. However, a welcoming fire glowed from the grate, with hot and cold-water basins beside the bed, and clean baby garments on a nearby table – all the work of two neighbors and the attending grandmother. With smiles and nods, they frequently asked, "Can we help you, nurse?"

Molly's helpful gathering of women waited for three hours till the sun peeped over the top of a ridge and shone through a crack in the wall. Still they waited with anxious expressions. "What can we do, nurse?" Mindful of their concern, I allowed the birthing committee to change the bed linens as labor advanced.

At last, when the sun came up in full strength, the waiting silence faded as their faces broadened with reassured smiles when they heard the wail of a baby girl. Joy broke loose in the cabin.

"You got a name child, now!" cackled the grandmother as she thumped me on the back. "Molly always said she was going to name it after you if it was a girl baby!"

Molly looked at me, beaming. "Miss Mitchell, this here's Hanner Druciller!"

I looked at the women. They could tell I was flabbergasted. Professionally, we nurses practiced not telling the mountaineers our first names; they only knew us by our last names. I recalled a conversation with Molly, when I had said, "Oh, you don't want to name your baby after me. Besides, you don't *know* my first name."

"But won't you tell me?" she had pleaded.

"Oh, no. You should name it after someone else you like well." How she found out my full name I'll never know, but I carried my namesake to the fireplace for her first bath and hugged her snugly on the way. "Well, she's a little darling," I crooned.

When they heard the baby cry, Molly's other children raced over from across the hollow where they had waited at a neighbor's house. When they ran inside, one of the little tykes asked in astonishment, "Where'd this baby come from?"

Molly smiled and bit her lip to keep from laughing. "Why, Miss Mitchell brung it in her saddlebags."

The children's eyes shone while they watched me bathe their little sister by the open fireplace. I answered all their questions while I dressed Hanner, and at the same time I kept noticing a persistent tug at my shirtsleeve. I finally looked down at a little face looking up at me anxiously.

"Miss Mitchell, Billy Gene lied to us."

"He did? How did he lie?"

"He said you warn't kin." Her little chin quivered. "Is you kin?"

I glanced quickly at the smiling mother watching her daughter from the bed. Because the child's expression desired so badly that I be related, I fleetingly prayed that I wouldn't also lie.

"Well," I said with a tender look. "I'll be kin if you want me to."

Her face lit up and she skipped across to her mother, whispering loudly, "She said she'd be kin!"

One of the neighbor's children came over to see the baby after I left. His folks had sent him to check out the baby, hoping for a favorable reception since they expected a new one at their house soon. Molly told me that when the child returned home his mother quizzed him.

"What did it look like?"

"Oh, it was red and cryin'."

"How big is it?"

"It's a scrawny little thing!"

"So what did they name it?"

Four-year-old Paul couldn't remember, but he kept scratching his head, shifting from one foot to the other. Finally his eyes danced. "I know! It was Han-me-th'-scissors!"

CHAPTER 25

A Little Watchdog

When Betty Lester went back to England she left behind a small thoroughbred collie named Barrie. I had often watched fondly as Barrie ran ahead of Betty's horse when they went out on district, and had thought about how nice it would be to have the companionship of a dog. Since my district was isolated she offered to give Barrie to me before she left. Too, she had recognized our friendship. He would often sit at my feet, laughingly waiting for a word of attention or praise, with his tail wagging when I spoke his name. I liked his even-tempered nature.

At first he didn't understand to come with me when Lady Ellen and I started off down the hill for a delivery, or regular visits to my patients. He would sit by the barn and whine, or come a few feet and then sit on his haunches. "Come on, Barrie, it's okay. Come on, boy." I kept coaxing till he came. Then, once on the trail he was happy, sometimes running ahead or lagging behind to chase a rabbit, or prance alongside me proudly displaying his white ruff.

I wondered what he might do if something unusual happened on the trail. Would he just bark if I took a fall? Would he go for help? I might have found out had he been with me the time I got into trouble along a creek bed. I had been forced to swim my horse across part of a creek, and then, not familiar with the area I dismounted and started walking up the creek bed. It looked solid when I stepped on it, but I was quickly mired up past my knees in quicksand. Within seconds I had sunk to my waist. I called and called to a house that sat a few hundred feet up a hill, but the noise of rushing water along the creek drowned out my cries. Where were those peering mountain eyes when I needed them?

"Oh, Father. Help me!" I screamed. It was then I discovered a limb hanging overhead. With one arm I managed to reach it and hold on. I pulled and tugged with all my might, until my other hand broke out of the sucking mire, and I reached further up the thin little branch, praying it would hold. Finally, hand over hand I gradually pulled myself out with mud and sand clinging to me. I lay exhausted on the creek bank, thanking God for saving me from a terrible smothering death.

"What would you have done, boy? Could you have alerted the people in the cabin and directed them to me?" Barrie barked in reply and chased a squirrel up a tree.

He loved the mountain children. When we went in the cabins and Barrie sat by the chair that held my saddlebags, toddlers often grabbed his tawny fur and pulled up on his beautiful white ruff. Some of them even took their first steps toward him; only when they became too rough would he whine or move away. While I moved around the room making preparations for delivery, he stayed by the chair with the saddlebags, and sat beside me as I bathed the baby. He never snapped at a child, but when an adult came too near the saddlebags, he would growl and show his teeth.

"Ye got ye'erself a watchdog," a surprised father said one day, when he jumped back after Barrie had warned him about coming too near the chair.

"He does seem to like me all right," I agreed. "It's okay, Barrie." The friendly collie wagged his tail at the mention of his name, and nudged against me while I re-packed the bags.

"Where's my stethoscope?" I wondered out loud while I felt in the bags and looked around the room. Over by the fire Granny sat peacefully rocking away, wearing two sweaters with a shawl over her head. Over the shawl was the stethoscope attached to her ears and heart while she listened intently. "I jest wanted to see how my heart was acting", she said with a toothless grin. We all laughed, and I let her listen while I finished caring for the mother and baby, then put my instruments away so I could saddle up.

"What's ye'er hurry?" asked the family. "We got dinner ready for ye." One of the older girls escorted me to a table in the corner with a white cloth and one chair pulled up. Fresh fried chicken, some green beans and cornbread lay steaming on a plate. Families usually saved back a chicken to fry in celebration of a new baby's arrival.

"Have you already eaten?" I asked as she shyly offered me the chair.

"No'm. We'll eat in the kitchen."

"But, can't I eat with you?"

The family looked astonished. "Well, the overseas nurse always liked to eat by herself."

"Well, I want to eat with *you*."

"Why, you're plumb welcome to!" they grinned. "Come on out in the kitchen!" Thereafter, they treated me like a family member, chatting in everyday conversation while we ate the meal.

"Folks talking 'bout you, Miss Mitchell," the father said, winking across the table at one of the boys.

"Oh? What are they saying?"

"Word's out that you're uncommon good with birthing. The old granny of the mountain is telling mothers to paper their cabins and get their baby clothes ready."

"Good!" I laughed. *So! The nurse passed the matriarch's inspection. She can catch the babies now!*

After the meal Barrie and I started for home. A fresh rain had loosened the soil of the mountain trail, so I decided to walk and lead my horse. As we walked along watching rain drip off the trees in the afternoon sunshine, I heard a cracking noise from up high on the mountain, but I paid little attention to it. Barrie had run ahead, but he returned at once, walking close beside me, and then he suddenly placed himself right in front of me on the trail, obstructing the path.

"Move, Barrie! I can't walk, you're so close."

Suddenly, I heard the cracking noise again. Looking beyond me and up the mountainside I saw a cliff give way, loosening boulders and mounds of wet dirt. It all came roaring down the hillside, large stones cracking trees like matchsticks, with mud and dirt oozing behind. The mudslide crashed across the trail up ahead with the woods echoing this roll of destruction. Then, as quickly as it had begun, the woods settled into quietness again. The whole time it was happening, I stood frozen in shock. Barrie still pushed his back against my legs.

It was then I realized his intervention by slowing me down, for had I been in its path I could not have reacted in time to escape. His warning of the slide had saved me from either certain death or injury. "Good boy!" I said, bending down and hugging him. "You saved me from being crushed!" He remained close beside me as we backtracked and took a different route home, with me praising him all the way.

"I never heard of such a thing!" exclaimed one of the couriers when I shared the story back at the stable. "He wasn't trained for it. I know that for a fact!"

* * * * *

I took the nursing exam and received my diploma as the First Graduate of FNS Midwifery School in August 1940. It should have been Burt since her name came first alphabetically, but she became ill and had to postpone her examination. I found it difficult to believe that I had been in Kentucky for almost two years. The work had kept me very busy as Barrie, Lady Ellen and I picked our way up and down icy trails in winter and slippery banks in summer, at all hours of the day and night.

It didn't matter to Barrie, which horse I rode either; he adapted well. I had noticed a large horse in the next stall that usually whinnied a greeting when we returned from district. He seemed very lonely to me because he was never ridden; his only exercise was when Clint walked him around the yard.

"Oh, that's Traveler and he's bad, Miss Mitchell," Clint said, eyeing the horse warily. "They've brought him here from Wendover. He's the horse Mrs. Breckenridge rode the night she fell and broke her back. It was raining and her raincoat flapped across his eyes and scared him into a run. She held on long as she could while he bolted along the trail, but she finally lost her balance and fell. He's plain skittish now every time it rains."

"But he's such a beautiful animal! And he needs more exercise."

Clint gave me a cautious look. "So ye'd like to ride him?"

"I'd be delighted! Anything to get him out of that stall!"

I started re-training Traveler to carry a baby or child, like I had trained Lady Ellen. Beginning with a rolled up newspaper the weight of a baby, I worked up to a child's weight, took him out on district in good weather, and he did fine. Once, a woman on district gave me a watermelon so I took it home on Traveler, holding it between the saddle and me. He didn't object, so Barrie and I alternated between him and Lady Ellen.

The days I traveled long miles I really appreciated being able to switch horses. On Lady Ellen I went to see a baby one day eight miles away, then two miles further to a clinic that I held all day. After being home only a short while, long enough to get my boots off, a man came for me on delivery, ten miles away from the hospital. I switched to riding Traveler this time, because altogether it made a forty-mile day, too far for one horse. But somehow Barrie endured it all, although by nighttime he collapsed beside my bed too tired to eat.

One morning I had many visits to make with new babies and mothers, so I started out quite early on Lady Ellen. White frost sparkled along the mountain trails where sunshine filtered through the overhanging trees. Lady Ellen felt frisky in the cool mountain air that held a touch of fall, and Barrie ran ahead sniffing the damp ground, darting back to me with his tail wagging. "Looking for a rabbit, huh?" I laughed, enjoying the ride. He took off again with his nose to the ground.

When we came within about two hundred yards of the first cabin, I tied Lady Ellen, for slippery beech leaves covered the narrow path down the mountainside. I put my saddlebags over my shoulder and started down the path, looking around for Barrie, who was again out of sight.

Suddenly my feet slipped, and I lost my saddlebags as I started tumbling head over heels down the steep hillside. I snatched at saplings and twigs in my plunge, but I fell too fast to grab hold. I hurdled downward faster and faster, with the forest a topsy-turvy world of trees, and the ground and sky all in a whirring blur. I clawed at the ground frantically, trying to dig my fingers into the mud and leaves in an effort to slow me down. When the world up-righted itself I panicked, realizing that I was headed for a twenty-foot drop over the creek bed, where cruel unyielding rocks lay. I shut my eyes as I neared the drop-off and held my breath.

Then I felt something solid against me, pawing at the ground as it slid with me. I grabbed and hung on as we slipped and oozed down the bank toward the precipice. The furry creature braced itself against my weight, and stubbornly continued pushing and digging, till at last we slowed to a stop just above the creek bed.

I lay on the hillside covered with mud and leaves, heaving and crying with relief while a wet tongue continuously licked my face, crying with dog joy because I was all right. Somehow Barrie had gotten back and placed himself in my treacherous path. I hugged him close and cried into his fur. When I managed to sit up I opened my hands; in each one I held chunks of Barrie's beautiful ruff.

"Oh, Barrie. My lovely Barrie," I cried again, hugging him. At last after I felt around and decided I had no broken bones and could get up, he didn't run ahead anymore; he stayed very close until we reached the cabin.

I called out to the woman and she came running out. "Why, Miss Mitchell! What in tarnation happened to ye?" She sat me in a chair and sponged off my bleeding hands and examined the knot already forming on my forehead. "And ye're uniform is sure ruined, too."

"I almost fell off the cliff back there," I explained in a quivery voice, petting the dog. "But my Barrie saved me."

She looked at the bare spots in his fur. "It'll take months to grow back. But he shore watches after ye good, don't he?"

After the visit, I limped back up the hill to head back to the hospital for a bath and change of clothes before I tried to continue riding district. Barrie proceeded slowly, glancing at me with a watchful eye. Still weak and shaky, I managed to mount Lady Ellen.

On the way home I praised him again for his good deed and told him how beautiful he was. It didn't seem to bother his dignity that his ruff was damaged, but we both took the return trip slowly. As the feeling gradually began to come back in my bruised arms and legs, I realized with a grunt how sore I would be the next day. I shuddered when I thought about the unmerciful rocks at the base of the cliff, and alternated between praising Barrie, and praising God even more, for giving my little watchdog to me, and for saving a life that could hopefully be used for Him.

Chapter 26

Fun Times

Sometimes on a Saturday night or Sunday noon, when I neared the hospital, I could smell delicious roast beef cooking in the oven. The British nurses had made a cultural mark in the hills. I even came to enjoy their menu of very rare beef, Yorkshire pudding, watery vegetables, and especially, trifle - a sponge cake spread with jam and sprinkled with macaroons, or sometimes soaked in wine and served with custard. I couldn't wait to get into something casual and gather around the dining table with everyone – nurses, Dr. Kooser, his wife and children.

"Good evening, Mannie," I called in passing as she now and then sat in gardening attire on the front steps, holding a hoe, or rake, as though she had just finished yard work. I didn't pause for her reply because she never returned a greeting. "What's wrong with Mannie tonight?" I asked whoever happened to be in the living room or clinic area.

"Oh, she's probably tired. I hear she's had a rough day," they replied with mock concern. We never knew where we'd find Mannie. She could turn up anywhere. For a month at a time, everywhere we looked she was there, often at the dining table all dressed up in Sunday clothes from the grab room. She sometimes waited for hours before a meal was served. I didn't find it particularly funny to enter my room at day's end after a hard delivery, and find Mannie in my bed with a nightgown on. It was then; deciding enough was enough, I would hide her carefully, and pretending I had nothing to do with her disappearance, would frantically join the search for her.

"Mannie, come on out! Where are you? Stop that pouting and come out here!" We searched in closets, under beds, in the attic. At times we almost tore the place apart looking till we found her. Periodically I returned the prank, dressed the soft floppy mannequin in a uniform, and sat her on the toilet with a roll of toilet paper in her lap, or placed her on an examining table in the clinic and covered her with a sheet, like a corpse.

Late one afternoon, after posing her in the bathroom, I sneaked back to my room and watched through a crack in the door to see if anyone came down the hall. Sure enough, along came a nurse, with towel and toothbrush in hand to enter the bathroom.

"Oh! Excuse me!" she said when she saw the room was occupied, and waited in the hall. Peeking through the crack I snickered in the dusky twilight while she waited patiently for the person to finish. The sun had completely set when she finally figured out the prank as she eased open the door. I believe she left Mannie reclining in the bathtub, waiting for the next victim when she finished.

Until I went to the mountains I had never gone frog gigging. One night a group of us, including the doctor, went down to a creek where we heard loud croaking bullfrogs. Wearing our worst clothes and long rubber boots, armed with flashlights and long poles as spears, we waded into the creek. The lights shone on swimming snakes that quickly disappeared when they saw the flashlights' beams, but mate-calling frogs froze in the light until we gigged or speared them.

"Whoops!" yelled Dr. Kooser, dropping his flashlight. It waved like a wand in the darkness, and then lay submerged in the water while the doctor struggled to keep his balance, only to splash into the creek himself. We all burst into giggles, but forced ourselves to hush so the frogs would re-gather and start croaking again. All of us came out soaked with mud, but with several frogs, knowing the best was yet to come. Dr. Kooser knew how to dress the frog legs, and keep them from jumping out of the pan while they cooked. Rolled in corn meal and fried in hot fat they made a delicate meal, and in between mouthfuls we laughed about the snakes and spills we endured trying to gig them.

We celebrated both American and British holidays at the hospital. The first weekday after Christmas was called Boxing Day, and was a legal holiday in many parts of the British Commonwealth. We marked it by giving Christmas boxes to postmen and hospital employees.

Days before New Year's Eve we would sneak up to the attic grab room, where boxes of clothing for all ages and sizes waited for the choosing. People from large northern cities sent all kinds of casual or informal wear, work-clothes, and suits. Very useful for the mountainfolk, some outfits looked new or only slightly worn, including French evening gowns that were just right for our dress-up occasions.

On New Year's Eve the entire nursing staff, the doctor and his family, would gather in the clinic waiting room for a Ball. We danced with stark white chests and arms blaring, and dark rings outlining our necks where our high-throated riding habits had come. Even with masks, loaded with costume jewelry, and some of us fortunate enough to find elbow-length gloves, we didn't fool anyone as to our identity.

Luxuries and necessities that we wanted, the local drugstore could not provide. We all flocked around the Sears Roebuck, or Montgomery Ward catalogues for wish book sessions, then what a hassle when a package came, and someone had to receive the delivery and keep the tab straight for various ones purchasing on that order.

I sent off for a wildflower book, which started everyone hunting unusual blossoms and they brought them back to the book to learn its name. Sometimes a flower hung in a buttonhole for eight miles or got squashed into a wallet before it arrived at the authoritative little book. Most of the flowers pictured in it we actually found blooming and growing in our mountain valleys.

* * * * *

"Mitch, why don't we go camping in my pick-up truck?" suggested Audrey Dyer, soon after she bought it. "I'll get one of the men to make wooden bows, covered wagon style, and we'll cover them with canvas." Within a few weeks we had the details worked out for our camper. At the bottom of the canvas sides we attached a broom stick horizontally, so that in the summer we could roll them up at night for ventilation, and drop mosquito netting down for protection from insects. We put a firm mattress on the truck bed that fit tight against the back of the cab. At the tailgate we stored cooking utensils, a grate to place over stones wherever we stopped to cook, a Dutch oven for cornbread, biscuits, or cobblers. I pre-packaged ingredients in jars, except for the fluid, and tucked them around in the bed of the truck. We included a scout axe, butcher knife, and cups, plates, and cutlery.

In our first jaunt we covered parts of six states! On one of those nights we went to sleep by a lake to the sound of jumping fish. Another time, we drove up a side road in the mountains beside a water tank. The truck paused while Audrey changed gears. "Listen," I said, holding up my hand. "I hear water leaking from the water tank." We decided to camp at the spot and took a refreshing shower under the drip. Later, I found a patch of blackberry briars covered with dead ripe berries, and the best part of our dinner that night was blackberry cobbler.

Hooked on camping, Audrey and I couldn't wait for our next time off duty to head out in our covered wagon, each time improving on our camping skills and ways to pack food. We bumped along flapping and rattling like old prospectors with clanging mining pans.

On one trip we arrived in North Carolina park country around four o'clock in the afternoon. We settled in where a huge muscadine vine hid a lovely parking spot, and a cold clear stream provided a bath. That night after dinner we stretched out on the bed to sleep, but I suddenly remembered seeing a sign that said, *Don't Feed The Bears*. Uneasy, I crept out and locked the bacon, jelly and other tantalizers in the cab, then crawled back into bed.

"Audrey, what will we do if a bear comes?"

She yawned. "I'll grab the scout axe, and you take the butcher knife."

During the night I awakened to a smelly creature sniffing outside just even with my face. I didn't dare move and scarcely breathed. After a few minutes he left to sniff around the cab of the truck, and then ambled off. Next morning I said, "Audrey, we had a visitor last night." "You were dreaming!" she guffawed. But when she saw huge paw marks in the dust around the truck she was convinced.

Our last stop that trip was Cumberland Falls, where thousands of mosquitoes swarmed around the camping area, but we felt secure behind our mosquito netting, so we paid them no mind. But Audrey unknowingly had rested her arm against the netting during the night, and next morning it had dozens of bites. She was already shivering with fever, so we cancelled the rest of the trip and headed back to FNS so she could recuperate.

We arrived clanging and banging at the hospital around ten at night, waking the entire countryside of dogs. But the compound was dark as nurses and patients slept on and no one came out to greet us or complain. Only a light from a living room lamp welcomed us, and faithful Mannie in a chair, all proper and ladylike, in a smart black suit and white blouse with a veiled hat adorning her head. Ready for tea the next afternoon, she stared blankly as we stepped into the clinic for medication, and didn't even nod when we told her goodnight.

CHAPTER 27

It Was God's Will

"**G**rannies usually catch my younguns, but one of ye're nurses birthed my last one," stated the prenatal patient I was interviewing at the Bull Creek clinic. I praised her for coming in to register, and questioned her about her previous obstetrical history.

"You have two living girls, don't you?"

"Yes'm. But some of mine have been born dead. One like to bled me to death. I've had a good many bad lucks, don't rightly know how many. I had wasting with some and miscarriages, but I reckon I'm about six months along this time," she said with a hopeful expression on her face.

I commented, "You seem to have a hard time having children."

She dropped her head forward on her hand. "It's queer. My man says I can't fetch him no big family. I guess I'm just drinlin'," she said, referring to her poor health.

"I don't get a drop of milk, except once or twice a swallow of sour milk. I'm a fool about shucky beans with fatback, though," she said, and added, "but if I had my druthers, I'd have them dopes all the time." I jotted down her fondness for soft drinks.

Palpation of her abdomen disclosed an apparently normal fetus in a flabby abdomen that had lost its muscle tone. I approached the subject of hospitalization. She drew back with, "Why, I'd never go there! Lots of folks have died there!"

When I discussed her with Dr. Kooser, he shook his head as though he had heard such stories many times. "You could try talking with her husband," he suggested.

In training, we were taught three purposes as nurse midwives: to offer complete obstetrical care under medical direction to a normal pregnant woman, to recognize any deviation from normal in time so the physician could correct it, and to exercise good judgment and careful evaluation of each patient.

In my evaluation of Sary Osborne, she definitely deviated from normal with her pregnancies. A poor obstetrical risk, her chances of a normal delivery this time looked slim. Through the remainder of her pregnancy, she stayed on my mind. I visualized her going into premature labor, alone in a cold cabin, and possibly hemorrhaging to death. If only I could convince her to spend the last weeks of pregnancy at the hospital, we might possibly save both her and the child.

One day, I met her husband in the road as he rode a mule toward town. I coyly asked about his welfare, the two children and Sary. He looked down at his hands resting on the mule's back. "She ain't never done well, totin' a baby."

"Then why don't you bring her to the hospital ahead of time to have this one? We could watch her carefully. Besides, Mr. Osborne, she could hemorrhage, you know." I spoke in a serious tone.

Sary's husband raised his head and fixed his gaze on the twitching ears of his mule. Turning to me, he said with finality, "Sary don't need to go traipsin' to get a young'un." He kicked up his mule and they headed on to town for supplies.

Sary continued coming to the clinic for visits and listened to my questions and instructions. Her diet had improved. "Our neighbor's cow's fresh and I'm getting sour milk. Been eating soup beans and poke salad," she bragged.

Her hemoglobin had improved and I began to have hope for her. Even at term, however, she still adamantly refused to come to the hospital for delivery. Dr. Kooser had even talked with her husband.

One afternoon, Sary's husband came for me. "She's having miseries," he stated. "I better get on back."

I quickly saddled up. Fortunately they didn't live far away, three or four miles, in case she needed to be brought by stretcher to the hospital. Lady Ellen, knowing the difference between a regular twenty-seven pound saddlebag, and delivery bags that weighed forty, stamped impatiently while I tightened the girth. Either from the extra weight or my tension, she took off when I put one foot in the stirrup. Barrie stayed at home, since it was getting toward evening, and he never accompanied me at night.

By the time I arrived at the cabin, Sary's contractions had become irregular and had almost stopped. The fetal head was not deep in the pelvis, and the baby sort of floated in the uterus. I couldn't get a fetal heart tone.

"Have you felt the baby move this afternoon?" I asked with dread.

"No'm. It was pert the day before, but today it didn't move a heap."

We passed the time chatting about their house plunder. "Some of the furniture was made by my Grandpappy," she related proudly, while I glanced around the darkened room. Straight-backed chairs with hand-woven seats were lined up around a kitchen table, where generations of family members had propped their elbows and forearms. Even the bed slats under her lumpy mattress were hand-sawn years ago at the same time the bed was pegged. The late afternoon grew old while we waited.

Just before dark, I said, "Sary, I need to use your new privy."

"Well," she grinned. "It's plumb full of corn in the ear. Ye'll jest have to take to the woods." The mountain families developed worms from this practice of using the privy in the summer and then storing corn in it during the winter. When the WPA had come in and built outdoor toilets for the mountaineers, it only multiplied sickness for them. Although we told the people constantly to store the corn in another area, they wouldn't. Besides Sary's inadequate diet, I suspected that she also had worms.

After a few hours of waiting for the baby's birth, I had about decided it was a false call. On the other hand, I felt quite uneasy. Her strong contractions came and went with irregularity, and the baby's head was not descending, as it should. Checking again, I still found no fetal heart tone.

Sary's husband came to the doorstep and asked how things were going. I went out and quietly said, "Would you mind going back for the doctor?"

"I ain't never unsaddled for fear of fetching the doc. He knowed she was uncommon piedy." When he left, I prayed for his and the doctor's soon return.

Sary rested some. Flames from the stone fireplace sent rays of hope into the room as we continued our quiet vigil. Occasionally, I walked out on the uneven porch boards and squinted at afternoon shadows in the silent trees, hoping to see Dr. Kooser and Sary's husband. Then I went inside again and returned to her bedside.

Suddenly, she awoke with a strong contraction. With one sharp yell, she pushed hard, and out came the baby with a bloodless cord tightly wound around its neck. I hastily cut the cord, clamped and wound it, while I watched for any sign of life in the perfectly formed little body. I scooped mucous from its mouth and tried to resuscitate it, but I used all my knowledge in vain.

A small gush of blood recalled me to the mother. When the placenta came out it was torn, and the remaining short cord stripped thin. Sary knew it was hopeless.

"It's another dead one," she moaned.

"Yes. The cord was too short. I'm so sorry, Sary."

Grief and despair welled up in her eyes, and then an expressionless mask came over her face. She didn't cry. Resignedly, she said, "It was God's will."

I was holding the fundus to tighten up a boggy uterus so she wouldn't bleed, when I heard the clatter of hooves on the creek bed stones. Dr. Kooser bounded in. "The baby's here, Doctor. But it's dead. The cord was apparently too short and was around its neck. See what you think."

When he saw the torn placenta he whistled under his breath. "She could have easily bled to death," he said. We carefully inspected the semi-circles of the placenta, interlaced with blood vessels. Called cotyledons, if one of these remains inside the mother, she will bleed. After fitting them together we decided no pieces had been left inside the uterus.

I bathed the dead baby, dressed it, and set it aside. The father came in to look at it. "What was it?" he asked, and then dejectedly walked outside to sit on the doorstep. Dr. Kooser went out to explain what had happened, but the father didn't understand, or didn't want to discuss his failure to have sired a live son.

When all was done, Dr. Kooser and I left them to their grief. We emerged from the grieving tomb of the cabin into a living night forest, yet I carried with me the loss. We mounted our horses in the light of a full moon that flooded the countryside, bathing everything in fairyland splendor. Even the stones in the creek bed shone. The leaves on the cow cumber trees danced when a slight breeze flitted by, exposing their silvery under-leaves.

A short flat area gave us a chance to ride our horses alongside. Traveler and Lady Ellen, equally matched, raced home to their supper. We could hardly restrain them and were so busy handling our horses we didn't get a chance to discuss the case. The only other sound besides the pounding of hooves was Dr. Kooser's frequent chuckle, at being out from the hospital and on horseback again. However, exhilaration from the ride had no effect on me; I just wanted to get home.

While we unsaddled in the barn I offered to rub down the horses, but the doctor sensed I needed his opinion. "Mitch, this is one you'll just have to chalk up as a loss. You tried to get her to come into the hospital. Even there, nothing you could have done would have made a difference."

"I know," I admitted with a catch in my voice. I gave Lady Ellen a firm rub down that night while I tried to follow his advice. After all, we seldom lost a baby in childbirth anymore. I should be thankful.

But even two days later, when I went back for Sary's postpartum check-up, I nearly fell apart emotionally, as I prayed all the way about how I could help her deal with grief and guilt.

A neighbor woman opened the door for me and I entered the room that would ordinarily show signs of a baby's presence, with diapers hanging on a chair by the fire, little grunts, or wails, as it demanded to be fed. Sary nodded at me from the quietness of her bed. I gently gave her postpartum care, and she touched my hand like I was part of the family. Silently, I shared their grief while I jotted down nursing notes.

After I finished she said, "I want to show ye something." I looked up at the neighbor who was bringing me a pillow, which I recognized as the one where I had placed the dead baby. Carefully preserved was the indentation made by the weight of its little head – their only reminder of its brief presence. I smiled sadly at them both. The neighbor, then gently, so as not to disturb the pillow, placed it back on top of a primitive clothes press.

Sary began to talk then. "The preacher'll come next spring for big church at the burying ground and people'll come for miles around." Her voice faltered, and then grew stronger as she continued. "We'll have a baby buried there now, so kin are bound to come. There'll be a big dinner on the ground."

She began to plan the memorial service, her thoughts easing grief and guilt for the present. The service would be a time of belonging in the community, with social prestige. Later, alone in the long, dark hours, when her house was still and her family asleep, she could remember her baby again, and ponder God's will.

I marveled at the inner strength of these hill-folk, and their acceptance of personal loss as 'being the Lord's will'. I saw them express it time and again after the death of a loved one, or a house burning, or when they went hungry. It was possibly their way to remain sane as they struggled to survive in poverty and ignorance.

Barrie and Lady Ellen seemed to sense my mood as we slowly picked our way along the ridge back to the hospital that afternoon. Along the way, as the trail wound up and down hills, through the creek beds, and on toward the hospital, I thought of the Osbornes.

Then I was similarly reminded of those people who never make their spiritual birthing cry in the Lord Jesus. Just as its own cord had choked the beautiful baby in the cold cabin, so do their own bonds of self-centered righteousness choke them. Like the baby who never saw life, they too are dead, lost forever from the loving arms of the Heavenly Father. How He must grieve for all the children that will never know Him, or come out of poverty of sin into the riches of His glory, and the life that He prepares for His family.

Chapter 28

Stanley Jones

During the early days of colonization in the Kentucky Mountains, settlers claimed property near the creek beds. Eventually, the creeks were named for the families who lived on them; for instance, Ashers Branch, or Jones Mountain and Jones Creek. As a man's family grew up and left to make homes for themselves, each child received a parcel of land on the same creek bed that bore their family names. It is around the area of Jones Mountain and Jones Creek that Stanley Jones lived.

Stanley had earned quite a reputation in that part of the country. Twelve notches cut on his revolver identified the number of men he had killed during feuds or fights with revenuers. Evidently he always got his man.

Stanley's wife had developed high blood pressure during her first pregnancy, and the nurse at that time advised her to register at the clinic early if she became pregnant again. So, when she came in early in her second pregnancy, there was some question in my mind whether she really was pregnant. She was, however, and did quite well until her eighth month when she developed cloudy urine and erratic blood pressure, signs of toxemia poisoning.

"You know, it would be wise if you had the baby in the hospital," I suggested.

"Oh, no'm. It's too far away. Besides, I couldn't leave Stanley or my little boy."

Unable to convince her that she would receive better care in the hospital, I started visiting her at home. Each time, she showed me something new that she had prepared for the baby's coming: either crude bed pads made from newspapers she had picked up at the hospital, or rough homespun baby clothes she had pieced together.

Whenever I went out to pay them a visit, I knew to let Stanley know when I approached a certain point on the mountain trail by singing, or whistling, or talking loudly to my dog Barrie, or my horse. Stanley operated a still, making off mash in the daytime and selling moonshine at night, and I didn't want to chance getting shot at by stealthily arriving near the vicinity of the still. Sometimes his tall, lanky frame would suddenly appear in front of me from behind a tree. Honed down like a razor strap, with every muscle like iron, he would nod, or say howdy, then wait until I passed. After his brief greeting, he would again vanish into the forest. We never mentioned the still or any danger about sudden appearances.

The Jones' cabin roosted at the top of his mountain above the creek bed, and a torturous winding path led up from the creek among huge rocks. At times, after I had climbed up the path, I would find Stanley sitting on the porch, his gun resting on his knees while he scanned the area below from his bird's eye view. Had he spotted revenuers he could easily frighten them away, or pick them off before they could climb up the path.

Early one evening, after I had just gone to bed a call came from the hospital yard. "Halloo. Halloo. Hello there!" Someone went to find out who it was, and then appeared at my door. "It's Stanley. He's come for you to deliver his wife."

I had ridden Lady Ellen all day so I saddled Traveler and we started out, with Stanley on a fast mule trotting beside me. About two miles along on the eight-mile trip, a sudden mountain storm came up and quickly developed into an electric storm. Lightning flashed and ran along the ground from low hanging clouds, and played all around Traveler's feet, accompanied by an immediate explosion of thunder that preceded a downpour of rain. Traveler reared in panic, threatening to lose both the saddlebags and me in his terrible fright.

"It's all right, boy," I kept saying soothingly. "Calm down. You're doing fine." My patting him on the neck and talking did nothing to calm him. Sweat became foam, and the foam got thicker and thicker. Finally, realizing I couldn't hold him or keep pace with Stanley, I let him out.

"I'm going on ahead!" I called out. "Pick up the pieces if you find them by the wayside!" I heard Stanley laughing as Traveler charged into a terrified run.

I knew we were coming to an area with a steep grade so I figured he would tire out there. In the daytime I always led him up this steep incline but now I didn't dare, for fear he would tread on me and injure me terribly, so I stayed on. He climbed with all his might, his sides heaving. I again tried to slow him down to help his difficult breathing, but deep in his memory lurked the stormy night when Mrs. Breckenridge's rain cape had swept across his eyes, frightening and blinding him. Just when he seemed pacified, another bolt of crashing lightning sent him in another hurdle up the next incline. We arrived quickly at the foot of Jones Mountain.

I walked Traveler around for a few minutes to cool him before I dismounted. Though it still rained hard, the thunderstorm had pretty well passed. I tied him with his bridle reins and a spare halter before I started the long climb up to the cabin, so I wouldn't find myself stranded when I returned.

At last, with the help of my flashlight guiding me around the boulders, I arrived. "Helloo," I panted. No one answered and I went in. My patient lay on her bed in a dark and quiet room with a child asleep beside her. The fire in the grate was only a bed of coals.

I glanced in her direction while I turned up the lamp, and momentarily froze when I made out her form. Her head was thrown back, eyes bulging. Saliva oozed from her mouth as her body stiffened and jerked with one of the worst convulsions I have ever seen. I quickly dashed out to the lean-to kitchen for a pail of water to wash my hands, then grabbed a needle and syringe out of my saddlebags, and gave her a first injection of magnesium sulfate, to begin bringing down her high blood pressure.

Stanley arrived at the foot of the hill just as I finished. Before taking his mule to the barn some distance away, he only tied him and rushed up to the cabin.

"Stanley, your wife is very sick," I said when he entered the room. "She is having continuous convulsions. It's too far to go for another woman to help me, so you'll have to be my help tonight. Do you think you can do it?"

He went to the bed to confirm what I had said, and his face blanched. "Yes, Miss Mitchell," he said in a hushed tone. "I'll do whatever you say."

"All right. Hold this tongue blade in her mouth, and don't allow her to bite down too hard on it. Try to keep her from chewing her tongue. And watch your fingers!"

He followed my instructions, soothingly talking to his wife while I prepared things for delivery. Stanley held her hands still so I could take her blood pressure and get her ready for the birth. Throughout the entire night we worked, holding her in the bed protectively during convulsive labor, giving her medication at intervals. Stanley moved his sleeping son to a pallet in front of the fire that he had built up with fresh logs. Each time I asked, he did everything I wanted.

Just at dawn she had the baby, then her blood pressure promptly returned to normal, and she came to. "How's the baby?" she asked weakly.

"She's fine," her husband answered in relief. "Did ye hear me, darling? We got us a girl baby!"

While I worked with the baby, I motioned to Stanley. "Sometimes women with toxemia bleed severely. We want to prevent this." I showed him how to press hard with his fist on the lower abdomen to keep her from hemorrhaging. This he did, while I cleaned out mucous from the baby's throat, tied and cut the cord, and put silver nitrate in her eyes.

After the baby had a proper bath, and was dressed warmly in one of the homespun receiving gowns, she went to sleep, so I relieved Stanley. Soon afterwards he disappeared, and pretty soon I heard a chicken squawk.

"Sounds like we're having fried chicken for breakfast!" I announced to the new mother. Stanley soon had the chicken in the pan and set about frying apples in lard, and cutting out huge biscuits like an expert cook. I raved about his cooking between mouthfuls, starved after the stormy trip and laborious all night nursing.

After breakfast, and after I was satisfied that the mother's blood pressure remained normal, that she had no excessive bleeding, and that the baby nursed well, I packed to leave. I instructed Stanley on caring for the two. "And if you're away from the house tomorrow, get a woman to stay with your wife. I'll return day after tomorrow."

A couple of days later I found Stanley sitting on the porch, lovingly caressing his old gun. "Howdy," he nodded, evaluating me as I came up on the porch. For the first time, I noticed with a shiver, his steely blue eyes that could turn cold and stare a man down, but they smiled at me from the porch shadow. A quirk of a smile played in the corner of his mouth. "Wife and baby doing fine," he responded to my inquiry about their health.

When I came outside after the visit and started down the rocky slope, I paused and turned to the husband. "Stanley, if I ever leave the mountains and go back to the city, I'm going to apply for a new kind of job."

"What's that, Miss Mitchell?" he asked curiously.

"Back in the city are people who scale tall buildings, going right up the sides as they cling to them all the way. They're called human flies." He smiled because he knew what I would say next. "I'm having good experience here in the mountains as a human fly, just like the ones in the city." We laughed while I carefully picked my way over the stones, and down the hill.

After skipping a day, I returned the next. I gave my usual warning on the trail, but the forest stood silent as I passed through, so I noisily dismounted at the foot of the mountain and peered up at the porch, but it was empty. No Stanley anywhere. I heard the baby crying, so I knew the mother was occupied. No one welcomed me as I started the climb, but something else did. Carved through rock and dirt, from the creek bed to the house at the top, lay an impressive flight of dirt steps. I ascended the hill as easily as walking up an ordinary stairway, pausing frequently to marvel. Fascinated with what one man could accomplish in a day's time, I voiced my compliments to Barrie, in case keen eyes and ears observed from a hiding place.

"Oh! I'm so glad he fixed the hill, so you can bring your water up more easily!" I said to his wife.

She smiled in her impassive mountaineer way. After a moment she replied, "Well, it weren't for me he done it, Miss Mitchell. He done it for you."

"He didn't!"

"Yes'm. He was laughing because ye was talking about being a human fly, and decided he'd better fix his hill so ye could get up more pert like." She paused, twisting her sandy red hair up at the back of her neck. "'Course I'm glad it was for you, 'cause it's for me too, after I get up and start doing things and going down to the creek."

So! Stanley and I had become friends. Although I still didn't approve of his moonshine still, I felt bound professionally not to turn him in. Just as a minister or doctor wouldn't reveal secrets about their clients, I couldn't either. Stanley knew my main concern was the health and welfare of his little family, regardless of how he earned a living.

Years later, I learned that he had drowned while swimming. I'm sure that he had carried a dread that eventually he might get shot and killed by one of the feuding men, which, according to the mountaineers would have been a shameful way to die. But death by drowning was peaceful, even admirable in comparison to death by a gun. In time, whenever people spoke of Jones Mountain they would mention Stanley, the man who was a sure shot with twelve notches on his gun. But he was also a peaceable man they might say; he took good care of his family. "Why, he even helped birth his second young'un." In his death he had preserved the honor of Jones Mountain, passing on a legacy to his children.

"Weren't you ever afraid out there on the mountain, alone with Stanley?" people sometimes asked. "Especially the night his wife was so sick?"

"No," I honestly replied. "I had no fear whatsoever. Not at any time." I had already committed the night of the delivery into the Lord's hands. It never entered my mind that Stanley might do something evil, either that night or afterwards. I reflected on his kindness to his wife when she was in labor, his desire and willingness to care for her. No woman had ever been as conscientious as he in following my instructions. He surpassed all female help in ability. Looking back, not only was I unafraid, I believe he was the best help I ever had.

CHAPTER 29

Red Bird Center

I suspect that Mrs. Breckinridge had heard that I could cook and had the gift of gab, so she asked me to move sixteen miles from the hospital to Red Bird Center. It was located near the Ford property, which had a short runway and a small plane, so the center had developed into a popular guesthouse for people who flew in from the outside. Many of Mrs. Breckinridge's society friends wanted to experience the routine of the frontier nurses' activities, and the nurse in charge of the clinic also served as a hospitality receptionist.

A courier rode Lady Ellen and brought Barrie, while I rode with the driver in the truck carrying my possessions. These couriers were excellent horsewomen. Some had received veterinary training; others came from wealthy, influential homes in the East. They came to FNS to serve in many ways. If a horse became lame or had some other ailment one of the couriers treated it professionally. They delivered messages or medicines to outlying centers, and performed many other important duties for us. As friends of Mrs. Breckinridge, they considered it part of their charity work to help us at Hyden.

Of the nine outlying centers, Redbird was the most attractive. Situated on the Red Bird River, it was so named because large flocks of cardinals nested and frequented both the river and the center. The mountaineers had constructed the building using substantial creosoted logs notched at the corners, and caulked it with mud and straw, so it was free from drafts or leaks. It sported a roof of hand split shingles that had weathered gray, and nestled on a plateau, its smoke from a sandstone chimney welcomed people from a distance.

On a slope above the house sat a barn, chicken house and small garden. A deeply bored well at the summit of the slope brought water by gravity to the barn and house. Like the mountaineers' homes, it lacked electricity and relied on kerosene lamps and candles for light.

A little mountain girl whom I was to train to cook and clean met me when I arrived. "Ye'er Miss Mitchell," she said with her eyes to the floor.

"Yes. And you're Annie," I responded. "Tell me what you know about me.

She tucked her head. "Ye'er a nurse from way off."

"That's right. You may have a hard time understanding what I say and do for a while, just as I'll need to get acquainted with you. Would you like to show me the house we'll share?"

From an open porch we entered the clinic waiting room. "This is where the sick folks or expecting mothers come. The nurse takes care of them in the other room. Here's the bathroom," she said, pausing and musing out loud. "I jest wish when they had to go they wouldn't make such a mess of the paper."

The stone fireplace in the living room was a thing of beauty, and could hold large logs, creating not only warmth, but also myriads of pictures in the flames. On it hung a ninety-seven inch mantel of hand-polished black walnut three inches thick. The fireplace stood in the middle of the house and separated the clinic area from our living area and heated both sections of the building. I bragged on the clean hearth rock.

"I scrubbed it jest this morning," she admitted modestly. While we toured the building she remained silent and submissive until I offered to move to the next room.

I noticed a screened-in porch that opened off the living room at the other end. The front room contained a desk and hand-planed dining table, also of black walnut. Usage had given the wood a priceless patina, and homemade chairs around the table displayed backs and seats of woven splint or bark. Two floral wingback chairs were drawn up to the fireplace for conversation. Looking around, I imagined pillows on the window seat, a gigantic bouquet of wildflowers on the mantel with large brass candlesticks. A crackling log fire seemed to wait for the few personal touches that could make the room homey and inviting.

Two bedrooms with two single beds in each slept guests and nurses. Handmade clothes presses completed the furnishings, and scattered throughout the building lay rugs hand woven at Big Creek.

Annie showed me her bedroom and then the kitchen, her territory, complete with a coal or wood burning stove, cupboard space, a sink and work table. "Are ye hungry? I've fixed us a bite, but I can't cook much," she offered. "They say *ye* can cook good!"

I put an arm around her shoulder and said, "I'll teach you to cook like my mother taught me, all right?" She nodded, and smiled warmly.

Soon in the swing of things, I held clinic on Wednesdays for prenatals and postpartums, and on Saturdays held general clinic. On the other days I rode circuit, a territory of over a hundred families, and supervised any student nurses who came to observe for the weekend.

One day while I held clinic several people told me about a man whom a rattlesnake had bitten. They wanted me to go up and give him some snake anti-venom. "Did he send you to get me?" I asked.

"No'm, he didn't. He shore is sick though." I debated going, because the mountain folks handled snakes in their churches as part of their religion. They interpreted literally the verse in the Bible that says you can walk on coals of fire, and handle snakes without being harmed. I realized I might be intruding if I went.

However, at their insistence I took the medicine up to his cabin. When I entered, I sat down on a chair near the door.

"They tell me you've been bitten by a rattlesnake."

"Yes'm," he said tersely from a swollen and feverish face.

"Would you like for me to give you some anti-venom for it?" I didn't move an inch.

"I'm not about to have it!" he blurted out. "And furthermore, I don't want you around!"

"That's perfectly all right," I said quietly. "I only wanted you to have the opportunity to take it if you wanted it." I carefully stood, and slowly eased out the door. I had already noticed the bulk of a shotgun underneath his sheet, so when Lady Ellen and I rode out of gunshot range I breathed a loud sigh of relief.

Annie told me about a woman in a church service who was handling snakes, and she was bitten twice on the breast, and once on the arm. Her family waited a couple of hours before taking her to the hospital, and she died a horrible death.

Upon hearing the news, I shuddered. "Annie, do you ever handle snakes in your church?"

"Oh, no'm," she replied, big-eyed. "It don't seem too smart to me."

Patients came to clinic with the usual ailments of colds and sore throats, but we also routinely treated hookworm, roundworm and tapeworm. I never grew accustomed to seeing adults and children infested with worms. Hookworms went right through the soles of barefooted children who often played in the same area where they had used the bathroom. Or children with dirty hands ate unwashed berries containing roundworm eggs, which grew in the same area. If only we could convince the parents to use their privy for what it was intended, instead of storing corn in it, much of this infestation could be prevented. Too, people ate pork that was half-cooked, causing tapeworm.

One little girl came in with all three kinds of worms. She was so frail and thin we took her to the hospital, and on the first try we got over a hundred roundworms. They came out by the fistful, still alive. We got rid of the hookworm, but couldn't get the entire tapeworm. After we sent her home to fatten up, she returned, and treatment got the remainder of the tapeworm, but by this time she already was infested with roundworms again.

On another occasion we admitted one woman to the hospital with worms all inside her. Before she died they came out of her mouth and nose.

Although their carelessness about health and hygiene was discouraging, they often surprised me with their human concern for one another. Mahalia, one of my little mothers with two small children, became pregnant again. Poor even by mountain standards, her family had little food to eat, at times only what neighbors brought in. Any milk they were given, Mahalia gave to her children, and she looked pale and undernourished throughout her pregnancy. When the baby came, he was tiny and inactive with a pitifully weak cry, and when he tried to nurse he whined in frustration because the mother had no milk.

When I returned two days later another complication had appeared, in the fact that the baby's skull had overlapped on top. "Mahalia! Has anyone dropped the baby?"

""No'm," she replied from a meal brought over by a neighbor. "It cries a good bit, but nobody been near it to hurt it."

"I'm bringing the doctor out here. This doesn't look good."

When the doctor examined him, he decided the baby was probably post-mature. Because of the mother's weak and undernourished condition, labor didn't begin when it should, and the baby's skull had been in the birth canal long enough for the bones to start growing on top of one another.

"Mahalia, this baby will die unless you get it some milk. Eat as much as you can so you can feed him," pleaded the doctor.

A couple of days later I went out with canned milk and some bottles to make formula. Mahalia's milk still had not come in. I examined her while the baby slept, and when he grunted and started moving around, I decided to look him over and give him a bath. When I picked him up milk ran out of the corner of his mouth.

"Where did this come from? You have no milk!"

Mahalia smiled. "I wasn't to tell ye. Ye know Clarinda that lives up the holler from here, her baby's still nursing. She come down here and set down over there and fed my baby." As if she expected a reprimand she continued, "Miss Mitchell, that baby been crying till he can't cry no more. But soon as he got that bit of milk he went right to sleep. Been sleeping all morning."

"Well, that was good of Clarinda to feed him," I assured her. "But do you think you could learn to make formula for him?" I tried to explain about mixing the milk and boiling water and bottles, but it became a lesson in futility. Giving up, I said, "I'm going to ride on up and see Clarinda. I haven't seen her baby for awhile."

She lived at the end of a long hollow. "Clarinda," I said after we'd chatted a bit. "I've tried to explain how to make formula to Mahalia, but she doesn't comprehend. That child won't live if he doesn't get proper food. And, have you noticed his head? It's already developing wrong," I fretted.

She said, "Now, Miss Mitchell. Don't you worry about that no more. Jest take them bottles home with ye. Leave the milk. The other young'uns need that. I'll go down least once every day and give that baby a good bait. Maybe Mahalia'll get some in her breasts so she can feed him too." I left Clarinda's cabin relieved. I knew we could send the baby to a children's hospital in Cincinnati to repair his skull when he was old enough to send away, and he would probably heal, but we had to keep him alive till he was strong enough for surgery.

Back at the center I told Annie about Mahalia's friend and her willingness to wet-nurse the baby.

Annie turned this over in her mind while she prepared a hearty dinner. After awhile, she came out to the living room where I sat on a window seat. "Miss Mitchell, I been thinking about what Clarinda done. Ye know, that was the real milk of human kindness, to feed Mahalia's baby."

I looked up in surprise. "Why, you're right, Annie," I agreed, with a warm smile.

With her bit of mountain wisdom she had endeared herself to me, as had so many others. She was a good student and had learned to cook well, and she also took pride in keeping our home spotless.

Sometimes I overheard her talking to my patients about her responsibilities at the center. She often added, "Miss Mitchell and me. We're friends." She claimed my friendship with great self-esteem and envy from the visitors. Annie was right. I considered her my companion and friend also, and a valuable asset to Red Bird Center.

Chapter 30

Mrs. Henry Ford

hey arrived around four in the afternoon, hot and thirsty.

"Since it's our custom to serve tea, would you prefer yours hot or iced?" I teased as they dismounted.

"Iced!" Mrs. Ford and her friend shouted together as they brushed trail dust off their clothes and wiped perspiration from their faces. The friend and Mrs. Breckinridge had just finished visiting all the other centers on horseback and had arrived at Red Bird for dinner.

"Why don't you freshen up while Annie prepares your tea?" I suggested, handing their horses over to the barn man to be groomed and cooled before feeding.

We lingered over the refreshing tea, chatting. Mrs. Ford gave me news from all the other centers and they all filled me in on details of their trip that day.

"How's Henrietta?" inquired Mrs. Ford.

"Oh, she's dependable as usual! Come out to the barn and see for yourself."

I pulled open the large doors at one end of the barn and we walked in, inspecting Henrietta while we walked around her, patting her shiny black parts. At his wife's encouragement, Mr. Henry Ford, Sr. had improvised a Ford car that drove very much like the jeeps of today. Other than the body frame that he had elevated off the ground, it looked much like a Model T. Because of the rough terrain and bad roads in our area we relied on Henrietta, especially in bad weather. Sometimes we nurses used her when we wanted to get away for a few hours to Hazard for a meal or to buy personal accessories not available at Hyden.

"You should see my driving," I gestured, climbing in the driver's seat. "I've accomplished a real feat in approaching the Center. After much practice I can now come up the steep slope, stop the car, reach out the window here, and pull the short pole that opens the Kentucky gate. I then drive through and pull the other short pole, closing the gate."

"That *is* an accomplishment," agreed the friend as she looked down the hill while we walked back to the Center. "I'm not sure I could do it."

Annie had cooked fresh chicken, cornbread, and vegetables for dinner. We also ate congealed salad and fresh peach ice cream which I had made earlier in the day. Also, my two visitors couldn't seem to get enough iced tea.

"Mitch, how did you ever learn to work the Kentucky gate with the car still in gear and the motor on?" asked Mrs. Ford's friend, still analyzing our earlier conversation.

"I'll take you for a demonstration ride sometime," I said, "but I'm glad you didn't see me learn, because all the animals tried to escape when they saw the gate open, and I had to watch to keep from running over them. A few times, I thought Henrietta would roll down the hill and crush me against a tree while I leaned out the window to catch the pole." We all chuckled. They seemed to enjoy my story and the meal, from the blessing to the end.

I can still see Mrs. Ford push back her chair, cross her legs, and turn to me, rattling the ice in her tea glass. "Now, Mitch. Tell us how much ice you brought in over the mountain from Manchester to put on this meal!"

"Why, none," I smiled.

"But...," she stammered, glancing at her friend who also looked stunned. "You don't have any electricity!"

"No," I grinned. "I have a *kerosene icebox*."

"We never heard of such a thing!"

"I owned a little second hand Plymouth before we got Henrietta but it wasn't built for these mountain roads. So, after Henrietta came along I sold it and used the money to buy the icebox. Come, I'll show you."

I embarrassed Annie by bringing them into the kitchen cluttered with dirty dishes, pots and pans, but they weren't looking at utensils. Their eyes went to a huge metal appliance that reached almost to the ceiling. On top sat a container of chemical liquid. At one side on the bottom, four burners were attached, much like on oil stoves.

"To make it operate," I explained, "I pull out these burners and fill them with kerosene. After adjusting the wicks and lighting them, I push them back into their compartment. As they burn, the liquid on top runs down the pipes. Ice is made, food is frozen, or cooled, at very little expense, about twenty-five cents a week."

"Well! I never!" they marveled.

"Butter was oil at the other centers," grumbled the friend, still eyeing the icebox.

"They didn't offer us iced tea, either!" added Mrs. Ford. "Everyone complained about the hot weather and how easily meat and milk spoil."

"Oh, we've saved on our grocery bill because of it, haven't we, Annie?" She nodded quickly, furtively glancing at the dishes, implying that she wanted us to leave.

"But don't tell Mrs. Breckinridge that the men had to cut down a tree in order to bring it into the house," I joked, guiding the ladies out of the kitchen.

Mrs. Ford waved a hand and snorted, "Don't worry. I won't. I know her, the way she cherishes each tree. In her eyes, it's a crime to cut one down."

Just before the edge of dark the women announced that if they didn't ride on over to the adjoining Ford property they would have to spend the night.

"That would be fine. Tomorrow is clinic day. Patients arrive early, so you ladies could have some more experiences by helping me with the clinic." They looked at one another, and quickly decided they could make it home before sunset.

Weeks later, I received a phone call from Miss Lewis, the business manager at Wendover. Scarcely audible because of the poor connection on the wall telephone, all I heard was, "Thanks,

Mitch. Sending you a check." I hung up, thanking her for I knew not what.

Within a few days the postman delivered a note confirming our conversation. "Thanks, Mitch. The husband of Mrs. Ford's friend owns a hardware business in Dearborn, Michigan. She and Mrs. Ford decided to donate iceboxes like yours for all the Centers. Thanks to you, we can all drink iced tea now! They're sending you a check to repay you for yours."

Chuckling, I remembered our hot afternoon visit. Not only did Mrs. Ford turn out to be one of the most noted and charming visitors I ever entertained at Red Bird, she displayed a generous spirit as she returned my hospitality, benefiting us all. I laid the note aside on the window seat and picked up my Bible for a few minutes of quiet time.

Outside, the rest of the world was in turmoil because of the war raging throughout Europe and the Pacific, but here in the mountains, life continued at its usual peaceful pace. I loved sitting in the bay window, watching the cardinals flock around the native hollies while they fed on the profuse red berries. At intervals during the week I would sit there and read my Bible, my only opportunity for worship. While I meditated on scripture, red birds darted from bushes to the ground where berries had fallen, or to their nests down by the river. I felt content with my life as I attempted to count the colorful red cardinals.

CHAPTER 31

A Time to Root Up...

"Telegram for ye, Miss Mitchell," grinned the mail carrier. "Them folks in Washington don't calculate such a letter takes long as the regulars out here," he said, as he fumbled with mail in his pouch.

The telegram was from a nurse midwife on the staff of Children's Bureau in Washington, D.C. Puzzled, I began reading it while the nosy mountaineer peered over my shoulder. "Hope it ain't bad news?"

"Oh, no." I smiled, closing the telegram. "Just business." I thanked him, and to his disappointment went inside. He badly wanted to know the contents, so he could spread the news about a telegram arriving at Brutus, and elaborate on what was said in it. I was working at Brutus Center for a few months, filling in for someone on leave.

Just business. But what a business! "Central and South America have asked the Sanitary Bureau to contact and provide a nurse midwife to set up temporary nurse midwifery school in Panama City, Panama. Purpose: to teach experienced and intelligent nurses from various countries to staff a school and continue the work. Will you come?"

In a quick reply I graciously thanked the midwife, stating that I couldn't possibly leave my position in the States, my excuse being the severe need for nurse midwives in Kentucky, due to the wartime shortage. I stated, that at present I worked twenty miles from the hospital at Brutus Center, where I trained student nurses on a one to one basis.

Within two weeks I received a second cable, pleading with me to accept the position. It promised I could return to the States after a couple of years. Again I declined, and then dismissed it from my mind.

One evening the telephone rang. Even with interfering static on the line Mrs. Breckinridge's tone sounded crisp and formal. "Mitch, I want you to come over and see me."

"Certainly," I responded, but I tried to put her off. "As soon as we get a break. We have several mothers about to deliver now."

"Come day after tomorrow, Mitch. Two o'clock." Without waiting for a reply, the phone went dead.

I slowly placed the phone back on its hook. Outside, squirrels chattered and played under a hickory tree. *Your play will soon change to toil, little friends. You'll need to gather and store nuts for the winter.* I shuddered when I thought of the cold and sleet to come, since Brutus Center was not as well constructed as Red Bird. Gaping cracks between the logs collected leaves and allowed insects and field mice free homes as they looked for dry places to live. Snow and ice would soon collect in the air pockets if I didn't get one of the men to board up the holes. Crickets droned in the last rays of an Indian summer day that denied the coming of autumn, singing as though summer would last forever. *If only it could. If only favorite seasons could last without changing.*

Just as I had dreaded, the day of my appointment arrived without any interruptions. In vain I had waited for the phone to ring, hoping Mrs. Breckinridge might change her mind. Apprehensively, I had hoped for a mother to begin labor. But the phone hung silent on the wall and babies waited indefinitely. So, after lunch, Barrie, Lady Ellen and I started on the trail for Wendover.

* * * * *

I knew full well what incident had provoked the invitation to South America. During my work at Thousand Sticks I had diagnosed a patient as being pregnant with twins. Dr. Kooser had confirmed this and we advised her to enter the hospital when she neared term. All went well throughout her pregnancy, so I was to deliver her when she came in.

When she arrived at the hospital she was already in second stage labor. I immediately notified Dr. Kooser and he came up and scrubbed. We had no sooner scrubbed and prepped the patient, when two nurse midwives arrived from Washington, D.C. When they heard that a nurse midwife was delivering twins, they excitedly asked if they might come up and observe. In fact, they came without waiting for a reply, and stood outside the delivery room door anticipating arrival of the babies.

I didn't approve of their presence. With the tiny room already overcrowded with the patient, the doctor, two cribs and myself, I considered the women rude and intruding.

While Dr. Kooser spoke with them, I attended my patient. Ready to deliver, with only a tiny rim of cervix left, she cried out and pushed down hard, but nothing happened. Meanwhile, of all things, I heard Dr. Kooser introduce me to the women.

"Mitch is our first graduate of Nurse Midwifery School," he crowed. I listened with one ear but really paid them no mind. The patient, a multipara, or a woman who had delivered several babies, concerned me. Her efforts to expel one of the babies were ineffective, although the large woman had a roomy pelvis.

Reaching over, I did a vaginal examination. The cervix, though completely dilated, was totally obstructed. "Dr. Kooser!" I said in a low voice with my back to our guests. "This woman has locked twins!"

He shot me a look that said he thought I had been reading the textbooks too much. This complication occurs in only one of about a thousand deliveries, and is seldom encountered even in the lifetime of a busy obstetrician. To cover for me, he loudly said, "Okay, Mitch. We'll wait a minute or two, and then you go ahead and deliver the babies."

The patient pushed with another strong contraction. Again, nothing happened. I nudged the doctor. "She's in trouble! Do a pelvic exam and you'll find that the twins are locked!"

Somewhat embarrassed at my alarm, he turned from our visitors to the patient. After carefully examining her, he somberly turned to the guests and announced in a grave voice, "Miss Mitchell has just correctly diagnosed something that few people have ever seen. We have locked twins. For that reason the patient is no longer her responsibility. If you will excuse us, I must take over." Gasping, the nurses stood back and hurriedly left the room.

Dr. Kooser discovered that the first baby had come down into the birth canal correctly. Its head lay right in the pelvis ready to come out, but the second baby rested just above it with its head on the chest of the first. With both heads crowning, neither could deliver, creating the patient's difficulty.

Locked twins are managed only by displacing the second child upward, hopefully so the first infant can be extracted. But if this cannot be accomplished, the first child must be decapitated, since attempts at extraction would lead to its death anyhow. Forceps then deliver the second child, but this doesn't always work out either.

We administered an anesthetic to the mother. Dr. Kooser attempted to push the second baby upward, but in so doing he crushed the chest of the first baby. It never breathed. Then he went in with forceps and delivered the second one, but its head was mashed and bruised so that it also died. However, he did manage to save the mother's life.

One of the nurse midwives present at that delivery evidently felt that I qualified as an instructor, and remembered me when the call for assistance came from South America.

* * * * *

"Mitch, you know why I've sent for you," Mrs. Breckinridge maintained in a businesslike manner, after we caught each other up on routine news. "Our work here in Kentucky is progressing nicely. Most of our centers are becoming teaching clusters for new nurses, and our eventual goal is to expand the school, attracting nurses nationwide."

"And I enjoy the work here, Mrs. Breckinridge. I don't want to leave," I contended.

"I know, Mitch," she said, her eyes softening. "Believe me. I know how attached one can become to the mountaineers, but look at it this way. The women in South America are much in the same predicament as the people here, before we came in. It will be an act of good will from our country for someone as qualified as you to help them set up a school."

"Then you could send someone else who is also qualified," I protested.

"But they asked for you, Mitch. As bad as I hate to see you leave, I feel you must go. Look at it on the brighter side. You'll be our first student to teach in a foreign country."

At Mrs. Breckinridge's insistence I finally relented and agreed to go, although I couldn't interpret why I was being uprooted and pushed out of the nest again.

I started back to Brutus Center late in the afternoon. Barrie and Lady Ellen obligingly slackened their pace to match my forlorn mood. The trail led abruptly into the forest where a slight chill earlier in the day had sharpened for want of sunshine. Weakened rays of a late summer sun did little in the deep woods, and at the heart of the forest deep shadows hung, long and uninviting. Here, summer had already ended, with mounds of slippery leaves piled deep in canyons and along the creek beds. Like it knew a well-kept secret, the deep woods prepared itself for advancing fall and winter. Streams had slowed to trickles waiting for ice to form, and mountain flowers slept under blankets of pine straw and leaves. Although sunny hillsides ignored the coming change and basked in latent sunshine, the forest knew and waited.

As I regarded the ageless forest changing its dress here and there, and how each season clings until another season overlaps, I began to realize something about myself. In the same way I also hold fast to lovely seasons in my life, clutching at time and not wanting it to pass. Begrudgingly I watch it mature and fade from the present, until finally I am forced to relinquish people, jobs, areas, and locations, and then move on. Sad as it was for me to accept, I faced the fact that time had matured and it was now time to leave. I needed to face whatever the Heavenly Father had in mind. As it says in the Bible, eventually there is a time to uproot what seems securely planted. *Pull up your roots, Mitch. Your season is over with the mountain folk.*

Thunder rumbled in the distance as I put my horse in the barn at Brutus. Clouds formed on the horizon, swift and heavy rain clouds that blocked the setting sun. Barrie joyfully sniffed the breeze blowing across the ridge that carried away the mugginess of the afternoon; with his head back, nose in the air, he took in the fresh wind. I, too, breathed deeply and smelled the rain coming to drench the mountain during the night. A hidden sunset brought a lovely day to a close as I slowly walked inside the house to make myself a cup of tea.

Chapter 32

Saying Goodbye to Friends

"You mean....ye won't be our *nurse* anymore?" whimpered the little girl as I stooped to take a look at her bandaged arm. Wide blue eyes looked up at me and her mouth trembled. Other patients in the clinic stopped chatting to listen while I explained about being needed in South America. An uncomfortable silence hung in the air as though the mountaineers felt betrayed.

"But ye'er *our* nurse, Miss Mitchell," the blonde tyke managed to whisper.

"Audrey, take Missy into the examining room while I wash my hands," I croaked, my eyes filling up as I hurriedly went to the bathroom to wash.

I had tried to keep news of my leaving quiet until the last minute, but the mountain grapevine had quickly spread it over the hills. I knew that in time the folks would come to accept my departure with their unique stoicism, but preparing to leave, saying goodbye to them, the nurses, and our doctor, became extremely difficult for me just the same.

173

About that time a veterinarian from London, Kentucky came over to routinely check the horses. After looking at Traveler he said, "This horse is dangerous for anyone to ride. Arthritis in his knees is so bad that they could give way and make him fall, injuring whomever he's carrying." For some time I had noticed stiffness in the horse's knees, and especially when going up a rocky path, he groaned and grunted while I coaxed him up. Although in obvious distress, he always responded while I good-naturedly called him an old man. Even though he showed a tremendous will to work, his years of box-stall confinement before I started taking him out had stiffened his joints. The vet suggested that the big horse be put to sleep or killed.

On the morning of the vet's return for Traveler's destruction, Audrey volunteered to stay at the clinic and give him anything he might need. "Besides, I have a patient I want you to see while you're visiting your own." I showed visible relief that I wouldn't have to be around until the end for my horse.

While I saddled up Lady Ellen, I looked through a crack in the barn at the mountain men who were already digging a large hole for Traveler's body. I knew that during my absence the vet would come and blindfold him, lead him out to the hole and dispense with his life with one pistol shot. Before I left for the day, I went over and patted Traveler one last time, leaning on his shoulder and talking to him. He turned and snorted affectionately.

I stayed away as long as possible. After seeing Audrey's patient, I revisited favorite views of the mountains where wildflowers grew in patches along the trail. By the time I returned, the men had filled back the hole, so that all I saw was fresh dirt and a lonely, empty stall.

Traveler's death hit me doubly hard because the vet had also told Audrey that Lady Ellen didn't have much time left either. He recommended that after I left the hills, they should put her out to pasture for a lovely summer, and then end her life in the fall, so she wouldn't be limited to a box stall during the winter, and also become crippled with arthritis.

I wasn't prepared for this, because she had never slackened her gait, or let on that she experienced any difficulty in walking or running. Just the opposite, she displayed great sensitivity to her rider and tried to keep me comfortable in the saddle.

I remember one particular incident that happened one night when a student and I went to deliver a patient. About halfway through our eight-mile trip, an uneasy nausea that had begun shortly after we started out suddenly became unbearable. I soon found myself leaning over the saddle and retching from sharp pains that shot through my abdomen each time it knotted up. Lady Ellen, sensing my discomfort, moved and swayed her body each time I did, as if to ease me when I felt a pang of nausea. Every now and then she looked back over her shoulder like she was saying, *are you all right?* The student also looked back apprehensively while I lagged behind.

The baby had already come when we arrived at the cabin, but the placenta had not. Later, after expressing the placenta, when I put my hand on the mother's abdomen I discovered that she was hemorrhaging, so we gave her a shot to stop it and held the fundus tightly. All the while, waves of nausea and abdominal pains gripped me, until I finally went outside and gulped cold mountain air. After the student bathed the baby we finished all the after-delivery duties, packed the delivery bag, and started back to the hospital.

Anxious to get back to their feed the frisky horses competed with one another in the early morning air. Each time they stretched out, I thought I would die in the saddle.

"Are you going to make it?" the girl asked.

"Why don't you go on?" I gasped. "I'll just take it a little slower."

Lady Ellen calmed down after the other horse left. She walked graceful and cat-like whenever I leaned over in the saddle, but it finally became so horrible to ride that I dismounted and walked the rest of the way.

I tried to sleep after I got in bed, but the pain worsened so that I went over to the hospital where they waited for me. When I walked in the clinic door the nurse greeted me with, "We're having two appendectomies this morning, Mitch. How about you being the third?" As she said this, she made a motion like she would hit me in the abdomen. I fainted. Instead of the third appendectomy scheduled, I became the first.

I shall always be thankful to the Lord for giving me patient and gentle Lady Ellen to ride that day. Her response to my agony in the saddle probably prevented my appendix from rupturing and causing a much more difficult convalescence.

The day soon came for my departure from the hills. I had already said goodbye to most of my patients in all the districts I had covered during the six years I worked among the mountaineers. I walked out the clinic door with my Gladstone bag in hand. Audrey waited with her truck motor running, while I quickly said goodbye to people who waited around to see me off. I had given away most of my things, the rest rode in a wardrobe trunk in the back of the truck, along with the two dogs – hers and mine.

I looked back at the hospital and clinic when we started down the hill, remembering the first time I had climbed its rocky path one snowy, icy morning. As I looked, the little group of people disbanded to go about their daily routines. We rode past men who nodded in farewell, women and children here and there, who stood and watched dispassionately until we drove completely out of sight, and away from Hyden, on the road to Lexington.

The dogs struggled to keep their balance in the truck bed, and tried to stay clear of the bouncing trunk, while Audrey fought to avoid deep holes in the washed out road. I kept looking back at Barrie until Audrey offered to let the dogs up front. I smiled weakly as Barrie curled down around my feet on the floor. I particularly wanted him close by on this, our last trip together. We had one stop to make before Audrey put me on the train in Lexington.

Nothing much was said as I reminisced about my animals, but after about an hour I blurted out, "Did I ever tell about the time Barrie saved my life at Red Bird Center?"

Audrey jumped, darting a glance my way. "Well, uh...no, I don't guess you did." Barrie responded with a sigh and grunt at the mention of his name. He kept his eyes closed, feigning sleep except for the wag of his tail.

"I expected guests for dinner that night. After I came in from district I decided the living room needed a bit of color. Remembering some Sweet William or wild phlox up in the woods just back of the Center, I went out to pick them. As usual, when I stepped outside the door Barrie came running to go with me. I had changed from my riding habit into some low oxfords and slacks, which offered little protection from briars, but we playfully picked our way up the rocky path to the flowers."

Reaching down in the floor of the cab, I patted Barrie and stroked his ruff while he nuzzled my hand. "I spotted a splendid cluster of phlox just over a large log and started to step across. When I did, Barrie jumped in front of me and began lunging up at me. 'Oh, you want to play, do you?' I said, picking up a stick and throwing it, but he only stood very tense.

I took another step forward, pushing him aside. He growled at me. Shocked, I stepped back. 'Why, Barrie! Why are you doing this?' I then tried to go around the dog and the log instead of stepping over it. As I started around I saw a large rattlesnake, lying coiled, with its head ready to strike. He was where I would have stepped. He looked bigger around than my arm, with over a dozen rattles. I almost fell down the hill and over Barrie, getting away."

Barrie whined and looked up at me from the floor of the truck. "Yes, you know you saved me again, don't you, boy?" He lolled his tongue laughingly, and then settled back down again. Audrey drove and I lapsed into silence the rest of the trip.

When we stopped the truck, Barrie sensed either from my attitude or odors when we opened the door that something was wrong. He whined and backed away, trembling at the recognition of smells of a vet hospital.

My collie was nine years old, and with his many long runs in the cold and icy rain, he also had developed arthritis. I had managed to care for him to a certain extent, giving him medication, but because I loved him and knew that no one else would ever have the joy of his early years, I felt it unfair to leave a sick dog on someone else's hands. I had planned to have him put to sleep just before boarding the train.

His whining and shaking while I attempted to snap on his leash completely undid me. The tears began to flow.

"Do you want me to take him inside?" Audrey asked.

"Oh, Audrey," I sobbed, holding my dog. "You've already seen to Traveler. I'll do this."

"I don't mind," she said, gently taking the leash from my hands. I hugged Barrie close, then she led him inside the hospital, with him obediently following. Crying openly, I waited for it to be over. I felt guilty, like a Judas betraying one who had looked to me for friendship and protection. When Audrey came back outside carrying the empty leash I really broke down.

"Barrie seemed to suspicion death in the air, but when they put him on the table he became very subdued and obedient. I told him to lie down and he did. He behaved so well, Mitch. I kept my hand on him while they gave him the shot. He felt no pain."

When we arrived at the station, we checked my trunk and I boarded, clumsily thanking Audrey again for everything she had done. "I'll write you about news from the hills," she promised, waving me off.

The train lurched forward and pulled out of the station, away from the familiar craggy canyons and hills, the shanties and impoverished people. From my seat by the window I viewed the contrast of the unique blue-green grass of the Lexington countryside with its immaculate white fences and mansions, huge barns and caretakers. Racehorses peacefully grazed in sunny pastures or rolled in clover, sometimes galloping alongside the train, flaring their nostrils in competition. I found myself envying their life of ease while one of my horses lay buried on a poor hillside, the other soon to follow. Now I felt even more incomplete without my working animals, for I terribly missed my dog who would no longer lie by my bed at night or wait attentively until I signaled him to accompany me on a mountain trail.

My spirits sank to an all time low as the train chugged further away from the people I had grown to love. To strangers, their non-committal howdys and Chaucerian-spiced conversation only identified their proud and ancient heritage, but I had known their kindness and affection shown in small ways, from shearin' a flower pot for their nurse, or naming one of their cuddly infants after her. I shall never forget those people of the Middle Fork and Red Bird Rivers, Bull Creek, Thousand Sticks and Hell-fer-Sartain Mountains. True, mine had been a job with demanding needs, but their friendship was a valued reward.

I thought of Missy, the little girl with the bandaged arm who had tearfully objected to my leaving, the bandage the result of a burn when she had fallen against an open wash pot in the yard. I hoped her little arm would heal and not leave a scar on an otherwise perfect body. Names and faces of other hill folk came to mind as the train took me further away.

While mountains and valleys leveled out to open plains, I still saw folks sitting on their porches or waiting in cold cabins for their nurse – *her* touch, *her* advice on bathing the new baby or giving medicine to a sick grandmother. Probably today or during the night Alma's husband will saddle up his mule and ride to Hyden to fetch the new nurse and catch their baby....

I must stop thinking about my friends and patients. Instead, concentrate on a reunion in St. Louis with your Mother. Think of her and how truly glad you will be to see her and hear about your brothers and their families.

The mountaineers are no longer of significance in my life, I kept repeating as telegraph poles turned pink and amber, and then blazed with the brilliance of the setting sun. As long fingers of night stretched across the sky I continued reasoning with myself. *After all, I'm not the mountaineers' nurse anymore.... I'm not their nurse anymore.*

Martin and Sarah Mitchell
Kenneth and Paul - standing
Russell and Mildred
James - not born
Mary Evelyn not born

Mitchell family (above)

St. Luke's Nursing
School Graduate

Clockwise from top left: Joe on trip,
Hannah on trip, and trip to California with
Joe to meet his parents

Clockwise from top: Hyden Hospital and annex, 'Wee hoose' downstairs morgue, and Bridge of Shivers

Hannah and Traveler

Hannah on Mary Ellen with
Barrie (above)

Nurses on horseback

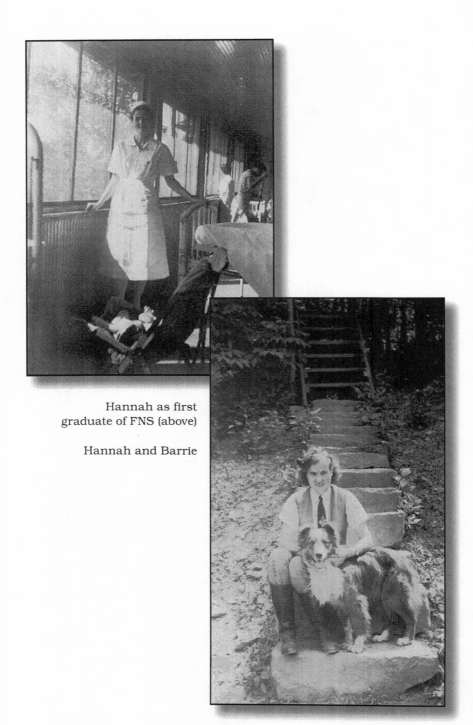

Hannah as first
graduate of FNS (above)

Hannah and Barrie

Red Bird Center
(above)

On steps of St.
Thomas Hospital

Hannah at
her retirement
luncheon with Dr.
Brackett (above)

Pat Clements, Bible
study hostess,
with Hannah
(center) and
Shirley Ferguson

Hannah's Haven

Front terrace

HANNA'S 83RD BIRTHDAY

HANNAH'S JOURNAL, JULY 1990

It is early morning as I sit on the upper slope of my garden here in my Atlanta home. In many ways Hannah's Haven has been like Red Bird Center. A place of my own, just minutes from downtown Atlanta, it has been a calm buffer with my garden of shrubs and trees. I have spent many contented hours watching cardinals, redbirds and robins. Whether dozing in a lawn chair on the upper shelf, or preparing Bible lessons, this landscape has ministered to me, and so many others, who linger during a visit.

But just like nature's seasons, I have counseled and taught that life has seasons of its own. I know that my season in Hannah's Haven is ending. Just as in early spring I have pulled weeds and thinned out plants, I realize that once again I will soon be uprooted from here, just as I was forced to leave the mountains and head for a foreign country....

1944-1946

CHAPTER 33

Alone In The Canal Zone

My plane left New Orleans at night, as most of the planes did because of the war. Circling the city, it then flew out across the water and moved away from the shoreline. With the city spread out below, its unmasked outline resembled a brilliant emblazoned shield along the coast, reminding me of the armor of God and the shield mentioned in the Bible. I imagined similar sights bordering all waterfronts in our country as battle stations of protection from invasion, but I acknowledged that our true protection came from the Lord Himself through the faith and prayers of many people.

I swallowed hard as the plane roared into the night like a noisy cumbersome bird leaving its nest. Although I had been away from home for several years and went back periodically to see Mother, I dreaded not being able to visit her now for almost two years. She had seen me off in St. Louis where I had taken a plane to New Orleans.

"Now you be careful in that foreign country, Hannah," she kept reminding me.

"I'll be in safe surroundings, Mother. Don't worry."

"Isn't it good that you already had your birth certificate?" she chortled, nudging me.

"Yes. I must thank you for that," I smiled tenderly.

A couple of years previously, Mother had suddenly decided that all her children needed a proper birth certificate. It wasn't required in those days, so we hadn't bothered, but she nearly ran the attending doctor and me ragged about it. So from time to time I had made efforts until we all had our births recorded properly, and the paper to show it.

"I couldn't possibly have gotten it now, considering the little time I had to prepare for the trip," I laughed, hugging her waist as we walked along.

"Evidently you were intended to go. God must have put this strongly in my mind so you would respond," she said.

"You're probably right." I nodded soberly, facing her for a reluctant goodbye.

Many of the sleeping passengers on the plane were headed for Guatemala or Panama, including a few army and navy personnel on their way to the Canal Zone adjacent to the Republic of Panama.

At dawn, we neared the country of Guatemala. It appeared to be nothing but vegetation, but surprisingly, when we dropped in close to the landing field I discovered we were in Guatemala City. Some of the trees were only camouflage, with tops and sides of buildings painted in greens and browns.

Girls met our plane with huge trays of gardenias that they either pinned on us or handed to us in bouquets. A group of us decided to see the sights during our hour and a half layover and hired a limousine. When we came out of the airport the altitude of the city and its invigorating air reminded me of Denver. People hurried along the streets carrying things on their heads, including great baskets of coffee beans gathered form plantations surrounding the airport.

The gardenia fragrance almost overpowered us as we rode around the city wearing our corsages or still holding bouquets in our laps. In the market we saw abundant food for sale, hand-woven clothing, cloth, with stacks of leather goods hand tooled and made into shoes and bags. Still, the flowers appealed to me most, baskets of gladiolas - four, five and six feet in height and in full bloom. Varieties of orchids, more gardenias, jasmine, ginger, all variations of roses and flowers I didn't recognize lined the marketplace in a riot of color and smell.

Among the magnificent buildings stood extravagant Catholic churches with layers of gold on the altars and throughout the ceilings. The interiors revealed skilled craftsmanship in their statuaries of gold, silver and precious stones.

Time passed quickly and we raced back to the airport, where we entered an atmosphere of excitement and fear. Soldiers ran from all areas, converging on a small man, while people screamed and shoved one another trying to escape the guns of the soldiers. An agitated voice on the intercom commanded: "All passengers for Panama City quickly board the flight. It is leaving early." Sure enough, the plane engines revved while we scurried on board; the stewardesses quickly pulled in the steps and we took off, still wondering what was happening.

When we arrived in the Canal Zone we saw even more camouflage. Many buildings were covered with wire and wood on top and were painted in camouflage. Army personnel saluted one another dressed in camouflage, including their helmets.

We went through customs on the Republic of Panama side and were rigorously examined for cameras or weapons. The officials, noting uniforms and books in my luggage drilled me with questions until I showed them all my credentials.

Next day, I noted in the English section of the paper that a small revolution had taken place in Guatemala City, with some of it occurring at the airport where I had been. *What had I told my Mother? That I would be in protected surroundings? Not to worry?*

That same morning I received a brief telephone call from the Policia Nationale of the Republic of Panama. "We suggest that you come at once to the station downtown, and bring all credentials, plus any extra pictures from your passport." I cautiously made my appearance at the station, and they left me nervously sitting for quite awhile, until someone came to inform me that the purpose of my wait was for an interview with the Chief of Police!

I was finally called, and warily entered his office. To my surprise, the police chief stood and extended his hand. "I want to officially welcome you to our country!" he said graciously. "We greatly appreciate your coming to help set up a school for nurse midwives." He motioned for me to sit.

"I must warn you that we endure constant revolutions; therefore it is our desire to protect you at all times. We are preparing a little photo album for you to carry everywhere you go." I nodded my head and thanked him for his concern. *Oh, my! Washington didn't warn me about all this.*

In the days to follow I used my new credentials to good advantage. I was uptown one day and suddenly heard shouts and saw soldiers running through the streets. I tried to hail a taxi to return to the Santo Tomas hospital, but I couldn't get one so I grabbed the first bus. Part way down the street soldiers halted it and entered, coming straight to me, the foreigner. They roughly grabbed my arm and I frantically fumbled for my badge from Policia Nationale as they attempted to dislodge me from my seat. When the soldier read it, he immediately loosened his painful grip, and escorted me up to a seat behind the bus driver, where he gently sat me down. In commanding Spanish he instructed the driver to make no stops until we arrived at Santo Tomas, probably insinuating that he guard me with his life. So, with a sigh of relief, I began to see how my initial interrogation and delay that first day in the country would pay off.

It is difficult for me to express my feeling of aloneness when I first went to Panama, unlike any isolation I have ever endured. By myself in a foreign country, without any friends to converse with or depend on, I particularly felt my foreign identity. I occasionally attended the Catholic Church when not on duty, but I didn't feel at home there because of the differences in beliefs. The people, also engrossed in their own activities, paid little attention to a lone woman in their church.

The dormitory quarters at the hospital were nicely arranged in private apartments for the executives. The building, surrounded on all sides by screened-in areas, made for very cool sleeping quarters. I had a clean room and bed; the only problem was with mildew that coated any shoes and clothes when left outside the closet. A large light inside the closet burned night and day, preventing too much buildup, so I made sure any articles of clothing were shut up inside. That is, everything except my Bible, which I kept by my bedside, and every morning it was coated over with mildew and had to be wiped clean.

Perhaps the Heavenly Father wanted me to realize there was none I could depend upon like Him, so He removed all my crutches of human kindness, love and support. Without anyone to call my own, my only consolation in Panama City was my mildewed Bible and the assurance of His presence. My little badge provided by the police department protected me from the revolutionaries on the streets, yet I discerned a larger protection around me that kept me from total solitude and delivered me from fear in unfamiliar surroundings.

During the night I sometimes awoke to strange noises. Quickly sitting up in bed, I instinctively said, "It's alright, Barrie. Lie down, boy," just as I had said at Red Bird on the sleeping porch where he and I had slept all year. Then, coming fully awake I realized I had no dog. And I was no longer in Kentucky, but in South America, alone with people who didn't understand my language. At that point I sometimes reached over and put my Bible under my pillow, not only to keep off the mildew, but also to have its familiar words nearby.

CHAPTER 34

La Enfermera de Santo Tomas

I taught seven students from various countries of South America, which involved much of my time in class, and supervising practice in nurse midwifery. In addition I held a class once a month for sixty local midwives. My Castilian night school Spanish proved a barrier at first, but my students patiently explained the language idiosyncrasies. Although their culture, climate and companionship differed from what I had previously known, I noticed similarities in nursing demands and rewards.

One afternoon, as I walked down a hospital corridor to supervise a student, a maternity patient called to me when I passed her door. "La enfermera! La enfermera!" She gestured wildly, waving her hands when I entered the room. I hurriedly responded by rushing to the supply room and produced a bedpan, only to see her frown in disgust when I dashed in with it. Pointing and chattering away in Spanish, she at last made me understand when she handed me a coin that she wanted a popsicle from the street vendor going past her window!

I often ate an early breakfast across the street from the Maternidad with a lovely, brilliant, obstetrical resident who was from the States. We then walked over together to begin our day's work. One morning as we strolled along the palm-lined walkway, inhaling fresh salty air that smelled of seaweed, down the street came a loaded chiva, or little bus. We laughed at its cargo of coconuts, mangoes, pineapples, plantains, chickens and leafy vegetables, with the passengers added as an afterthought. Its small wheels groaned to a stop at the curb, its weight shifting as stifled passengers squeezed together to allow a couple to disembark.

Our smiles froze when we saw a very young pregnant woman crawl out on her hands and knees, assisted by her husband and the driver. I ran up the sidewalk and grabbed a stretcher on wheels, on which we quickly loaded her and rushed her to the examining room. While I yanked on surgical gloves, she told me repeatedly that during the night she had 'mucho dolor', but they ceased suddenly, and ever since she had felt nauseated. I noted two longitudinal mounds in her rigid abdomen.

When I examined her rectally, I concluded that her uterus had ruptured. "Do you wish to confirm my diagnosis?" I asked the resident.

"No. Yours is good enough. Let's get the surgeon and prepare the operating room for immediate surgery."

After a hasty preparation, surgery revealed my diagnosis as correct. The lower segment of her uterus had indeed ruptured and she should have hemorrhaged, but the baby's head had moved into the gap of torn tissue, with the size and hardness of it acting as a tampon to close off the torn vessels. We found only one clot in the viscera. Although the baby had been dead for hours it had saved her life. We performed a hysterectomy and she survived after a stormy convalescence, during which time we became well acquainted. We talked about her other children, the care she gave them, the health of her and her husband.

Even if a woman has given birth to several children without any complications, this case confirmed my instructions to the students that there is no such thing as a typical obstetrical patient. Each pregnancy, labor and delivery is uniquely different. Although most proved uneventful, I also told them to remain alert for any unexpected turn during childbirth.

And the unexpected happened one day when a patient entered the hospital in normal labor. I supervised the student who attended her and everything progressed nicely as the baby's head crowned and the baby was delivered. But it lay still, without moving or breathing. The student, recognizing asphyxia pallida, the limp and dead-like condition afflicting some newborns, looked at me with dread. Hesitating momentarily, at least she knew not to spank the baby in an effort to make it breathe.

I reached over and grabbed up the infant, at the same time scooping mucous from its mouth and nose, and alternately placing my mouth over his, breathing into its lungs. After several long minutes of resuscitation the baby quivered, took a breath on its own and let out a wail.

The mother, awake during the whole ordeal, had watched anxiously while I fought for her son's life. She wept in gratitude when at last he cried, then squirmed and yawned in my arms. She soon spread over the Maternidad the story of how her newborn had been dead, but the Americana angel of mercy had given it life.

On rare occasions I took time off. Once, at the invitation of Dr. Clark of the Gorgas Research Laboratory, another nurse and I accompanied him into the interior. We cruised by cutter across a placid lake, and up the Piscado River to a little country store, where Dr. Clark often conducted research work on malaria.

We entered the thatch-covered building, and when the owner saw me he shouted, "La enfermera de Santo Tomas! La enfermera de Santo Tomas!" We all looked at one another while the storekeeper rushed over with a chair. He gestured for me to sit down. Grabbing a bundle from a nearby hammock he placed in my lap a black, howling curly-haired baby, several months old. All the while, the father smiled and repeated, "Es su bambino! Es su bambino!" Then he fled from the building.

Dr. Clark said, with a wry grin. "It looks like you have yourself a baby!" I sat bewildered, looking at the baby, seeing myself returning to the States and presenting my Mother with a young Panamanian child.

I had scarcely quieted the baby, when the father returned with the mother and several neighbors. He gathered them around, and with great expression gave a lengthy Spanish explanation, about how this was the baby that had been born dead at the hospital in Santo Tomas, but the enfermera had worked with it a long time and gave it life. Now, as a token of gratitude to God, I could have him, although beautiful and precious as he was to him and his wife.

While he spoke, the mother's eyes grew wide with horror at the realization that she was losing her baby! I did some fast thinking.

When he finished, they all waited for my response. In stumbling Spanish I launched into my own speech, making it as lengthy as I could, about how lovely a gesture it was for them to offer me the baby, his beauty, their obvious love and care for him, and how honored I felt. But I realized that God had only allowed me to be the *instrument* of life for their son. He must have wanted them to parent such a charming child; therefore I found it impossible to interfere with God's will and to keep their treasure as a gift!

I then stood up, and with a dramatic sweep of my arm, offered the chair to its mother. She came, timid, but smiling, and took her seat. I kissed the baby and placed him in her lap. Anyone who is a mother knows how eagerly she held out her arms when I returned her son to her. With relief, she looked at me and cuddled her baby, and to my relief the vision of me presenting my Mother with a very black little baby receded.

As time went by I became more acquainted with Spanish and the customs of the people in Panama. I developed real affection for many of the patients that the students and I delivered. I remember keeping count, beginning with the first delivery I had made at St. Luke's, and continued counting while in Kentucky; then at some point while in Panama, I totaled that I had delivered one thousand babies.

After that, the nurse from St. Thomas stopped keeping count.

CHAPTER 35

My Life is Hid With Christ in God

One time a group of American nurses from the Canal Zone and I toured the neighboring San Blas Islands in a small boat with a crew of three men. We started out from Colon on a typically gorgeous, sunny day, basking in the tropical sun's rays, laughing and enjoying the exhilarating sea air. Then, without warning, a gale wind came up, bringing clouds that obliterated the sun with a blinding, driving rain. It churned the ocean into huge waves that dwarfed our boat, permeating even the calmness of the crew.

"You women get on the bunks!" yelled the captain. Terrified, we frantically climbed into the bunks, and hung on with all our might, while the fury of the storm threatened to capsize us. The men had not yet told us to put on life preservers, but when a huge billow took us down into a trough and back onto the crest of the wave, things looked desperate. To my dismay, when I counted the life jackets above the bunks, I added up one less vest than nurses. In paralyzing fear, I realized that someone would be without a vest should we swamp or overturn.

The crew had strung ropes around the deck much like a banister on a porch, which aided them as they walked from one side of the boat to another. Without warning, we hit another jarring wave, and although I gripped the side of my bunk, I lost my hold and went skidding through the cabin door, and across the deck. I grabbed at a rope that my legs had brushed against, but I went on through and hung upside down over the side, caught between the ocean and deck. For some reason the boat didn't dip into the trough, but paused in its descent into the water. I faced the foaming waves thinking I was a goner, when from out of nowhere I felt a crewman pulling me by the legs back onto the deck. At the same moment, another rising wall of water came crashing toward us. I took one wild glance out over the churning ocean, and as I looked, a great saw-toothed shark appeared at the crest of the wave, his cold unblinking eye staring right at me. I realized with a shudder, that had I gone over I probably would have been his next meal.

"Thanks!" I sputtered to the seaman after he drug me across the deck and threw me back into my bunk. I was shaking all over, soaked from the rain and the sea, but somehow found the strength to hang on. While we rode out the storm until the winds subsided, I couldn't forget the picture of the shark staring at me from the ocean.

A mellow moon hung in the sky six or seven hours later when we finally arrived in the peaceful harbor of Governor's Island. It was the only island that protected and housed tourist groups, the authorities permitting travel to the other islands during the day, but discouraging anyone from staying the night. Not too long before, a white man had docked at an outer island for the night, but he never returned – evidently eaten by the cannibalistic Indians.

Our hosts had almost given us up, but they brought out a sumptuous meal. Most of the seasick nurses looked queasy again at the sight of food, waved it away and went to bed. Only one other nurse and I felt like eating. We sat down with the crew to a banquet of turtle meat cooked with coconut, several different fruits including fresh pineapple, papaya and mango. As the cooks plied us with more and more food, I ate ravenously.

We later went for a stroll along the beach, the night was what I had always imagined in the tropics, with white sand shimmering against the darker waters' edge. Coconut palms dotted the island, their leafy limbs heavy with huge nuts. We at last put an end to an exciting day, after one of the coconuts fell and almost landed on our heads as we walked under a grove of palms.

The next day we went to sea again, going from place to place among the islands, looking at the different cultures among the San Blas Indians. A guide paddled us around in groups of four or five in a lightweight, long, and narrow wooden boat. Fascinating marine life looked deceptively close beneath the clear water, when really it was over a hundred feet below. When we neared different islands, many of the children greeted us and begged for money, which they would later fasten on a necklace with other coins.

On one of the islands I entered a thatch-roofed hut. After my eyes adjusted to the darkness I spotted an albino child, then saw two or three more huddling pitifully in corners, their pink eyes pouring tears because of their inability to take light. I was told that the highest proportion of albino births in the world occurs among these Indians, with about seven out of a thousand congenitally deficient in pigment. With their milky white skin, and colorless, thin hair on their heads, they were weighted down with silver coin necklaces, and were objects of worship by the other tribesmen. The albinos only pastime was that of making molas, the delicate and unusual embroideries, appliquéd with one color cloth hand-sewn over the top of another. As some of us approached, they held up the molas for us to examine in the semi-darkness, and hopefully purchase.

I bought two molas that were intended to make small children's dresses, thinking I would make them into pillows. But I knew they would get destroyed from use so I had them framed, as a reminder of the time the Lord allowed me to see these San Blas Indians. When I look at them I also thank the Heavenly Father for saving me from the shark and a watery grave.

From that time on the verse from the chapter in Colossians took on new meaning – "Your life is hid with Christ in God." I already knew the Lord was with me as he directed my steps, rearranging my circumstances to work out His will, but in a stronger way I saw another truth. Christ is in me. I am in Christ. Christ is in God. Nothing can penetrate those layers of protection if it is against His will.

Thank you, Heavenly Father, I prayed again and again, for His Providence, by hiding me in Christ. My life had changed direction many times, most of the changes contrary to my plans and painful for me to accept. But I probably will never know of the numerous times that a Providential God has shielded me from deeper hurt, and real calamity, even an early death.

CHAPTER 36

Front Page News

The longer I practiced nurse midwifery the more I realized I needed and wanted more formal nursing education. That need became an almost insatiable hunger while I was in Central America. I had saved almost all my salary, and months before my return to the United States, had sent application forms to several universities, including Columbia University in New York City, which appealed to me most.

Yet I felt doubtful about returning to the States because of my feelings about a man I had met the first year in the Canal Zone. The parents of the woman resident in obstetrics lived in Panama City, and they had invited us to dinner one evening along with other guests. I sat next to her father, and on the other side of me sat a handsome fellow a little older than me. All during dinner I enjoyed the conversation of the talkative father, but recognizing my discourtesy to the shy man on my left, I turned to him and drew him into the conversation. From then on, he became very attentive.

More than six years had passed since my broken engagement with Joe. On vacations away from the Kentucky Mountains I had often dated men, but they were very casual acquaintances. Now a man had become seriously interested in me, and I found that I also liked him greatly. He came from a middle class background; he treated me kindly, and with his shyness displayed a clever sense of droll humor. However, we never went on a date that I didn't compare him with Joe. I really did the man a disservice because I couldn't accept him for his own good qualities. Although I laughed at his jesting, playfulness and ability to play jokes on someone else or me, I caught myself remembering Joe's seriousness and dedication to deeper spiritual things.

The two men differed in their appearances also, one dark haired, and the other brown headed. Joe's hair tended to curl and John's straight hair had a cowlick on top. Joe's thin lips parted with a generous smile accentuated by deep brown eyes; John's full lips laughed heartily and his steely grey eyes twinkled with humor. Joe, always particular with his clothes, approved of my getting dressed up; whereas John, in casual tropical clothes, often looked a bit sloppy. John's interest lay solely in me, and not my clothes. I scarcely believe that after an evening with me, he could have told what I wore.

However, as we dated, I felt drawn to John's good-natured affection with others and his honesty in revealing to me how much he cared. I kept praying for the Lord to give me insight into His will for me in this matter. *Was it right for me to still hold on to the memory of Joe as mine when the Lord had so definitely removed him from me? Did He want me to accept John's advances, or hold him at arm's length?* My time in Central and South America would soon end. I changed my prayers. I began to ask God to give assurance that additional schooling was right in His eyes. I prayed for Him to smooth the way if he purposed more education for me, otherwise I wanted Him to firmly shut the door, and I would accept rejection from the universities as the go-ahead to pursue marriage with John. I knew He could make it plain what I was to do. Just as He had answered my prayers in the past at the proper time, I knew He would answer me now in His marvelous way.

In his amiable way, John never pressured me verbally, but I picked up on his longing for me to remain with him when I caught him giving me lengthy looks, or when his mood changed to quietness. Shortly before my term expired at the hospital, he became less and less jovial as we waited to hear from the colleges. For me, the answer came at last.

At dinner that evening I showed him the letter I had just received from Columbia University. He looked puzzled.

"Don't you see, John? It's all too obvious. Out of all the schools I applied to, it's the only one to accept me, the one I wanted most to attend."

With a nod, he replied huskily, "And you'll be leaving in a couple of weeks."

"You know what they say, 'sometimes absence makes affection grow even stronger.' Why don't we see what happens?" After a lengthy silence, I sensed his resignation at my plans. Pensively, he said, "Describe the outfit you'll be wearing when you leave."

"And why do you want to know?" I smiled.

"You'll see."

Out of the abundance of flowers in Panama and the Canal Zone I knew they grew enough orchids to make me a corsage, but John wouldn't have any of them. Instead he ordered a gorgeous, huge corsage of tiger orchids from Columbia, a gold color with chocolate brown throats. It perfectly matched the only suit I owned, a nice gold wool I had worn on the way down to the Tropics, and which would be very appropriate for cooler fall weather when I arrived back in North America.

"Now you'll go home in style," John murmured, as he pinned it to my shoulder.

I'll admit I weakened when we drove up to the airport, and was having second thoughts about the wisdom of separation. He reluctantly put me on the plane, and I can still see him waving to me from behind the fence until takeoff.

I removed my flowers during the long stretch while we flew across the open water, and handed them to the hostess to be placed in the refrigerator. When she pinned them back on they still looked fresh.

"My," she said, admiring them. "I'll bet you're someone special."

"Yes, I am," I smiled, thinking not only of John, but the new challenge of continued education that awaited me because of the Heavenly Father's provision.

I deplaned in New Orleans around two in the morning, and as I started down the steps flashbulbs started popping all around me. I shielded my eyes at the blinding light and looked behind me to see who was being photographed. Then, as I turned back I saw reporters swarming towards *me*!

"Senora," they called. "Senora, we'd like an interview!"

"Well, okay," I stammered, totally confused. "But first I have to go through customs."

"Customs can wait," they contended. "First an interview, Senora."

"Wait a minute. Did you call me Senora? Who do you think I am?"

It turned out they thought I was the wife of a prominent political figure in South America, who was also to arrive that morning in the States.

"You've made a mistake, boys," I laughed. "I'm Hannah Mitchell."

They looked chagrined. "Oops, sorry," one of them said sheepishly. "But you're dressed so nicely with the corsage and all, you look the part."

"And now, you don't have a story."

"Well, maybe a little story," they joshed.

"After all those wasted flashbulbs, I think you should have a front page and so should I!" I went on through customs and to the charming old St. Charles Hotel, where I fell across the bed in my room, to rest a few hours before taking another plane to New York. It felt so good to be back in my native country again that I fell into a deep sleep. From far away it seemed, I heard a faint knock at the door and roused myself enough to groggily answer it.

A bell captain handed me a folded newspaper. "I've been instructed to tell you to look on the front page," he grinned.

"Okay," I mumbled. I shut the door and sat down on the bed again, trying to wake up enough to look at the paper. *At five in the morning? What could be so important?* I looked all over the front page, reread the headlines a couple of times, but none of it seemed pertinent to me. As I folded it back up to turn out the light I noticed a tiny article down in a corner. A little three-line column stated:

Hannah Mitchell ...Arrives... Back In The States!

I collapsed on the bed in giggles. *Those crazy guys and their front-page news! Tomorrow, I must write Joe... I mean... John, about the impression his beautiful corsage made. Yes, I'm definitely back in the States. Not only did the Heavenly Father will it, but He also arranged a little welcome party for me.*

I snickered till I went back to sleep, shaking my head in disbelief at the zany reporters.

Chapter 37

A Room With A Three-Quarter Bed

When I left the airport in Panama City, South America, quite a different atmosphere prevailed than when I had arrived in the country two years previously. Just prior to my work termination the war had ended and truces had been signed. President Truman had declared Victory Over Japan Day as September 2, 1945, the date the Allies and Japan signed the surrender agreement. As the plane climbed into the clouds, I got my first look at their buildings stripped of camouflage. When I arrived back in the States, soldiers were shedding their uniforms to tuck away in closets, hopefully never to be brought out again.

None of my brothers had served in the armed forces. Marcus, because of an accident at the cannery in college years had lost his trigger finger. Russell held a strategic position in U.S. Public Health Service in San Francisco as Director of a tumor clinic. Paul's previous stint in the Army exempted him, plus he had a family. And James, still in high school, was considered too young. Although many brave men had fought and died for their country and I felt indebted to them, like any mother, sister, wife or daughter I breathed thankful prayers when it all ended.

When I arrived in New York City to enroll at Columbia University I noticed several army nurses among the new students. In fact, so many returning nurses had enrolled in colleges that Lucy Barton, also a nurse, went to Congress and persuaded the congressmen to provide monetary aid for these women. For them, it became the equivalent of the veteran's bill for men.

The women came back from the war front in the same condition psychologically as the soldiers, because exposure to bloody deaths, gross amputations and endless bombings had left them emotionally wrecked. Some often chain-smoked or drank excessively, and they shook visibly from exhausted nerves, while others managed to present normal exteriors, although their eyes reflected emotional trauma.

I wondered how I would be able to study with so much evident anxiety among the women. I recognized their small talk and overt friendliness as nervous chatter, so I started praying for suitable living quarters so I could concentrate.

Our residence dorm, Whittier Hall, was a fourteen-story building accommodating two women to a room. Those who had requested their roommates moved in as soon as they received their assignments, while the rest of us waited.

"Miss Mitchell, here's your room number," called a hostess and handed me a blue slip. I rode the elevator to the eighth floor, carrying my bag. When I reached the room, I turned the key in the lock while I knocked on the door, calling softly, "Hellooo. Anybody at home?" To my surprise the door opened into a small cubicle no larger than an oversized closet. In one corner sat a lavatory, toilet and tiny shower. Two windows looked out over the city. And over on one wall sat a three-quarter bed and desk. I smiled. *Well, Lord. You've taken care of my needs again! It's tiny, but I'll be by myself, so I can really hit the books.*

As school convened, war shock became more obvious, because the army nurses were unable to remember some of the easiest assignments given us. I began my courses taking fairly good notes in class and asking questions until I understood the instructor. I also started immediate work on papers that were due weeks later, while the army nurses procrastinated. During study hours they roamed the halls, visiting with each other, unable to keep their minds on the books. As time went by, a steady stream of students found its way to my room, as they asked my view of the assignment, or leaned on me for my notes. I sometimes even outlined things for them.

An old acquaintance from St. Luke's was also at Columbia, working on her Master's degree. We took frequent walks in the neighborhood, while she commented on how crowded my room had become, saying the bedsprings could collapse any day.

I often heard hysterical crying from down the hall, as fragile nerves gave way when time for first quarter exams came. Recognizing they couldn't cope so soon after time on the battlefront, a few nurses left school with plans to return later, but some never came back, thereby forfeiting their government aid.

We weren't allowed to know our grades, only if we passed, or failed. Discouraging for some, it helped foreign nurses, blacks and Canadians who were unable to make perfect grades, due to language difficulties or educational backgrounds.

Toward the end of my year I received a little scholarship, left over money from the Lucy Barton Act. Although not army attached, they decided I qualified because I had gone out of the country to work for the government, so the financial help loosed me from working on weekends, and permitted me to attend church again.

Since I had worked for years in cultures where I didn't feel at home in church, I was like a beggar from a land of famine, listening hungrily. On Sunday mornings I attended the famed Calvary Baptist Church where Dr. William Ayer was pastor. His was an open pulpit, with many worldwide speakers, and scores of visitors. On Sunday evenings I went across town to the Presbyterian Church.

The college also had speakers, but none so inspiring as the ones at church. Among the topics and speakers listed on the hall bulletin boards, were positions offered with job descriptions, and addresses available after we graduated. As it neared time for me to receive my Bachelor of Science degree I wrote to several places. The Pan American Sanitary Bureau in Washington, D.C. called me in for a personal interview with the thought of sending me to Paraguay or Uruguay. The Episcopalian Missionary Board also approached me about foreign mission work.

As opportunities came open I often retired to my room where I knelt beside my bed and prayed. "Heavenly Father, I want my future in your hands. Shut doors where you don't want me, and open the door where you do." I knew only one door could remain ajar for it to be the Lord's leading.

I finalized that I couldn't honestly go with the Episcopalian Board because I didn't agree with some of their doctrines. I wrote Mother about the Government asking me to work in foreign countries.

Her return letter said, "Hannah, I know it's your life, but this grieves me. As long as I live, I hope you won't ever leave the United States again. I just don't think I could bear it." So, I took as a sign from the Lord, my Mother's counsel that I shouldn't leave the country. *What would I do? Where would I go?* I wanted a strong, direct call as offers came in from many areas.

Years before, while I was at FNS, Georgia Public Health sent a student nurse to Kentucky by the name of Jo Kinman, for a degree in nurse midwifery. Afterward, she returned to Georgia, and set up a small, nurse midwifery clinic in the town of Clayton, in Rabun County. A pioneer project, its clinic was sponsored and backed by physicians in her county. She reported to Dr. Guy V. Rice, head of Public Health in Atlanta. As she set up the clinic she would repeat, "Mitch did things this way. Or Mitch said to do that, etc."

Exasperated about this 'Mitch', Dr. Rice finally said, "Well, where *is* this Mitch?" By then I had left Kentucky, so they kept tracing me until they found me at Columbia University.

One day after classes, I returned to my cramped little room, and opened a letter lying on my desk. It read: "Dear Miss Mitchell. Would you please come to Atlanta for an interview with Georgia Department of Public Health? I tried to get the administration to pay for a round trip. They finally agreed on one condition. If you will come to work for us they will pay, but if you refuse, they will only pay for one way." It was signed Guy V. Rice, M.D., Director of Maternal and Child Health, Department of Public Health, Atlanta, Georgia.

My giggle caught the attention of a passing student in the hall. She stuck her head in the doorway and saw the letter. "Got some news?" She snatched the letter out of my hand and plopped down on the bed. "Well, I'll be! This sounds like what you've been waiting for!"

She and several others were aware of my Christian approach to many things, like the fact that I never studied on Sundays because I felt the day belonged to the Lord. I believe He continued to bless me for observing this practice that I had begun at John Brown University, because, after a day of rest from the books I had stamina, and my grades stayed up, while some of the others wilted. They were also aware that I had specifically prayed for the right job opportunity, so the classmate knew what I meant, when I said aloud about the invitation from Atlanta, "Well! May the Lord be praised!"

HANNAH'S JOURNAL, MID-JULY 1990

Heavenly Father, I know it was in your plan for me that I live a long and fruitful life. As I prepare for bed during the final days in my home that you have provided, I know once again that nothing can penetrate my life and safety if it is against your will. In my night terrors, while the dark closes in, you are there; and even during the day, though I am still frightened knowing that my memory is slipping away, I still have the confidence that you are with me.

Like the writer of the old hymn, I know whom I have believed. I am persuaded that He is able....to keep that which I've committed....unto Him against that day. Against that day when I can no longer quote scripture....or sing praises to You.

Just as you have protected me throughout my life, you will shield me from calamity and death, before you decide that it is time for me to come to Heaven. I am thankful for so much - for healing my broken heart many times, for my education, the places my career has taken me, especially my home here in Atlanta.... I rest in thankfulness...

1946-1967

CHAPTER 38

At Home In The Land of Cotton

*I*n the middle of a busy street in downtown Atlanta stands a statue of a woman draped gracefully in a long dress. Her arms are stretched upward as she assists a bird about to take flight. The statue is called The Phoenix, inspired by a legendary bird which lived a long time, burned itself to ashes on a pyre, then rose youthfully alive from the ashes to live another period.

During the Civil War when Sherman and his army swept across the South from Chattanooga on his way to Savannah and the sea, they brought a new kind of war with them. They destroyed civilian property and laid waste to everything that might help the South continue fighting. They burned Atlanta to the ground, stripped houses, barns and fields, ripped up railroad lines and left in ruins anything they could not use.

However, Atlantans refused to let their city die. During the long, anguishing years of Reconstruction, they rebuilt, preserving some of the fire damaged walls and retaining only memories of the plantations, southern belles and aristocratic gentlemen in their heritage. The ashes had long since settled when I went for my interview in 1946, although it had been just eighty years before, when Sherman had made his fiery sweep through Georgia. At this time, the population of Atlanta was similar to the other small cities in the South, although I noted a throbbing restlessness in the spirits of people on the streets. Merchants talked of enlarging businesses, building shopping centers; city officials spoke of attracting outside revenue. With vigor and youthfulness Atlantans looked to the future, determined to grow, to go forward. Like a graceful bird, the city was poised to rise again, and live more gloriously than in the past. Atlanta's history of new beginnings appealed to me, since my own plans had also often begun afresh.

I had sensed an open mindedness in the Georgia Public Health office during my interview with Dr. Rice. His small physical appearance belied a big brain with vision and practical sense. Years ahead in his thinking about public health projects, he had the reputation of being far-out to some, but they said once he exploited an idea and found it worthwhile, he delegated authority until its accomplishment. He got right to the point soon after I sat down in his office.

"Miss Mitchell, I'm sure you are aware of the statistics in Georgia regarding maternal death rates, infant morbidity and mortality." I nodded. Indeed, I had looked up the facts before I came. They were deplorable, as were figures from other states.

"We want to change these figures," Dr. Rice said, stroking his moustache pensively. "We want to save lives by educating expectant mothers, black and white." He sighed. "And somehow we must also salvage the premature babies and give them a good start in life."

He struck a responsive chord in me when he spoke so strongly about saving lives of mothers and babies. I had a feeling of camaraderie with him throughout our conversation, a positive nudge about his attitude about Public Health.

"Well, when do I begin work?" I asked, catching him off guard.

"Then...you'll come?" he asked, leaning forward in his chair.

"I have no choice," I grinned. "I can't afford to pay my own way back to New York."

I looked forward to the transition from school to work, because it would be a continuation of caring for mothers and babies like I had done with Frontier Nursing Service, and my work in South America. Only now, it would be on an administrative level where I could have more clout.

So, in 1946, shortly after receiving my Bachelor of Science degree, I moved to Atlanta, and soon became certified in Georgia to practice nurse midwifery.

Nevertheless, when I first started working in the office, the paper work, something I was not accustomed to, was mind-boggling. There were numerous reports to file with the Children's Bureau in Washington, state forms to complete in detail. It also fell to me as my job, to involve all the counties in projects, ascertaining the value of nurse midwifery service in home deliveries, or the county hospitals. Did they need maternity shelters or clinics exclusively practicing obstetrics and deliveries? When answers from questionnaires came flooding in from all over the state, I thought I was in over my head. *Lord? Are you sure about this job?* Many a night I asked for his help in conquering the paper mounds on my desk.

On the other hand I looked forward to times when I visited the offices in the counties. Jo Kinman, the former FNS nurse who worked in Clayton grabbed me the first time I visited her midwifery clinic.

"Oh, Mitch! Now I can get some support! You know all my problems!"

Ruth Davis, also one of my students from FNS, had worked in Georgia for years in a private physician's office. After she retired, she came out to Monroe, in Walton County, and helped with my first research project. We established a demonstrative nurse midwife program, training nurses for home deliveries, maternity shelters and hospitals. The study evaluated the expense of hiring nurse midwives, and also their effect upon the health and welfare of mothers, and babies.

Another reason for my being hired was to help prepare a new teaching aid for mother and baby care that would replace an old outdated pamphlet. About twenty consulting nurses came to Atlanta from the regional offices for a meeting to discuss the project. As the new nurse present, I listened, while the others spoke.

At a pause in the debate, while he reflectively smoothed his moustache, Dr. Rice said, "Miss Mitchell. What kind of cover would you like on the booklet?"

I quickly replied. "One so attractive in color and appeal, that a pregnant woman would eagerly pick it up, and look inside."

"Go on," he said, his eyes narrowing. I continued with a description of an endearing mother and baby picture in blues and pinks with the photo completely covering the back and front pages.

He nodded, catching my vision. "Good. You take care of the project."

With this, he pushed back his chair and walked out, signal that the meeting had just concluded. The other nurses laughed at my dumbfounded expression, as though they knew this to be the typical, decisive conclusion to one of Dr. Rice's meetings.

* * * * *

Also, part of my job was to stimulate interest among doctors, and public health people statewide, in our attempt to upgrade health care. This put me gladly out in district again, promoting enthusiasm and public relations.

One day at the local health department, down in Thomas County, we were discussing the need for getting orthopedically handicapped children into clinics, for diagnosis and treatment, or corrective surgery. Nurse Williams commented that several handicapped children lived in one part of her district, but after repeated attempts on her part, still they didn't come in for treatment.

I thought for a minute, the situation sounding familiar. "Who is the matriarch in the area?" I asked.

"Matriarch! What are you talking about?"

I explained that in some cultures, and probably among the Negroes in the South, frequently, the person in authority was a woman who demanded considerable obedience, not only through her command of women, but men as well. She was, as the name implied, commander in charge of the community.

At this new revelation to Mrs. Williams and the other nurses who were listening, she said, "Well, while you're down here I wish you'd go find this matriarch for me!"

So the next day, we drove her car through the district, making home visits to postpartums and their new babies. Interestingly enough, in two of the homes when I asked who had delivered their babies, it was the same midwife.

"Is she any kin?" I asked casually. She was.

In the last home I met a talkative woman who knew a lot about the community. "Are a large group of you kin?" I probed. She told me about interactions regarding blood kinship. This gave me names of several families. Not showing much interest, I said, "I noticed several families have Mandy's last name, and she delivered their babies. Are they kin?" They were. I felt we had found the matriarch.

On the second day in that area I said, "Why don't we pay Mandy a visit?" Nurse Williams smiled knowingly as we schemed about her casual introduction of me, not as someone from Atlanta, or the State Health Department, but just another nurse.

When we drove up in her yard, Mandy watched from behind her screen door. We walked up the rickety steps to the porch, past several buckets of flowers that hardly left any room to walk. Rusty tin cans sat on the railings, and around the porch, sometimes two deep, filled with varieties of plants.

As we approached the screen door, Mrs. Williams said, "We've been visiting some of the new mothers you delivered, and stopped by to tell you what a nice crop of babies you have." The old midwife smiled appreciatively, and we discussed babies through the screen awhile, nothing about crippled ones.

I changed the subject, looking around the porch admiringly, and bending over a lard bucket. With a love of flowers cultivated since childhood, my comment was sincere. "I've never seen so many different kinds of house plants thriving so well!" When I said this, Mandy came outside and joined the conversation. When we left, I proudly carried bunches of cuttings to start houseplants of my own.

Two days later, I easily went back to report on the plant slips she had given me. After some flower talk and her advice on proper gardening, I sought her opinion on the children. "What do you think about Edward's club foot? He has difficulty in walking."

Mandy sighed in agreement. "It's hard for him to get around, all right."

"Will he be able to go to school?" I asked curiously. "When he grows up, will he walk like other men?"

"Oh, lawsy, no," she said with a moan. "I guess its God's will for him to always be this way."

"Well, do you suppose he'll have hard feelings about not getting that fixed? You know, in this day and time, he can get that fixed for free." She looked at me sharply. I knew I had touched metal.

Although the child's foot problem was from a birth deformity and not diet, I left there thinking about how old ways and habits still affected culture. It reminded me of the empathy I had felt for a small boned man I had heard speak years ago at a nursing convention. George Washington Carver had talked about the diets of poverty-stricken families in the South, and how he had tried to convince the blacks near his home in Tuskegee, Alabama to improve their diets.

With little regard for his own apparel he had looked like a rainbow, wearing an orchid tie and green coat, with a red shirt blaring from beneath his jacket. But when he spoke we forgot his appearance. His speech sounded surprisingly British, with his brilliant genius displaying itself in excellent grammar.

"It is difficult to persuade my people to change their ways," he said. "If only they would eat less pork, and plant greens and peanuts, a black family could not only survive, but their health would improve." I shared Dr. Carver's concern about their diets, but also hoped for real medical progress among the blacks.

I was strongly encouraged when it was later reported to me that the children from Nurse Williams' district had begun coming in to Atlanta for treatment, some to Ardmore, and others to the well-known Scottish Rite Hospital for crippled children. Some months later, Mrs. Williams informed me that all the handicapped children in her records had at last checked through. Mandy, and many other midwives were at last catching our vision of giving new and better health care to whole families.

As the song implies, old times in the South are not easily forgotten, but at the time I moved to Atlanta change had begun. True, as I drove throughout the state I saw men in overalls and straw hats stooped over in the cotton fields, the women in faded cotton dresses and sunbonnets, a scene from days of slavery. But their children didn't play away their childhoods under the trees anymore. They went to school. It would take years for prejudice to wane; poverty and ignorance wouldn't be erased overnight, but change was on the way.

I fell in love with Atlanta, the city of dogwoods and azaleas that blossomed profusely in the spring. The charm and friendliness of southerners made me feel at home, and anytime I left on business or to visit family, I was anxious to return to the city with the Phoenix in her street. Atlanta's population soon mushroomed after officials enlarged the airport, yet it retained warmth because of the genuine hospitality exhibited everywhere. In time, I came to know without a hint of doubt that at last I had come home.

CHAPTER 39

Hannah's Haven

"LOVE NEST FOR SALE" read the large print as I casually looked at the want ads in the Sunday Atlanta Journal. *How vulgar!* I thought, and I continued to think, on up into the next day at the office. But after I went home for the evening, I pored over the ad again, and before dark I called the realtor and went by to see the place. I looked around by myself while he spoke with some other prospective buyers.

Ever since I had been in Atlanta, one of my greatest desires was for a little house of my own with space for flowers. I had prayed for direction as I considered three places I had chosen. *Lord, if you don't want me to have any of them, just shut the door.* So He did, emphatically! One house sat in the eventual path of an expressway, another with a good garden area was sold right out from under me, and slums later surrounded the third. So, I thanked Him for preventing me from buying any of them.

But is this the place? It's so run down, although I can mentally picture what might be made of it. Is this the one of your choosing? While I prayed, an appraiser by the name of Orville Wainwright came to mind, and I asked the realtor to wait, while I went after him and his wife. We walked all over the grounds. Afterwards, he said, "You'd really like to have this place, wouldn't you?"

I nodded. "Yes. I realize it needs a lot of work but I think it would be good for me, and I hope I would be good for it."

"How much does the owner want?"

"9,600."

"Offer her $9,000. I think she'll take it."

"Okay. If she does and it works out financially, I'll know this is the place the Lord intends for me to have." Around two hundred couples had been on the property on Sunday, because of the wording of the ad, but the owner demanded large cash down payment, and young couples couldn't afford it. She wanted one-third in cash, another third for the mortgage while she held still another mortgage of the remaining third.

To my surprise, the owner took my offer of $9,000! I remembered the firm lesson in economics I had learned, when Dad owed the fifty dollars on our home in Norwood, Missouri. So, I paid one-third down as the seller requested, took over the mortgage she owed at the bank, and doubled up on the payments to her, until I had paid her and the bank off in a year. It became mine on May 13, 1959, and I moved in on June 13.

It wasn't until I moved in, that I realized what an undertaking for a lone woman I had assumed. The house's three shades of paint were peeling badly in several places. Ivy, wisteria and running honeysuckle ran berserk over the grounds. From the kitchen door, I couldn't even get through the tangle to the backside of the property, where wet weather springs had eroded a hillside. Felled trees with huge limbs and branches protruded from the tangle of underbrush, and three upright dead trees housed many woodpeckers.

Friends stopped by to see the place and remarked in dismay, "Why would Hannah ever want this?"

The property runs three hundred and sixty-eight feet up a sloping hill from the street; to the flat elevation the house sits on, then back along a gradual decline to the back fence. Under the tangle of vines I discovered a stone wall running the depth of the property from the street to the tool house. The house also sits on stone.

Beautifully intact, I discovered only one place on the right side wall in need of repair, which I paid a stonemason to fix. The realtor had estimated around $10,000 worth of stones lay in the walls, and each time I uncovered a bit of the stonework, I marveled that the original owner knew where to place them, with terracing for practical design and soil retention. I determinedly attempted to carry out this same design as I planted and transplanted with emphasis on unity, symmetry and harmony.

Underneath the peeling paint the house itself didn't appear in too much need of repair. Shotgun type, in that one can walk in the front door all the way through and out the back, it consisted of four rooms. I changed the entrance to the left side, which would open into the living room with the bedroom on the right, dining room on the left and tiny lean-to kitchen on its left. From the front door visitors face the tiniest bathroom in Atlanta!

I tried to hire help. I paid a black man to help me grub out the poison ivy. "Wear these gloves for protection, Sam."

He waved them off. "I'm not one of them folks that gets poison ivy," he assured me. He pulled it up without any covering on his hands and arms and promptly wound up in Grady Hospital. I decided this was a rather expensive way to rid the place of that toxic weed.

Friends who lived in apartments or had lost enthusiasm for their own places decided mine was a new challenge, so they volunteered to help. Mercedes Fischer started pulling some upright, thick stalks of what she thought was devil's vine.

"Mercedes! That's poison ivy!"

"Oh, no. It can't be!" she groaned. She broke out in a rash so bad it called for x-ray treatments plus internal and external medication.

After that I cleared the grounds on my own. I sprayed a spot of poison ivy with weed killer and waited until it died down. When some of it came back I dug around until I found the root. Without touching it I rolled it in newspaper, put it in boxes plainly marked and put it down front for the trash men. One of the men later thanked me for marking it and said they always handled the bundles carefully. They had burned trash from another place, and unaware of poison ivy in it, one of the men had died from inhaling the fumes.

Mercedes, Ruth Kern and Bernice Lyles, concerned about the dark path from my car up to the house, put in outside lighting for me. Ruth, a talented violinist, had an electrician father who suffered from severe coronary disease. As his assistant she had learned how to wire. The women put in two coach lamps and a tree floodlight that bathes the walkway in front of the house. What a comfort all these years to come home to welcoming light in the darkness.

Eventually I had the house re-wired to increase the capacity of the circuit box. After inspecting the outside wiring which lay safely under the soil in pipes, the electrician asked, "Who did your outside wiring?"

I bristled a little. "Why do you want to know?"

"It's one of the best pieces of three-way lighting I've ever seen," he said, shaking his head. "I was wondering which company did it."

"What would you say if I told you that three women put it in," I said with a grin. "One with the know-how and the other two as assistants." He let out a low whistle in response.

At first I didn't know what to do with the open areas in the yard that lay bare of ground cover or lawn. Except for weed patches, only a bit of furry moss about the size of a washtub lay under a tree. I experimented seeding other areas with this moss. I dug up a small portion and disposed of the weed roots, crumbled the velvety lichen over the soil and wet it down well. It spread out and grew! So, where ivy or large shrubs and flowers didn't grow, moss became my ground cover. Even today I don't have one blade of grass to cut.

Little by little the place took on a look of being loved and cared for. I transplanted two old and tired looking elaeagnus and spirea from the upper shelf to the back woods to prevent the soil from washing. Along the top of the stone wall I planted dwarf snow azaleas and fertilized them. Each year I have to trim them back to four feet in height.

I believe I have finally discovered all the stonework and displayed it as best I know how. Of course the renovation has been a continuing process, but everyone who comes by comments on the peace and tranquility of the yard. They stand in awe when they realize the width and height of the two white oaks that grow along the curb down at the street, or laugh good-naturedly about climbing up the many stone steps that wind from the drive up to the house. After about a year's work the same friends who wondered what I saw in the place, oohed and aahed and begged to trade mine for theirs.

Many a night I sank wearily into the bathtub to soak off the grime and ease my aching muscles. How often I had wished for a husband to help with my heavy task. Immersed in the steamy bubbles I reflected on the two men I had once taken seriously. For all time I had relinquished Joe, long ago. John's letters had come for about a year, but with little encouragement from me they had languished and then stopped. In my contemplation I had to accept again the Lord's will in guiding my life to remain an old, unmarried woman.

* * * * *

Just a few years back I had taken a leave of absence from my job in Georgia to study for a Master's degree in Public Health at the University of Michigan. While there I had gotten sick and the illness left me with a lingering problem with equilibrium. I went to the Health Service for an examination and some blood work.

Afterwards, the doctor had said, "Miss Mitchell, you are very fortunate that you never married and had children. Your thyroid production is so low, that had you carried a child it would have been a cretin." I recognized with a shudder what an awesome burden such a child would have been. Worse than mongoloid it would have been so severely retarded as to be vegetable-like with no mental response.

Of course, today we have medications for such thyroid disorders, but not back in my childbearing years. Whenever bitterness tries to surface about not marrying I thank the Heavenly Father for sparing me from the heartbreak of a child that could never know my love.

Although I don't have a husband or family to share my home and have lived all these years alone, I have a love nest just the same. Once, an artist friend of mine, Fae Allen, made a pen sketch of the front hillside and house on stationery. I made a thousand copies of the sketch and on the bottom put this inscription: *Hannah's Haven. Both Belong To The Lord!*

CHAPTER 40

A Church Home

I also church shopped when I first moved to Atlanta. For so many years my work had kept me from attending Protestant services that I enjoyed. The inspiring speakers in New York had only whetted my appetite, and I wanted and needed to join a church with a strong evangelistic outreach.

Dr. Donald Grey Barnhouse had held meetings at Westminster Presbyterian for awhile, the church where Peter Marshall had begun his ministry. When the meetings ended I continued going to church there because the pastor, Dr. Richardson, had impressed me with the way he taught. I visited sporadically at first, since projects kept me out of town. Also, in 1949 I had taken a leave of absence from work and enrolled in the University of Michigan where I received my Masters in Public Health. After I returned to Atlanta my job allowed me to remain in town more on weekends and I visited faithfully. Finally, on Sunday, January 7, 1951 I joined the church. I still have my certificate of church membership and the bulletin that introduced several others and myself the following Sunday.

I attended every service that I possibly could. It became a joke at work whenever someone asked me about my plans for the evening.

Either a special speaker had come to town I didn't want to miss, or it was Missions Week when the missionaries came and shared their lives, or I hurried to get to mid-week prayer service with supper served beforehand.

"I don't see why you don't just move into one of the rooms at church – you're there so much!" they teased. Or, "Do they pay you extra for all that over-time work?"

I enjoyed Sunday school where we discussed scripture. Pretty soon they elected me to an office in the class, and I often gave a quip about the lesson before the teacher began. Later I was asked to teach a night Circle.

The women in Circle enjoyed the object lessons I used in the devotions. Recently, one came up to me and asked if I remembered the one I had taught using keys. She was reminded of it occasionally when she removed her keys from her purse

I had held up my key ring and related how each one was a part of my life. "The ignition key transports me, one opens the door to my house, one fits my metal box with Deed and Will, and one key turns the lock to a house I own in Thomasville, my home away from home."

Then I showed them how keys are a picture of a Christian's life. "The ignition key represents the Holy Spirit as He moves me along in Christian activity, the house key is my rest in the Lord, and the strong box key holds the deed to promises that sustain me, and also the key to my Will after death where I will inherit heavenly experiences. The key to my home away from home really represents going to be with the Lord."

We needed a teacher for the college age class but no one wanted to take it. "How about Hannah Mitchell?" suggested one of the women I taught in Women on Missions Circle.

"Oh, I don't know," Dr. Richardson said, hesitantly. "We usually don't ask women to teach mixed groups." After a few weeks, however, with no response from the men in the church, they asked me. "Well, since you can't get anyone else, I guess you're stuck with me," I allowed.

The first Sunday in class, I said, "What would you like to study?" offering the students several books, but really leaning towards straight scripture.

"Let's just study the Bible," they said.

"Well, okay! What do you say we start from the beginning?" They didn't realize what I had in mind when I suggested Genesis, but after a few books later, they did. We began with a handful of students, and it blossomed to a few dozen with students coming from Georgia Tech, Agnes Scott College for Women, Emory University. After awhile, we numbered over seventy-five people on many Sundays.

One man dropped in frequently when he was traveling through Atlanta on business. "You were in Deuteronomy last time, now which book are you studying?" he asked before class began.

"You're telling on yourself," I teased. "We're in Judges now." We went straight through the Bible, all the way to Revelation. It took about eight years.

* * * * *

Many international students came to Westminster from Georgia Tech. On Sundays after church, I usually set my table for three or four guests from class, most of them foreigners and usually one American. One boy, a student from Valdosta usually brought a Taiwanese friend to class. I invited them to come the following Sunday to the house for lunch.

During the week I pulled out my cookbooks and decided on a Taiwanese dinner, with chicken walnut and oriental vegetables. Before I left for Sunday school I set the timer on the oven so lunch would be ready when we returned from church. When I opened the front door to my house the aroma hit the young man from Taiwan.

His face lit up and he said, "Smells like home!"

"Really?" I said while I finished setting the table. When he saw the table he started to cry.

"Miss Mitchell. Just like home!"

"Oh, wait till you taste it. It won't be like your Mama's cooking."

His tears stopped and he grinned. "All we need is tea."

"You'll just have to drink American tea this time," I said, pouring a cup at his place at the table.

The next week I went out of town on business. I returned to find a package of Taiwanese tea beside my front door. David Amurian called. "Miss Mitchell, did you get your tea? Our friend was disappointed that he missed you; he walked all the way from Georgia Tech to your house and left it for you. He had brought the tea from home because he knew he couldn't buy it in the States, and now he's divided it with you."

Next time our meal was complete, with Taiwanese tea. "*Is* like home," he nodded with satisfaction afterwards and patted his tummy. "Like home."

I knew how the boy felt. As someone who had traveled a lot, I had known real homesickness often. Hungrily I had responded to the warm-heartedness of friendly gestures, a smile or a cup of coffee with another human being, when I was far from home. At times, when I was alone at night in Hannah's Haven, I made myself a cup of Taiwanese tea. Looking around at my little house, now that my circle of friends had widened to those I most felt akin to in church, I felt like I had finally come home at last.

CHAPTER 41

All My Babies

*I*n one of the meetings to upgrade local midwife care, Dr. Rice spoke with concern. "According to our records 1,322 local midwives delivered 18,741 of the total live births in a single year. This shows that our population is still greater than the number of doctors we have in the state. Furthermore, our training programs aren't supplying enough certified nurse midwives in the rural areas." His hand worked with the hair on his upper lip while he spoke. For several minutes no one offered a solution.

"Perhaps we need a tool to aid the public health nurse as she educates the local midwives. Many of them can't read," interjected one of the staff nurses.

"Why not make a teaching film, like George Stoney did on venereal disease?" added another.

Enthusiastic discussion went around the room. In the midst of the clamor Dr. Rice turned to me. "Miss Mitchell, you worked with Mr. Stoney on his film. Should we attempt it, why don't you tackle being technical advisor?" His moustache twitched mischievously.

"Well, let's see if Mr. Stoney will do it," I stalled. When we approached him about writing another documentary script he agreed, provided we secure the necessary funds. So Dr. Rice went to Children's Bureau and received $20,000 initially, and convinced Mr. Stoney to direct and also produce the picture. So I was enlisted in a new project, unaware of the actual amount of preparation on paper and physical stamina it would require.

Before we began the script, I wrote a feeler letter to eleven other southern states, including New Mexico, asking if they needed such a film, and if they did, what specific problems should be stressed. Each state responded. In all, one hundred and twenty-five problems needed to be incorporated, either in the script, or visually! We tried to include them all from the beginning

We visited thirteen counties searching for a proper local midwife to play the starring role. We found her in Miss Mary, down in Albany. A ponderous black woman with a superb native intelligence, she was also deeply religious. When we got the script and cast together, she accepted my coaching readily.

Although it was an instructional film, the patients were actual cases filmed with their permission. Family members played themselves. The script begins with Miss Mary, a midwife who is greatly interested in her families, mothers-to-be and particularly the babies. A large photographic collection of babies she has delivered adorns the rough walls of her house. Two pregnant women come to see her; their separate visits are to engage Miss Mary to attend their future deliveries.

Miss Mary assisted Ida when her other children were born so she has a confident respect for the midwife. A healthy patient, she talks about the clothes she has prepared for the coming baby, pads for the bed and herself, to be used during the postpartum period. She registered early at the Health Department.

Maybelle, who has just moved into the area had a stillbirth, therefore she appears anxious and pessimistic. Neither has she visited the Health Department for examination by a doctor, as required for all midwife cases.

Later, due to Miss Mary's insistence they both go to the clinic, Maybelle for registration and examination, Ida for a routine checkup.

Ida's labor begins and her husband leaves to get the midwife. When they arrive Ida's mother is present to help. The husband tucks a quilt around his sleeping boy and girl. One child rouses and he takes her in his arms, quietly rocking her. When the baby is born, Ida smiles and the joyful laughter of her husband and mother are captured by the camera and sound. After Ida and baby are clean and presentable the father brings in the little girl, now awake to see the new baby brother.

An exhausted Miss Mary returns home and collapses on the bed, failing to prepare her bag for the next case. As she drifts off to sleep, she sees a flashback of the health officer at a midwife meeting, sternly telling of a baby's death. His repetitious *'something wasn't clean, something wasn't clean'* pricks her conscience till at last she rises, puts wood in the stove, and proceeds to boil her scissors and put all new clean supplies in her midwife bag.

Just as she finishes and gets in bed again Maybelle's husband comes for her. She scarcely has time to prep the mother before the baby arrives prematurely. Maybelle keeps asking, "Is it dead? Will it live?" Miss Mary, in soothing tones encourages the anxious mother with, "Shore. It's gonna be all right, honey." She sends the husband to the Health Department for a home type incubator.

Both babies do well, and the day Maybelle takes her little boy to the baby clinic the father proudly carries him into a photo booth. For twenty-five cents he gets a snapshot for Miss Mary's baby collection.

In the final scene, Ida brings her baby and little girl to visit Miss Mary, who points out the snapshot of Maybelle's little boy.

Ida exclaims, "I bet you're mighty proud of that little bitty baby!" To which Miss Mary says, "Why, yes, Ida! I'm proud of *all my babies!*"

We learned a lot in filming. In black and white film, a Negro looks comatose with white against his skin. We bought blue sheets, pillowcases and towels. Sometimes I had to use bluing on articles and iron them dry, so I went around all the time with cyanotic looking hands. First shots were often the last ones, and sometimes the last became first in the story, so as technical advisor I made diagrams about scenes, sometimes to a half-inch scale to make sure we included everything each time.

One morning we were about to begin shooting for the delivery sequence. Before the camera rolled, I looked around the room to make sure everything was ready, but I missed an article around the fireplace. None of the crew or actors had moved anything and I began to feel stupid holding up the work. Mr. Stoney went to the woman of the house.

"Oh, the insurance man came by last night to collect. I forgot to put the card back on the nail by the mantel!" With the payment card back in its place we were able to shoot the scene.

Before each day of shooting began, Miss Mary and I went off in a corner to pray for the film. "Oh, Lord," she prayed, with her eyes closed and face tilted upward, holding out her hands. "Use this picture to save many women and babies. And Lord Jesus, let it give *glory* to God. Amen!"

Typical of our busy day, we rose early with breakfast at seven o'clock, and arrived on location at eight. At noon we gulped down sandwiches, coffee and cold drinks delivered by a sandwich shop. Then, Lights! Action! I kept a good supply of bug spray in my car to nail the flies buzzing around the camera when we shot scenes inside the shack with no screens on the windows. They sounded like dive bombers on the sound track and I almost asphyxiated the cameraman as I shot them down.

The college girl who played the part of Maybelle looked too healthy, so we made a mixture of baby powder and molasses and painted a typical lesion from vitamin deficiency on one corner of her mouth. Under the hot lights it needed redoing frequently.

Some days everything went wrong. Just as we would start rolling a plane would fly over, so we waited. Or a dog would bark or howl till we convinced the owner to quiet the dog, or we would! The young preacher playing the husband wore his worst clothes, but we still had to rumple and dirty his neat shirt and jeans; to make him look older we plopped an old felt hat on his head. Attention to details made for a long day, and working past sundown gave us ravenous appetites for dinner.

During the evenings we discussed the film, the necessary corrections and instructions for the following day. If our rushes returned from New York City, we stayed up until after the late movie finished at the local theater, and there we viewed our pictures, commenting on the good takes and discarding those that needed re-doing. I fought sleep often in the cool darkness of the theater.

Back in my room at the New Albany Hotel, I often sat up doing cutwork embroidery on a tablecloth until the wee hours, because of noisy conventions being held. Even so, the crew assured me that mine was one of the quieter rooms.

Marian Cadwallader and I attended several baby deliveries with Miss Mary, to prepare her for any type difficulty that might occur during the film delivery. When Ida went into labor I drove her the five miles to our specially prepared room where the crew and Miss Mary assembled to meet us. Two cameras loaded with film stood ready to shoot from various angles.

All went well until the baby's head crowned and I realized the membranes were intact. A veil covered the baby's face.

"Mary, don't look at me," I whispered. "Reach over and place pressure on the bag of water just back of the baby's head with your thumb and first finger. Break the membrane and zip it off the baby's face." She obeyed instinctively and the camera caught a clear view of the baby as he entered the world.

Afterwards, I asked, "Have you ever delivered one like this before?"

"Yes'm."

"What did you do then?"

She grinned, "Why, I just lets it bust!"

Cutting the film and deciding which shots were best became laborious for the cutting woman, Mr. Stoney, others and myself. Actual shooting had taken two and a half months and near its completion, Dr. Rice had to get $10,000 more from Washington! I remained on location the entire time, except for two weeks due to a previous commitment, and then Marian Cadwallader filled in for me.

At last we gave a sneak preview for the state and territorial health officers of the association. Lou Applebaum's musical score was either highly praised, or declared rather weird. He had visited several black churches in Georgia, and midwife meetings, in order to capture a cultural musical pattern. A local Georgia woman who attended a Negro college in Washington, D.C. sang one of the spiritual lullabies while she held her own sleeping baby in her lap. This background music especially appealed to the granny midwives when we later showed them the film.

Miss Mary attended the showing of 'All My Babies' for Georgia homefolks at a theater on Peachtree Street where we heard special speeches, and the audience applauded with approval at the movie's conclusion. Later a woman came over and asked me about Maybelle. "How did you ever find someone with such a good evidence of vitamin deficiency?"

One week after the theater showing I flew to Washington for the Children's Bureau staff and guests to view it. My brother James honored me by coming from Silver Springs, Maryland, where he was doing dental research.

The film received nothing but praise afterwards. "This is the finest film of its kind, with excellent direction, acting, photography and evolution of the story. Best teaching documentary, ever. An extraordinary movie without a false note...true, correct and restrained," so read the accolades from professors of medical graduate schools, chief physicians at metropolitan hospitals, nursing educators, and someone from the film section of the U.S. State Department.

I believe the Lord answered Miss Mary's and my prayer for the film's uniqueness in its appeal to be used as a life-saving device. The year of its release it won the Flaherty Citation for Excellence in Documentary Filmmaking, an equivalent to an Oscar!

Years later, the World Health Organization cabled me to bring 'All My Babies' to a meeting in Geneva, Switzerland, and serve as a temporary advisor in maternal and child health and family planning. Many people came up to me after we showed the film, and commented on the possibility of its use in their countries, and asked for the address of Columbia Communications Center in New York, who handled it.

An interesting sidelight was the effect of the film on the crew. The cutting woman from England had been married eight or nine years without a child, because of her fear of childbirth; she and her husband had a baby. The film director Mr. Stoney and his wife had their second child. The cameraman and his wife added to their family, as did the lighting man and his spouse.

The only ones who didn't produce any offspring were Miss Mary, who had grown children and many grandchildren, and me, the technical advisor.....an old maid.

CHAPTER 42

Rider Of The Pale Horse

When I boarded the plane in Atlanta that day in January 1961, it was typically clear and cold, but the sun shone in a sky of deep blue. I was on my way to Kansas City, because I had received a phone call days earlier that my Mother had passed away. But a snowstorm aborted the flight in Little Rock, Arkansas, leaving us passengers stranded along with others from various airlines.

The ticket agent announced cheerfully that when the snow stopped, the snow ploughs would clear the runway and we could be on our way. Most passengers grumbled, but collected their luggage and found a place to wait. Only a few others remained at the ticket counter with me.

"We're doing the best we can, ma'am," the agent told me.

"Oh, I realize that, but I really need other arrangements. My brother was to meet me in Kansas City so we could drive to Norwood, Missouri and meet the train bringing my Mother's body for her funeral."

"I see," he said with a different inflection in his voice. "I'm sorry. Let me see what we can do." Eastern Airlines graciously paid my

241

way on the train that went to Mountain Grove, ten miles from Norwood, where I stayed in someone's home because all the hotels and motels were filled. Next morning, I took a taxi to Norwood, where Paul met me and we waited at the train station for James, who was accompanying Mother's body. James had wired ahead with funeral arrangements, so together we all went back to Mountain Grove for Mother to lie in state at the small funeral home.

In the years of the early fifties, although she was ageing, Mother had insisted on continuing work at a nursing home. But at our insistence, she had allowed me to take her by car to San Francisco to live with Russell. However, she didn't stay long because a persistent bleeding ulcer caused my brother to have ninety-eight percent of his stomach removed. Mother's sister Elvina in Nampa, Idaho, asked her to come there to live, so she moved once again. For several years she had remained in good health and raised a small vegetable and flower garden. One year I took James' ten-year old daughter Missy out on the train for a visit.

Later, we got word that Mother had suffered an embolic thrombosis in both legs. Russell sent an expert cardiologist to the hospital and he gave a poor prognosis for her. He thought she might need both legs amputated, and even at the most didn't expect her to live over a year.

James called Russell. "We want Mother to come live with us in Louisiana where it's warmer." At this, Mother stalled.

"What is it?" Russell asked. "You've been saying for years that you never see James. You know they'll enjoy having you."

"Oh, I know that," Mother said, prickling. "It's just that, well, I'm not having anything to do with those *wheelchairs* at the airport!" However, at Russell's insistence she gave in, and he accompanied her on the flight.

With Mother's resiliency, she had proved the doctor wrong about amputations and quickly recovered from the blood clots, but he was right about her life expectancy. Within a day or two of a year she died.

In addition to listing her relatives and survivors, the small town newspaper wrote a lovely obituary: '*She expressed her faith and hope in Christ in her teen years, and later united with the Christian Church here in Norwood. She lived faithful to the Lord until her death. She devoted her entire life to the welfare and progress of her children. She was a neighbor who always helped in time of need, and was loved by all who knew her.*'

Sometimes, when we lose a loved one, if it is by sudden accident, we are so numbed with shock and grief that we don't think we can bear it. Then, at other times we know ahead that a person doesn't have long to live and we make the most of the time, taking mental pictures and storing conversations in our memories to take out and savor long after they are gone. We hope by preparing ourselves that their passing won't hurt as much. In my parents' deaths, my Father's by accident, Mother's from a lingering illness, I can't say that the actual pain was any less. Either way I'll never see them in this life again. However, I have stood by open caskets and attended many funerals, some of them Christian and some not, and I can truly say that I had more peace at my parents' funerals, knowing they are in heaven with Christ, than I have had sitting with families whose deceased had no such hope.

It looked like the entire town had braved the snow and ice to come to Mother's funeral, with people lining the walls of the Norwood Christian Church. Two ministers preached her funeral and we took one final look at her while everyone else waited outside. She didn't look her age of seventy-four, with natural dark hair framing her face. Though somewhat wrinkled, she had pretty hands, with delicate fine bones that didn't reveal all the hard work she had done. After a brief graveside ceremony, we laid her to rest beside our Father and little sister, Evalyn.

* * * * *

Less than a year later Paul's wife, Lucille, called. "Hannah! Something awful has happened. Paul's car was hit by a train, and he's dreadfully hurt!"

A cold shiver went down my back. "Do you want me to come?"

"Oh, Hannah! Would you?"

At the hospital, nurses and doctors battled around the clock to save Paul's life. "Don't go in without these to protect him from infection," ordered a nurse as she handed a cap, gown and mask to me.

I went to the side of his bed. Severely burned, he lay swathed in bandages. With multiple internal injuries, including a ruptured spleen, he came and went into consciousness.

"Paul?" I said softly. All I could see were his eyes. They opened and he looked startled. "It's Hannah."

"Oh," he said through the bandages. "I thought you were Mom."

We called James and Marcus. Russell was on his way, but Paul died early in the morning before he arrived. Since we couldn't open the casket Russell didn't want to stay for the funeral, so after we made arrangements, and we all reminisced about our childhoods, he went on back home.

A couple of weeks later, back at work in Atlanta, I became concerned about my own health and went for my annual physical. I admitted that I hadn't felt well for some months but thought I was only tired and overworked, although I had noticed a rapid heartbeat that slowed then raced again.

When he placed the stethoscope to my chest, the doctor listened a long time. "Miss Mitchell, you have a lot of fibrillation. Were you a blue baby?"

"A doctor in nursing school asked me the same thing during a physical," I said. "My mother never mentioned anything about any abnormalities. However, at the time when I was a student nurse, the doctor said I had a hole in my heart."

"Well, your birth defect has caught up with you." The doctor sat down on a stool beside me and gave me a serious talking to. "I'm going to insist that you slow down and relax more. I know your job requires you to be out of town a lot. I suggest you time your appointments further apart, and when you're on the road, get out and walk around for ten or fifteen minutes, every couple of hours."

For awhile, I tried his suggestion of stopping along the roadside, but it did more harm than good, because I usually tensed up during the break, knowing I should be getting on. But I started noticing the abundance of wildflowers that bloomed year round in Georgia, and got the notion to take up photography. I imagined the beauty of close-ups done well. I knew of a dozen or so well-preserved covered bridges, and stately historic homes, and buildings that had escaped Civil War fires and mentally captured them on film.

I wrote my Aunt Vada Hartshorne, with whom I had lived in Tulsa, about my new hobby. As a national judge of colored slides, she also taught photography. She wrote back, advising me on the type camera to buy.

"Get a roll with sixteen film, and start taking pictures in order to get the feel of the camera. I'll take you on as a student for a year, critiquing your slides, with suggestions in the return mail. We'll see what happens."

At her encouragement I got my paraphernalia together and shot pictures of flowers, trees, buildings, anything that caught my eye, and proudly mailed her my first roll. She sent back a three-page, single-spaced letter of criticism and only an inkling of praise. "Continue taking pictures," she said.

I took the challenge. Instead of driving two hours and resting fifteen minutes, I sometimes drove fifteen minutes and rested an hour. With great care I planned my shots, tilting the camera at a precise angle. In the Spring I trekked across muddy bogs for a close picture of a dogwood against a boulder. In Summer I braved the heat along a roadside of wildflowers growing near a trickling creek. I sneezed my way across fields of goldenrods in the fall, to a tree about to change colors, and in winter, I chanced catching my death of cold for a snow scene. Whether my photography improved or not, I had great fun doing therapy, and I kept sending her rolls of film.

In north Georgia, I captured a picture of two charming goats, one white with little black on his coat, and the other black without much white. They were pressed against a delighted child in a red blazer. It was on a roll with several shots that I sent Vada, and this time she wrote back with more praise and less criticism. "I showed it to my photography class as an example. Another teacher and I commented on the luck of an amateur to get such good color changes, while the subjects looked altogether natural." After a few more rolls the praises really began, so I knew I was at last getting somewhere with my picture taking.

* * * * *

One day at the office, an employee commented on an odd AP wire photo appearing in that morning's Atlanta Constitution. "Under the picture the caption read, 'Woman in Tulsa on way to church killed by hit and run drunken driver'."

I stopped filing documents, a foreboding feeling coming over me. "I have an aunt in Tulsa. Hartshorne."

"Why, I think that was her name!"

I raced downstairs to the library. Snatching the paper off the table, I sank into a chair and stared at the picture. A shoe was laid in the foreground, further back a Bible, and in the background a sheet-covered body. It *was* Vada. A passing photographer had snapped a picture of the accident.

Days before, she had written me about a slide show she had enjoyed judging in Hawaii. As she neared the age sixty-five, she had spoken of retirement, so she could fulfill her dream of traveling and taking slides. While I sat recovering from the jolt, I thought how amused she would have been, as one recognized internationally for her photography, that in her death, the Associated Press would display her picture across the country.

Within three years of one another my Mother, my brother Paul and my Aunt Vada had passed away - an old and sick woman, a man in his prime with a family, and a woman nearing retirement and leisure.

Some people view life with a fatalistic approach, in that no matter what our accomplishments, ambitions, or value to society, Death is always leering in the shadows. Bringing ruin, he always has the last word, they say, as he locks us in our graves with a heavy key.

However, as a Christian, I believe Christ's words in the Bible. "Do not be afraid," Jesus said. "I am the First, and the Last, and the living One. I was dead, and behold, I am alive forevermore and *I have the keys of Death and of Hades!*"

Those of us who place our hope in these words know that at the moment of death our souls go to be with God. For as the apostle Paul says of our spirits, "to be absent from the body is to be at home with the Lord." Then, one day our bodies will come alive and be caught up to Heaven, where re-united with our souls, we will live with God forever.

At that time the saying will be fulfilled. "Death is swallowed in victory. O Death, where is your sting? O Death, where is your victory?" And Death will not answer, for he will have vanished forever.

CHAPTER 43

Statistically Speaking

During my years of service with the Georgia Department of Public Health, through the participation and cooperation of other people, we accomplished some worthy goals. In fact, Dr. Rice and I once tabulated them to one almost each year. A detailed description of even a small portion of two decades of statistics would prove cumbersome. However, a partial listing might be in order.

In the late forties we printed the Mother and Baby Care Booklet mentioned earlier. It evidently proved beneficial, for it went into eleven printings. Each state received a copy and many asked permission to use parts or ideas from the contents.

The study on nurse midwifery services for Georgia was the first reason for my being hired, and was funded by The Children's Bureau. It drew attention from various states and lasted for over ten years.

In 1951, we coordinated mother and baby care classes. A joint Public Health and Red Cross program for teaching parents, it enabled both agencies to educate more people than either could alone. A plus for the Public Health nurse was the opportunity to work with social strata other than the indigent.

With the Health Conservation Branch I reviewed and evaluated unmet health needs throughout the state, with emphasis on recognized medical problems. We took steps to phase out programs already completed.

Due to the tragically high premature baby death rate, the Health Department provided safe wooden boxes equipped with warm water engines to Crawford Long and large county hospitals. A total of 588 incubators went out until the commercial ones came down in price. This service lasted from 1941-1950.

We prepared a clinician's manual for prenatal and well-child conferences in 1951, for clinic personnel use, in upgrading physical exams of pregnant mothers and children. We also prepared a pregnancy summary card, and used it first in nurse midwife service, and the local health departments adopted it as they regarded it to be a time saver.

I helped with two films. One evolved from a study on venereal disease, a splendid documentary film entitled *Palmour Street,* which was distributed to the public for educational use. The other documentary, *All My Babies,* produced in 1953, was for the upgrading of local midwife care.

We studied handicapped children in Clark and Oconee counties, to evaluate their total care needs and cost. Since no organization sponsored help for epileptic children, we pleaded until Children's Bureau put $20,000 into the Crippled Children's budget, for medication and staff training. In 1964 we studied deaf children at Cave Springs, the state school for the deaf, as to the predominant cause of deafness.

We worked with representatives from the Education Department in preparing a School Health Guide, a classic outline for school health programs. This was in demand from many states.

I also wrote a dialogue on interviewing techniques to stimulate discussion on family planning with patients. "How Do I Talk – Family Planning?" was applauded in the American Journal of Nursing, January 1967.

* * * * *

Because my work kept me out of town so much, one year I didn't get around to sending out my Christmas cards. Friends from all over the world had sent them to me, and the number piled higher and higher. I placed them all in a basket, feeling obligated to respond; yet I did nothing about it. It just happened that one day I pulled a card from the basket and took it with me. I propped it on my desk while I worked, it rode the dashboard of my car, it nestled in my handbag at the grocery store, or was snugly hidden in my pocket when I went out to sweep the walk.

Throughout the day I thought of the sender. Short prayers accompanied my thoughts. *Lord, take care of this person today. Be mindful of his plans. Protect him from unforeseen disaster.* That night, in my quiet home, I sat down and wrote the person a letter, telling him how I had spent the day in spirit with him.

Thus began a habit that has continued throughout the years. Instead of sending cards, I simply pray sincere prayers for those people who send them to me. I write them, telling them which day I have lifted them up to the Father. Those prayers have been answered with power from God. Some people have yearned to know the Lord after receiving a letter in regard to the card they had sent.

A nun whom I had known for many years laughingly sent two Christmas cards and asked me to pray for her, two days out of the year.

One young couple that had been in a college Sunday school class I taught were fond of each other. One year, when he was Director of Westminster Camp for the summer, he called the girl every day from camp, asking her to marry him. She kept refusing. One day I drew her card, and felt led all day to pray for the right man to come along for her, that she would know when this occurred, and would accept. They told me afterwards that he had called from camp again with the same plea, and surprisingly, she accepted.

"After all this time," he asked. "Why did you say yes?"

"I don't know," she said. "Suddenly, I just felt it was all right." My reply to her Christmas card had come the next day and she could hardly wait for his call that night. "Now I know why I said yes! Miss Mitchell was praying for me, and that I would know *when* to accept the right man!"

Many others have written me, about how they had been moved to present the plan of salvation to someone on the day I prayed for them to be a true witness for the Lord Jesus Christ. One man on a business trip the day I had pulled the family card prayed that he might do a work for the Lord. He witnessed to someone traveling with him, and that person became a Christian!

* * * * *

Looking back over the work I did with the Health Department, we were able to gather some data to inform us of how worthwhile the projects were for the public. This encouraged us to entail even more plans for health improvement.

But until I see eternity, I probably will not know the heavenly statistics that have accumulated regarding my practice of praying over senders of Christmas cards. Through the years, it has tremendously blessed me, and I look forward in Heaven, to hearing of marvelous things that the Holy Spirit has accomplished in this life, through my intercession in this small way.

Hannah's Journal, August 1990

As I look around at my modest cottage and belongings, I realize that I am losing my sense of self-worth. I can only trust that my life has been of significance, and that I have been an influence for good.

The heaviness of grief presses down with a terrible weight. I have lost all my family member- first my parents, then Paul, Russell, James and Mark. As the oldest sibling, why am I the one remaining? Why has the Lord allowed me to live, the old maid, with no husband or children?

I face a future dependent on others; even my personal hygiene will be left to a caregiver. I am being stripped of pride, vanity and independence. Far from home, friends and church, my nightmare will come true. I will soon fade into obscurity, a statistic of a life lived.

My sadness is reminiscent of how I felt when I was forced to retire because of my health....

1967-1990

CHAPTER 44

An Unpromising Future

I awoke early that morning in the autumn of 1966. Even before I opened my eyes, I sensed something terribly wrong, like a menacing black cloud on the horizon. Was it a dream? I had hoped morning's light would make the ominous feeling vanish, but it had persisted. I suddenly sat up in bed in stark fear, remembering that today I was to go into Emory Hospital for an arteriogram.

Why panic now? Off and on, for a couple of years I had not felt well. Severe headaches, double vision, and sometimes - even numbness in my left hand had persistently warned me to lay aside part of my salary, in case I should have to retire early. Yet, on days when I felt better, I had shrugged off the idea. But then, occasional spasms in my left leg, or a sudden involuntary jerking when I walked, would cause my leg to buckle, and I would fall. My bruises were becoming more difficult to explain away, as I realized how accident-prone I had become.

My doctor had not found the source of my complaints, and once, I even went to a psychologist, wondering if I was either neurotic or psychotic. My eyes were examined, reflexes in extremities tested with pinpricks, ice and heat applied for reactions, until I was weary of it all.

Finally, my doctor asked me to stand on my head so he could listen to the blood vessels in my neck. I dreaded this, because anytime I bent over when working in the yard it would give me a terrible headache. When I turned upside down during the examination, my vision blurred and I felt like my head would explode. With a heavy weight settling on my chest, I couldn't breathe. After the doctor listened to my carotid arteries I had to lie down for a few minutes. The doctor helped me up, and said, "I think I've found your trouble. Your carotids are almost closed, particularly on the right side, and eighty-five percent on the left."

The morning of the test I had eased down beside my bed and committed it all into the Heavenly Father's hands: tests and results, doctors, technicians, and recovery.

At the hospital they rolled me into x-ray and anesthetized me. When I awoke to orders to lie flat, I felt the assurance of angels in charge, as I drifted in and out of sleep. The next morning the cardiologist came in. "Young lady, don't concern yourself about surgery on those blood vessels in your neck. They are like corkscrews! And because of that, they are inoperable."

When he left I thought of the future. *If no surgery, then what?* Now that I was the patient, I fumed in frustration, because sometimes doctors are so factual they forget the patient's reaction. I was frightened, thinking of my prognosis. Would I continue to worsen until I died? Trying not to break down I again sought the Lord. *Into thy hands I commit my body, mind, all. I'm so exhausted, Father. Give me rest and peace and joy in whatever you have for me in the days ahead.*

After I was dismissed from the hospital, a friend took me home. When I looked up the hill and saw my little yard and house beckoning me, it had never looked so inviting. When I had first bought it I didn't realize how it would embrace me over the years, and especially now as I weakly climbed the many steps from the drive to the house.

In his office several days later my personal doctor wore a serious expression. "I want you to try a new medication that hasn't been out long, Miss Mitchell. A blood thinner, it requires you to keep in touch with this office for as long as you take it; you must get a prothrombin time check every two weeks. Any activities such as travel will require permission from me." He then turned in his swivel chair and looked directly at me. "I also think you should stop working. What do you think about that?"

At last he said what I had dreaded hearing. I was surprised to hear myself reply, "You know, I really don't see how I can continue, feeling like I do now. In a few months I will have been with the Health Department for twenty years. However, they have a ruling that one must work that long before retiring and must be sixty years old. I'll be sixty my next birthday, April 6." I thought for a minute. "And in all fairness I should get some things in order before I turn the job over to someone else, so I should try to work a few more months."

"Good! Talk to your supervisor and we'll see how you hold up. We'll all keep in touch." With the interview at an end I was relieved that the future wasn't such a fog, and I still had something to accomplish in a given time.

Dr. Morris Brackett had replaced Dr. Rice several years before, bringing with him rich experience in army obstetrics. Soft spoken and fatherly, he had seen me through several headaches on the job. When I approached him about my condition and retirement, he expressed grave concern and even went with me to the retirement board. They suggested that if I could work until July 1, 1967, a few months past my April birthday, that my income would be a bit more. Even at that I was disappointed at how much I would lose in retirement benefits by retiring at sixty instead of sixty-five.

But I made it my immediate goal to find a replacement and orient her to the job. Lacking in energy, I still managed to finish my work projects while trying to regain enough strength to sustain me through it all. Every day that I worked grew longer, until ordinary problems looked insurmountable, as I found that mentally and physically I could no longer cope. Each night the climb up to the house seemed longer, and Hannah's Haven grew more inviting.

I had told Russell about my diagnosis and he insisted I have my doctors send the reports to a friend of his for a final opinion. But his doctor friend confirmed it all. So, in every way I prepared to die. I re-made my will, resigned my teaching positions in Sunday school and Women's Circle. I just wanted to rest and rest.

I began to understand how terminally ill patients could give up on living. In my exhaustion I began to say, like the apostle Paul, "to die is gain." If God wanted me to leave this world and come to Him, then it became less a dismal outlook and more a vibrant expectation.

I went to bed at night saying....*In God have I put my trust....the Lord is my strength....I will not be afraid for the terror by night....* When I closed my eyes I accepted that I could either awaken to songbirds outside my window, or angels singing around God's throne.

CHAPTER 45

Escape to Holly Point

"If we're ever going to spend a winter at Holly Point, now is the time," my friend Mercedes said, sipping a glass of iced fruit punch I had made, while she read the notes people had sent commemorating my retirement. It was September 1967. The elaborate tea and farewell party given in July was over, my desk was cleared and a replacement had taken over the job. I longed for time to rest and soak in the plant life in my half acre, listen and watch for birds, and enjoy the quietness of my little four room house. But it was not to be. Goodbyes had lasted only for a day and now the phone rang constantly.

"How nice," they said, "now that you're free for volunteer work." Several organizations called.

"Oh, no. I'm ill and I need to rest," I explained.

"But it would be *good* for you to be involved," they hinted, especially with *their* work. I even received offers of other jobs, inferior or equal to the one I had just left.

"I would have kept my own job had I wanted or needed one," I insisted.

Two doctors I had worked with at the Health Department in years past were provoked that I didn't jump at their offers. Also, people either called or came by to entice me to continue my same activities, but on my private time. This included making speeches, attending meetings and conferences, or helping with individual projects and programs. On sunny days, I tried to rest in a hammock in the woods away from the sound of the phone, but I eventually *needed* to go inside sometimes!

"Don't you agree it's time to escape?" Mercedes smiled with a twinkle, after I had excused myself for the third time to answer the annoying phone. I thought back to the time years earlier when I had first mentioned it to Mercedes. I visualized her place on Lake Nacootche in North Georgia, situated on a point that juts out into the lake with an excellent view up and down the entire body of water. Pines, mountain laurel and hardwoods cover the property, along with a magnificent wild holly tree.

One week-end when I was there marveling over it I had suddenly said, "I don't think you will ever know the beauty of this place until you have spent a winter. It must be enchanting in the snow." At that time I had no idea I would ever go, but the idea sounded appealing to me now as I finally just took the phone off the hook.

"That's over a hundred miles away," I had answered, turning the offer over in my mind. "I don't know what my doctor would say." But surprisingly, he had thought it a good idea, provided I return to Atlanta for a pro-time every two weeks.

So, we planned to leave the first of October. Mercedes had gas heaters installed to help the fireplace warm the cabin. We collected warm clothes, flannel sheets, electric blankets, boots and shoes for walking, cameras, stationery, and books for entertainment. I loaded my car and waited for Mercedes early one morning so we could follow one another. An air of expectation hung around the house while I waited. And then the phone rang!

"Miss Mitchell, I was present when you led a discussion on techniques of interviewing. Would you do so again with my staff?"

"Oh, no. I have retired. Perhaps you could call my successor."

"No, that won't do. I suppose I'll have to do it myself," she sighed. "Would you review what you said at the time I heard you?" So, while I withered standing at the phone I gave her some highlights of the discussion.

"I really must go. I'm leaving town immediately," I at last said, waving Mercedes inside.

"But I don't have near enough information. Where will you be so I can get in touch with you?"

"I'm going somewhere away from this phone! Goodbye!" I said emphatically and hung up. All the while, Mercedes had been pacing the room.

"Come on, Hannah. Let's get out of here." So we locked up and set out, me trailing her in my car. Should we get separated we had agreed to stop for lunch at a place in Gainesville.

It was only when we left the expressway and hit the country roads that I was able to view the delightful scenery. A few tall goldenrods still showed yellow sprays along the roadsides, fences and fields. Leftover Queen Anne's lace waved their brown flat-topped disks, and woolen mullein, two to seven feet high, only had a couple of yellow blooms left. I couldn't see the sharp white prickles on roadside thistle, but I knew they were there.

We soon drove into hills covered with mountain laurel, or calico bush, as the mountaineers call it, and sheep laurel, which was a bit smaller. Joe-pye weed and New England aster splashed purple in moist places, and I glimpsed a hardtack among them with its spirea-like pinkish flowers. Before long we were weaving our cars down a steep dirt road that ran for two miles to Holly Point.

At last we parked the cars and unpacked the basics. Although tired, I felt exhilarated in the crisp mountain air and I was starving, the first sign of appetite I had experienced in months. We made up our beds on the glassed-in porch, so we could listen to the lake and watch the moon make a path in the water.

In the mornings we awakened to fog on the water and mist on the mountains, anticipating the fall colors. But how slowly the trees changed! When at last the forest burst into color the hardwoods stood in vivid contrast against evergreen shrubs and trees. When they reached their peak the sun was setting behind the purple hills a little earlier each night. And at sundown I had to remind myself to take a little pink and salmon pill, difficult because I wasn't even accustomed to taking aspirin.

The first few weeks at Holly Point I had no motivation or energy. It took me all fall to send thank you notes for the many gifts and cards I had received at retirement, because I was continually distracted by either the view of the lake or woods as nature prepared for winter. Cardinal flower and an occasional blue lobelia reflected in muddy pools around the lake. One day, feeling somewhat rested, I ventured away from the cabin where I saw a ruby throated hummingbird plunge his long bill into the tube of a cardinal flower. What a picture, and no camera with me! From then on, either Mercedes or I carried one when we went for short walks.

"Feel like going a little further today?" Mercedes asked on a crisp morning during the peak of color. She nodded toward our hiking boots, so we both pulled off our shoes and tugged them on.

"Now all I need is a horse!" I laughed, setting out across the yard. On a receding bank we found a gentian with its intense blue club-shaped flowers closing up shop for the season. At the base of a cliff large foamflower leaves gave promise of frothy white flowers in the spring. In the sandy loam in the woods and mossy rocky places, we found dormant trailing arbutus.

Sunny afternoons after lunch found me dozing in a lounge chair under the pines, or reading a book. Soon my curiosity about the woods revived me and I started trudging up and down the hills alone at times, and at supper ate with a great appetite. Each time my friend and I hiked further away from the house exploring the primitive beauty of the woods and mountains.

My personal illness shrank in comparison to the grandeur of all the surrounding beauty, as I identified with the psalmist who lifted his eyes to the mountains, wondering where his help would come from. Like him, I knew my help truly came from the Lord, maker of heaven and earth. Although I had come to this place awaiting death, I found myself anticipating each new day as I sensed my strength returning in the surrounding mountains.

"I'm feeling much better!" I called to Mercedes one morning as I topped a steep hill. I inhaled deeply, looking out over a valley we were about to enter.

"I know!" she panted from below. "Wait up a minute, will you?"

Trips back and forth to the doctor with a night or two at home allowed me to swap things out. At first I tiptoed past the phone, but it had stopped ringing. Now, with Atlanta traffic my only stress, it made me anxious to return to the quietness of the hills.

We cooked Thanksgiving dinner for guests at Holly Point. Later we made Christmas dinner for the mountain folk on our side of the lake, complete with gifts we had made for the children. Together Mercedes and I also made gifts for family and friends in Atlanta. We got creative with our fixed incomes, fashioning evergreen wreaths with nuts and juniper and white pine. Using pipe cleaners we designed pixie dolls and gave them to children. A nephew of mine still has his, a gangly youth doll with a drum. Most of our fun was in gathering the materials, storing them on the porch, and smelling their pungent evergreen fragrances.

After breakfast one morning I started out to gather firewood and Mercedes came with me. "You are *really* getting stronger!"

"It's like a miracle, isn't it?" I said, while we sawed some larger pieces.

With never-ending interest we watched bird life that migrated to the lake and woods. We fed them liberally, particularly during bad weather. From inside the cabin we watched as a titmouse lit and fed on a window ledge from one of the crude feeders we had made. Soon birds came in droves, calling to one another and parading a variety of size and color.

One afternoon in January, snowflakes drifted down as we were returning from a short walk, increasing to a snowstorm during the night. Next morning we slowly ventured out and spied deer bedded down near our cars; bird tracks and paw prints led off in several directions.

When weather permitted, on Sundays we drove to church in Clayton; Mercedes to the Episcopal Church and I to the Presbyterian. Each time I thanked the Heavenly Father for the gift of life; for someone supposedly dying, I felt more exuberantly alive than I had in years.

In February, although we knew it wasn't possible, we looked for trailing arbutus buds. Instead, we found colorful mosses, lichens and mushrooms, and one day we saw a pileated woodpecker on a tree above the house. During our walks in places where the ground had thawed we found ourselves scooting down the hill on our backsides. Every rocky place became a waterfall; the cold air smelled of rotting leaves, a signal that spring was on the way.

Mercedes got chilled one day while we were out, and came down with a head cold that got progressively worse, until in a couple of days she was running a temperature. Coughing, and blowing her nose, she said, "I'm afraid I have the flu. I think we need to get home." I had already begun getting our things together, for the deep woods are no place to be should she get worse. I quickly packed my car and we left Holly Point, agreeing to return for her car when she felt better.

And back in Atlanta, Hannah's Haven was waking up to a few colorful early crocus, and the vivid yellow of jasmine on the wall. As I walked up the long hill, rejuvenated with restored health, I was anxious to clear away the winter debris that lay strewn all over the yard, so after I unloaded the car I couldn't wait for the next day, and grabbed a rake and started on the piles of leaves that lay beneath the oak trees. To my delight I discovered more crocus peeping out of their cold beds.

That night I went to bed with the good feeling that comes after a day of working outdoors, not exhausted and depressed, but just good tired. For some weeks in my bedtime prayers as I thanked the Heavenly Father for another day of life, I had felt that perhaps He wasn't ready to take me home just yet, for the little pink and salmon pills He had provided were working fine. Perhaps, I thought, He still had something left that he wanted me to do.

CHAPTER 46

Any Old Bush Will Do

Although at church I had taught the college class for fifteen years, someone else was now teaching that class. I had never taught pre-schoolers, and was delighted when asked to teach the two to four year olds.

To clarify a point with the children, I usually taught an object lesson using visual aids. I remember one Sunday I told the story of Samuel. I took a pillow with me and put my head on it, pretending to go to sleep right in front of the children. Then I awoke and sat up. "Somebody's calling me!" I said, looking around. Then I ran over in the corner where I had propped one of the dolls, pretending he was Eli. I had the toddlers act out the story and one of the two year olds did the pillow game constantly. Now he is an adult. One day he stopped me at church.

"I told Mother, 'that woman taught me in two year Sunday school.' You brought a pillow and told us the story of Samuel and his yielded life. It really made an impression on me. I'll never forget it."

I taught the little ones only about six months because they soon put me back in the college department. Over the years as I watched the toddlers grow up, some of them married and stayed in the church, while others moved away. One young man has remained dear to my heart. I was in the hospital and couldn't attend church for several Sundays once, so Terry Parker came and sat by my bed for about two hours. Sometimes we spoke, but I really didn't feel like it. He mainly sat to keep me company.

At the time he was concerned about his mother who didn't know the Lord. "I'll pray with you for her salvation," I said, and so we prayed for months. One Sunday afternoon, while in their rose garden Terry spoke to her about the Lord and she accepted Christ as her Savior. It was only a few months later that she died of lung cancer. How grateful he was for our answered prayer.

I had told all my students that if they would read the Bible through in a year I would give them a new one. Terry is a Christian lawyer now with his own law firm and a faithful member at Westminster. He still has that Bible I gave him years ago.

I asked to be relieved of the college department in the early seventies because of the many social activities required for this age group, and rejoined my adult class as a member. The teacher suffered a heart attack and moved away, so I substituted for several Sundays, and that position has stretched to six years now. We have studied Ezra and Nehemiah and other books in the Old Testament, we went through the book of Luke and discussed his outlook as a physician, and the life of Apostle Paul and his letter to the Romans.

* * * * *

I became a pal, or sponsor, in Pioneer Girls. Robin Clark, Donna McDonald, twins Janet and Carol Tozier, are a few I taught. Right after Thanksgiving one year I asked Janet if she would like to make Miracle Fruitcake with me.

"Miss Hannah, just what is that?" she wanted to know. So, while we got the ingredients together, I told her the story of how I had renamed it while we worked in the kitchen.

"One year a friend of mine, Audrey Dyer, came home on furlough as a missionary to Nigeria. She went to Africa against her family's wishes and one of her sisters practically disowned her. In fact, Audrey came to my house instead of going home to Minnesota. One morning after the postman had come and she watched me look through a few letters, she sighed. 'Hannah, what am I to do? I've written my sister all this time, and not one word has she written back.'

I put the mail down and poured us a cup of coffee. 'Just keep writing her as though nothing has happened. We'll think of something.'

Audrey was helping me make fruitcakes that December to send to family and friends. While we wrapped several cakes in foil, I said, 'Audrey, I want you to send one of these to your sister.' By now her feelings were really hurt because she hadn't heard from home and she didn't think it a good idea, but I insisted. So, she finally wrapped and boxed one, and after we prayed over it, she mailed it to their home in Minnesota.

In only a few days she received a letter. 'Dear Audrey, I have baked many fruitcakes in my day and given them to friends and family. But *never* has anyone baked one and sent it to me. Thank you so much! By the way, when are you coming home?'

"I would say that was a miracle, wouldn't you Janet - for the Lord to heal family relations in such a simple way? Since that time, I have called this recipe Miracle Fruitcake." Janet was enthralled with the story and took a cake home with her. Her family invited me over for Christmas dinner, and while I helped set the table, her mother told me how awed Janet was about the story while she had shared it with them.

Westminster runs a camp for boys and girls each summer, which is fun and beneficial. Six hundred children come from as far as eight states away, and many become Christians. Others develop a deeper walk as they ride horses, swim in the pool, and enjoy late night chats in the dorms with counselors in each.

Fae Allen, the artist friend of mine, promoted the camp with illustrations and was asked one year to put out a brochure. "Only if Hannah Mitchell does the photography," she said. So, for years we worked together advertising the camp. Once in awhile I taught Bible stories there, using visual aides.

* * * * *

I started teaching a home Bible class in Doraville in the late sixties. Seeing the budding interest of these women grow to full flower has brought me much joy. We started with Philippians, then First Peter. We examined the love story of Ruth and the reign of Queen Esther in her book. Joshua encouraged us to be strong and courageous.

We plunged into a study of David in First Samuel and then Psalms. We encountered the strong teachings of Romans, then guidelines to maturity in Ephesians and Colossians. It gives me satisfaction when those who move away to other cities remain in Bible study classes, and many become teachers themselves.

Through the years people that have been influenced and stimulated around me have gone out as missionaries. At one time I studied the Sunday school rolls from our old church. Seventy-five per cent of them are in full or part time Christian work, a marvelous blessing for the Lord. Some are included in the number I pray for daily, among them are forty-five missionaries.

My interest in Wycliffe Translators continued from decades ago when the Townsend brothers had first begun the project. Once, I sent a contribution and asked them to put it anywhere they needed it, so when Wycliffe sent it to a married couple in Mexico we began an ongoing correspondence. Though I have never met them I pray for them daily. One day I received a letter. "You sent five dollars fifty-six years ago and I wrote you back. You are the only one who has faithfully corresponded and I want to thank you for all the years that you have been our prayer partner."

* * * * *

The Holy Spirit usually nudges me awake at five a.m. to pray, but several years ago He started awakening me at four! *Heavenly Father, I said, I'd like some evidence that my prayers are being effectually helpful since I'm losing a lot of sleep being an intercessor.*

Almost immediately I received a thank-you from an organization overseas that helps keep nurses current in practice and technology. A second one arrived along with similar letters. One missionary made hers public by publishing it in Flying Figures, a publication put out by Wycliffe. Her husband and another pilot had developed engine trouble, but they safely landed in a grassy field without injury to them or the plane. "Keep on praying, Hannah. We really count on those early morning prayers."

Thank you, Lord for all those responses. Now when you awaken me from sleep, maybe I won't grumble so much.

The Evangelism Explosion Program at our church has been very meaningful to me. Other people train to go out and witness, as they visit homes of people who come to our church. I stay home and pray. On nights when Larry Enlow goes out he asked me to be his regular prayer partner. Each Thursday morning at seven he calls me before going to work, often to tell me who he will visit that night, or he just asks me to pray. We pray over the phone for the Lord to prepare that person's heart throughout the day and while Larry talks to them. If anything dramatic happens he rings me or fills me in on Sunday. I feel this is one of the most valuable things I've ever done in the way of prayer.

The Lord has blessed my life abundantly, through guidance, preservation of health, and materially. He even takes care of my wardrobe. I remember wearing my cousins' hand-me-downs in my youth. In high school my parents bought me an elegant silk dress with smocking on the collar and across the front. Mother was pressing it the day I was to wear it when my Father came in and said, "There's a string on it." He cut the string with his knife and accidentally cut the dress. He was so sorry, he all but cried.

Mother quickly glanced my way and said, "Oh, I can smock some across the front." She did, but the dress wasn't the same to me after that. My pride in the dress had fallen.

Today people generously give me nice clothes they have either outgrown or no longer want. Content and thankful, I am delighted with the Lord's provision as He gives generously on my modest income.

I came from thinking at retirement of a shortened life in 1967 to the present year, 1990 - twenty-three more years of sharing what God has given me! All my talents must be attributed totally to Him. Actually, I feel that anyone could open their lives and instruct people with even greater success. It all depends upon the person's dependency upon the Lord and his submitted will to Christ.

After all, the bush Moses saw burning on that mountain was not of any particular beauty or variety. So it is true with our lives. It doesn't matter our income, talents or beauty. All God wants is a heart willing to trust Him, His guidance, and even willingness of being uprooted by Him when we least expect or want it. Faith and trust are all He asks, because in the long run, any old bush will do.

Hannah's Journal, September 1990

A few days ago I woke from a nap on my sofa, groggy and disoriented. When I tried to stand I was unable to walk, so I crawled to the phone and somehow remembered Dot Townsend's number. She immediately rushed over and got me to the hospital, where the doctor said that I probably had suffered a mild stroke. After a few days of tests and observation, he sent me home. "She must remain on strict bed rest," he said gravely to Dot.

Totally drained of strength and unable to be alone, I have spent the last few nights at Dot's home. When she heard me crying during the night and came to my room, I broke down in front of her, and unlike my usual stoic nature, finally confessed my grief over what is happening to me. I spent a sleepless night, praying.

By the next morning I felt that my Heavenly Father had spoken clearly. I resolved to surrender my independence while it was still my decision to make, so I asked Dot to brew a cup of tea for us to sip while we talked.

I told her that I knew the time had come for me to once again give up what I called home. Would she please call my sister-in-law Nancy for me, and tell her that the time had come for me to accept her invitation to come and live with her. Dot's reassuring hug made me cry again and she showed obvious relief as she left the room to make the phone call.

This time, I realized, there would be no escape to Holly Point, no daily walks to regain my strength. Instead, there would only be declines in physical, emotional and mental stamina. How I wish I didn't have knowledge regarding the clinical symptoms and eventual outcome of my condition.

With increasing anxiety I have faced the fact that as dementia advances, damage to the brain occurs beyond the control of the patient. In the not too distant future I will lose my coordination in writing, walking, speaking. Paranoia will set in. My final stages will be confinement to bed requiring skilled nursing care....

In a few days I was strong enough to return to Hannah's Haven and friends have stayed with me while I go through my things. People from church have been kind to bring food and visit for a few moments, sharing fond memories of cheer and comfort.

When my minister from Westminster came to see me, we both cried. He gently asked if I wanted to say a few words at church on my final Sunday, but I cannot....I am exhausted.

This old bush is finally worn out and used up.

CHAPTER 47

In The Garden

Terry Parker, my lawyer, and Philip Florence, executor of my estate, are finalizing my finances. Dot, Audrey Florence and Janet Carpenter have been here for the past three days and are packing for me. I only want to take my Bible, a few clothes, some linens and the family silverware that Nancy has asked me to bring. The rest - all my furniture, lessons I have prepared, photo albums, everything, I will leave behind.

During some of the time, for the last few days while my friends packed for me, I was allowed to sit in my garden....

In my memory are many gardens. I remember my Mother's cosmos and zinnias she grew in the sunshine of our Missouri yard on the farm. Roses grew profusely along an old road that at one time had cut through our place. We used them on Memorial Day, gathering great baskets full that we took to the cemeteries for decoration.

Also, on the farm I enjoyed woodland gardens, although the woods were much sparser than some I have known since. My brothers and I made playhouses around huge stones, moving plants from other places and placing them among the stones, creating our garden. I particularly remember two varieties of birds-foot violets we transplanted – a lavender we called hens, another with the two top petals a deep and velvety purple we called roosters.

One day, Mother had sent Paul and me on an errand to a neighbor's home, a far walk from our house, but when we arrived we found it worth the trip. The Austin's yard looked like a picture book! Hollyhocks grew against the foundation, roses climbed a fence, and other vines grew in profusion.

Paul pointed out tiny birds we had never seen, drinking nectar from red and orange flowers. Mrs. Austin came out to tell us they were hummingbirds. She invited us to come back to visit, so I returned often to talk with her about her flowers; she shared their names, how to grow them, and seeds that particular birds liked.

When Mother had moved to her small city lot in Schell City she planted flowers. So many neighbors gave her seeds, bulbs or plants, that her yard contained hundreds of flowers. However, I provided her with some of her choicest ones. While in nursing school I discovered patients' wilted potted plants thrown in the trash, so I salvaged the spring bulbs, and then in fall gathered chrysanthemums. I sent them all to Mother, and she waited eagerly for tulips, white narcissi, hyacinths, crocus, acanthus, and mums to come up and bloom. She used her gardening as a ministry, giving away flourishing plants to people, sharing in their lives. Her visits became friendships as she frequently dug up a plant in bloom and carried it to a sick person. In turn they shared with her. Throughout town, people talked of her reputation with people and flowers.

Later, in Kentucky as I rode the mountain trails I often saw a miniature garden in a nook among the stones, trees, or sometimes a glade filled with flower varieties. Against a damp bluff one day, a foamflower caught my eye as it made a sheet of white. Another time I saw a bunch of lady slippers off to the side. I quickly tied my horse and knelt beside them to see every bit of their beauty. I didn't dare dig them because they were perfect in that little spot. One of the nurses had transferred some of them to a wildflower garden at the hospital, but they didn't live. This made me cautious when I later moved wildflowers and tried to keep them in their original soil and habitat.

After I bought my little house in Atlanta people often gave me plants, iris from a nurse, sedum from another, a start of peonies from a doctor. A nurse in South Georgia sent a small iron plaque engraved with:

The kiss of the sun for pardon,
The song of the birds for mirth,
One is nearer God's heart in a garden,
Than anywhere else on earth.

I learned two weeks later that the nurse had taken her own life. Thereafter, each time I passed the plaque I was reminded that one never knows the heart break that may be underneath the gaiety that people exhibit, and that I must constantly allow the Holy Spirit to lead as I talked and dealt with people. How glad I am that I had written her promptly and thanked her for the gift.

During my many trips to rural communities while I worked, I brought back loads of rotted sawdust and worked it around planted shrubs or used it to build up the soil to keep it from washing. I also hauled home a lot of South Georgia sand in the trunk of my car. I grabbed any good-looking stones by the side of the road, along with ferns and flowers that struggled in wayside places, and in my fertile yard they grew and multiplied. I even picked up two tortoises, male and female. Their little ones added interest to the shrubs and groundcovers.

I read library books on landscaping and even bought several on shady gardening, which I read and referred to often while I renovated and recovered the property.

I discovered deciduous ferns on the lower side of the stone wall at the upper shelf and mixed Christmas ferns with them. In front of these I crumbled seed moss that caught on and grew well. On the upper shelf I made a perennial bed of iris, day lilies, sedum and other spring bulbs. It was a damp area, so I built a stone walkway from one side of the upper shelf to the other, which joins steps leading down at either end. Now, the sight of the wall with moss in front, ferns along the base, azaleas across the top, and blooming perennials is a sight to see in the spring. I hope the person who buys Hannah's Haven will have the same love for flowers and shrubs, and will enjoy its splendor.

As a memorial to my Aunt Vada, Mercedes bought a birdbath on a pedestal with an angel on top; it stands in an alcove with a background of Boston ivy and a June beauty hosta around it. With the edge of the bath the same shape as the hosta leaves, it really is a picture when they bloom with their white fragrant blossoms.

My brother James, and his wife, Nancy, had surprised me with a white metal loveseat and table that they placed opposite the birdbath, giving balance to either end of the upper shelf. Two blue hydrangeas have at their base some orange day lilies and butterfly weed. Once, they bloomed simultaneously, blue against orange.

The woods took much longer to beautify. First, I laid out a circular path down one side, crossing over and then back the other side. James and his family made steps with stones that I had retrieved from the construction site of the Civic Center in downtown Atlanta.

In 1976, a landscape architect and committee for the Dogwood Festival came and looked over the grounds. They wanted my place to be shown in the Festival as an example for uniqueness, size and shady gardening. So I put out a plea for labor at the Doraville Bible study. "We'll help, Miss Hannah," they laughed, hearing the panic in my voice. For two days, we all worked getting the place in shape.

I made a plant lore list, naming the blooming plants and shrubs, and passed them out to guests along with the sketch of Hannah's Haven. Over a thousand people came through the property, and amazingly didn't harm one twig, plant or stone! They reacted in various ways to the sketch and inscription of *"Hannah's Haven: Both Belong To The Lord"*

Some thought it a testimony, one person thought it good material for her Sunday school lesson. For a long time I prayed for one of the men, who, during the garden tour read the inscription, and let out a deep sigh. Because of the crowds I was prevented from asking him if he knew the Lord.

Early in Genesis the Bible speaks about the Garden of Eden where God entrusted Adam and Eve as caretakers. Midway in the Bible it speaks about Solomon's Gardens, and at the end of the Bible is the garden where the tree of life will eternally grow. And our Lord sweated agonizing drops of blood in the Garden of Gethsemane. I'm sure gardens, then, must be dear to God's heart.

Hannah's Haven reminds me of the garden of our own hearts. God the Creator comes into our lives that are filled with the poison of sin and wild entanglements. We need a cleanup campaign by the Great Gardener, a grubbing out and casting away.

...And so, it has come to this. Now I must leave this small paradise that God has allowed me to cultivate. This plot of ground so dear to my heart. Out of all that I must give up, this is the most difficult task of all.

Hannah's Journal, September 1990

My friends have driven me to the airport, helped me board the plane and buckled me into my seat. On my lap sits my Bible, my journal, and the silverware chest for Nancy. The sale of my house, disbursement of furniture, photo albums, and other personal belongings rests in the care of loving friends.

I close my eyes. After a few short minutes the plane has taxied down the runway and we are in the clouds, with the view of Atlanta's growing skyline obscured from view...

I have left my church, friends, beloved city, and Hannah's Haven for the final time....I will not be returning.

CHAPTER 48

Leaving Atlanta

Once, I had gone by plane to Chicago, leaving on a Sunday afternoon. That morning I had taught a group of small children at church, and as I hurriedly threw my things together, I discovered my teaching materials were still in my purse, and had brought them on the plane with me. I always ask the Lord to guide me where to sit when traveling, and with this in mind I sat just back of the magazine rack, right up front where I barely had room for my legs. I sat looking out the window, when a tall man with wide shoulders came on board. He smiled and sat down beside me.

Just as soon as the engines revved up he grabbed the arms of his seat and started nervously twisting about. I watched him out of the corner of my eye for a few minutes, and then I said, "Are you frightened of flying?"

"Yes, ma'am!" he said, not the least embarrassed. "I've flown all over the world, but I have never enjoyed it. I don't know why, but it scares me to death!"

"Has anything happened to make you afraid?"

"No. I've never been in an accident."

"If you knew the pilot, would that make a difference?"

"Well, it might. Do you know him?"

"I don't know the man who's up front, but I *do* know the One who holds the plane in the air."

"You mean...."

"Yes, I mean the Heavenly Father."

"Oh."

"Do you know Him?"

"Oh, I go to church."

"I don't mean that. Do you *know* Him?"

"No, I don't. I wish I did. But I'm married to a fine woman, and she does."

By that time the sky had grown dark. I couldn't see to read from the Bible, but I reached my hand in my purse and hit upon the little wordless book that I had used with the children.

"I don't know if you can see these colors. This morning I spoke to a group of little children about coming to know the Lord, just like I'm talking with you." I went through the whole procedure of the wordless book.

"The first page is black, which shows that we all have sinned. Red inside represents the death of Christ and His blood, which covers all black sins when we confess them to the Heavenly Father. The white page is as clean as snow or wool, depicting how sin is washed away and replaced with Christ's righteousness. The gold page represents Heaven awaiting those who trust in Christ. The outside covering is green, that part of us which is constantly exposed to the world. As the earth is green, so we should continue to grow in our faith in God."

I had no more than finished when he said, "I believe!"

Surprised at his quick response, I skeptically said, "You do?"

He repeated, "Yes! I believe!"

"All right," I said with the same simplicity I had used in presenting the little wordless book. "I'm going to pray." I leaned over close so he could hear and thanked the Lord that he had found Christ. Then I said, "Could you pray, and thank Him too?"

He bowed his head. I couldn't hear what he said over the noise of the plane, but he prayed in earnest. I could tell he was pleading with God about his soul. Occasionally I caught a word that told me he was confessing his sins, that he had repented and received the Savior. Then we settled down and said nothing. To my delight, in just a minute or two he went to sleep.... like a newborn babe!

We got into the worst storm, one of the roughest I've been in, but he slept on. I kept chuckling - *Thank you, Lord, for showing me he has found peace.*

This is so true after we make our birthing cry in the Lord Jesus. Some souls, agonizing over conviction and trauma of indecision, react much like an infant in the birth process. The decision to emerge from unending darkness is not always a joyful experience at the outset. When God's new child suddenly finds himself liberated from captivity, his first new gasps often convulse into sobs. Some gurgle happily, and breathe a deep and peaceful sigh, but never before have I seen one just fall asleep. And in this case, a new Christian was healed from his fear of flying.

After our rebirth, God blesses us with evidence that we are Christians. Old habits are discarded; we receive love, joy and peace to help us grow in faith and fruit bearing. Then after awhile, with new growth comes pruning to make us more usable. This is often painful if we lose a job, or get disappointed in love, and are unable to marry the person we choose. Sometimes we are even forced to move to a new location against our wills.

My garden in Atlanta went through summer droughts at times; just so, Hannah the Christian went through dry and unfruitful times. Then came the heavenly watering that refreshed my life and started me growing to be like Christ again.

Throughout our lives our spiritual gardens accumulate many blessings from other people. A kind word is planted here, timely advice given there. In another spot a word of restraint is used. Our main nourishment comes from the Word of God that sustains us through all seasons. His Word becomes a light to guide us up the dark hills and around the upper shelves, and through wooded areas and valleys. We are often allowed tranquility as the Gardener attends to our needs while we grow and He cares for us according to His will.

As I used to sit and enjoy my garden, I realize that the purpose for my existence actually is for His enjoyment. I am to live in His shadow. He will be like the dew to me, I will blossom like the lily and flourish like a watered garden.

HANNAH'S FINAL JOURNAL ENTRY
SEPTEMBER 17, 1990

Even though I am moving into the shadows of my long life, I have the assurance that my Heavenly Father will be with me. Even when I can no longer pray or acknowledge Him, He will be there. At the age of eighty-three, I know that I am closer to going to my heavenly home now than ever before.

I know that when I sleep for the last time, the voice of the Lord Jesus Christ Himself will awaken me to a new world untouched by human hand. I believe that world will be filled with gardens.

And there, I will at last be a bride, His bride, and I will live with Him forever.

I am ready, Lord. Thy Will be done....

Epilogue

*"But blessed are those who trust in the Lord and
have made the Lord their hope and confidence."
Jeremiah 17:7 NLT*

To those who knew her well, Miss Hannah's dementia was slow in revealing itself. Lapses in memory were attributed to advancing age, and she carried herself with stately dignity.

In March of 1990, in honor of her upcoming 83rd birthday, Janet Carpenter escorted her to Stone Mountain for an early birthday lunch, where she was delighted in hearing the carillon play. Later, they went back to Hannah's Haven and walked around the yard to view the tulips in bloom. She seemed normal. Her house and yard were neat.

The year before, Janet had taken Miss Hannah to the governor's mansion for a tour. Janet had sent word to the governor's wife that she was bringing her own prayer partner. The governor's wife then invited them to her private quarters, where Miss Hannah prayed for her!

During the dismantling of Hannah's Haven, Audrey Florence asked her if she was taking her knitting with her. When Hannah had first moved to Atlanta, she had taught a college class at church. When the students married and had babies, she knitted stockings for their newborns, and she was still knitting gifts for other new parents in her later years. When Hannah replied, *no,* she was not taking her knitting supplies - that was another sign that she was giving up everything that she had ever done. So Audrey gathered up the yarn for herself as a memento.

During those last few days in Atlanta she bequeathed Janet her study books, penned by various authors, and the dining room table, where she had prepared Bible lessons that she had taught for so many years. Janet also managed to salvage her original study lessons from the curb where they had been placed for trash pickup. Although of no value to Miss Hannah, still, we who had sat in her Doraville neighborhood Bible studies considered them a treasure. I have those lessons in my possession.

I can still see her in one of our homes, standing beside the flip chart she used when she taught the lessons that she had meticulously and prayerfully prepared. I can hear her laughter that sounded so like a young girl's. I can see her genuine pleasure as she shared her faith in the Lord with us, hoping that we would become Bible teachers ourselves. She loved us. Like a mother hen she called us 'her chicks'.

Miss Hannah's departure to Louisiana was the last we saw of her. But one time, when Audrey and Phil Florence were on their way to New Orleans, they stopped by Opaloussas to drop off a box of linens that Nancy had wanted. Hannah, who greeted them, looked slightly disoriented, but seemed glad to see them after she finally recognized them. She and Audrey walked outside to look at the flowers, but she was visibly disturbed at not remembering names of plants.

Hannah had become so dependent on Nancy that she became her shadow, following her from room to room. As Hannah's dementia advanced, her elderly sister-in-law couldn't bear up under the burden of constant care. So, in the summer of 1991, Hannah was admitted to a nursing home where a sitter attended her for a few months. It was told that Hannah was a real sweetheart, and was able to participate in activities for a while, but as the dementia progressed she became reclusive.

Years before, Janet Carpenter and her husband had invited Hannah to live with them, but she wouldn't hear of it. Looking back, we have to trust that God spared us the grief of seeing her in the final devastations of dementia.

Hannah Mitchell passed away on October 27, 2000.

* * * * *

On a recent trip to Atlanta I drove to Miss Hannah's old address. To my dismay the cottage and gardens were gone, and a lovely new home now adorns the hilltop. Only a patch of ivy and a few stone steps remain where the drive begins, all insignificant clues to passersby of a home site that many people had once cherished.

I wonder what Miss Hannah's reaction would have been had she seen it. The new house is certainly an improvement over her three-room cottage. A large oak remains at the curb, but from the street, I couldn't tell if any flowering plants had survived on the back of the property, and I didn't feel it right to trespass in order to find out.

Had she been there, my dear old friend may have nodded in approval, once she recovered from shock over all the renovations. After all, she had always adjusted to profound changes as she was redirected from different places in her life. In all probability, within a few minutes she would have surveyed the house and grounds with a keen eye. If perchance the new owners invited her to come up for a closer view, she would have toured the place inquiring about their landscaping and gardening techniques. She may have even gotten around to mentioning the Heavenly Father, the Gardener with a Grand Design for their lives.

I can see her gracious smile and hear her compliment the present owners on their treatment of her former home place. She might exclaim: "Well! May the Lord be praised!"

And then, she would have signaled it was time to move on.

Miracle Fruitcake Recipe

24 oz. pitted dates
1 lb. candied pineapple
1 lb. whole candied cherries
2 cups plain flour
2 tsp. baking powder
½ tsp. salt
4 eggs
1 cup sugar
8 cups pecans

Cut up dates, pineapple, cherries in large bowl.
Lightly spoon baking powder, flour, salt into sifter.
Sift into fruit. Stir.
Beat eggs till frothy. Gradually beat in sugar.
Add to fruit mixture.
Mix with wooden spoon if you can, but at this point you may need to use hands.
Add pecans...mix well until batter is coated.
Line two 9x5x3 loaf pans or seven mini pans with parchment paper strips.
Pack fruitcake into pans with hands. Press down, filling empty spaces.
Bake @275 for 1½ hrs. for large pans, or 40 mins. for small pans.
Batter will look dry, but will not brown.
Do not overbake! Remove from oven.
Let stand about 20 mins. to cool.
Peel off paper. Wrap in foil.
Keep in fridge. Can freeze.

From Hannah Mitchell

Acknowledgments

THANK YOU: Rosemary Alinder, for your insight into the need for a Bible study in our Doraville, GA neighborhood back in the seventies. Although Miss Hannah had retired due to failing health, to our benefit she agreed to come and teach us. Thank you for hosting the study until you moved away.

THANK YOU: To the thirty-five women who attended the Bible study for the years we lived in Atlanta. We shared a special bond and you were a great encouragement to me personally. We were all privileged to be included as 'Miss Hannah's chicks' while we sat in her teachings about the Lord.

THANK YOU: Pat Clements and others for hosting the study; also my gratitude to Carolyn Holcomb and Janet Carpenter for your continued friendships. You are all my true sisters in the Lord!

THANK YOU: Janet Carpenter and Audrey Florence for your memories and input into Miss Hannah's final months in Atlanta. I could not have updated the manuscript without your assistance.

THANK YOU: Terry Parker, Executor for Miss Hannah's estate, for your permission to publish her story. I treasure your smile when we speak of her.

THANK YOU: My friends and family who have spurred me on with this project.

THANK YOU: Everyone at WestBow for your valuable assistance in making this book a reality.

THANK YOU: My sister, Jimmie Nell, for your comfort over rejected query letters and belief in this project.

THANK YOU: My husband, Mack, for your patience when I re-worked and tweaked the manuscript. For your encouragement to continue when my laptop crashed and I lost all data except what I had already sent to the editors, and for your provision for the whole endeavor.

THANK YOU: Miss Hannah for your testimony of faith and perseverance.

THANK YOU: Most of all, Lord Jesus, for your saving Grace of our entire family. We are truly blessed. I pray we will all make our lives count for You, and will one day ascend into Your presence in Heaven.

About the Author

Shirley is a free-lance writer with essays published in The Freshman Sampler, Department of English, University of Alabama in Birmingham. A former medical records librarian, her UAB research paper Midwifery Reborn, reiterates the value to mother and child of a nurse midwife attending delivery. Shirley is the daughter of a registered nurse and grew up with knowledge of medical terminology, developing an interest in the health and welfare of mothers and babies. Mother of four children, grandmother to seven grandchildren, she has continued her interest in safe delivery and development of infants and children. An avid reader, she works in her church library and writes a weekly article in the bulletin promoting the library. She and her husband live on a lake in Alabama where they boat, swim and linger in the porch swing.

You may contact Shirley at srferguson58@yahoo.com.

Part of the proceeds from the sale of this book
Will be donated to
The Hannah D. Mitchell Endowment Fund
For Christian Missions
National Christian Foundation
Alpharetta, GA

13363517R00196

Made in the USA
Lexington, KY
27 January 2012